NEITHER CARGO

NEITHER CARGO NOR CULT

Ritual Politics and the Colonial

Imagination in Fiji

Martha Kaplan

Duke University Press

Durham and London

1995

© 1995 Duke University Press

All rights reserved

Printed in the United States of America on acid-free paper ∞

Designed by Cherie Holma Westmoreland

Typeset in Galliard by Keystone Typesetting, Inc.

Library of Congress Cataloging-in-Publication Data appear

on the last printed page of this book.

To my parents,
Lucille and Lawrence Kaplan

CONTENTS

List of Figures   ix
Preface: Neither Cargo nor Cult   xi
Acknowledgments   xvii

1 Introduction: Culture, History, and Colonialism   1
2 Embattled People of the Land: The Ra Social Landscape, 1840–1875   19
3 Navosavakadua as Priest of the Land   46
4 Colonial Constructions of Disorder: Navosavakadua as "Dangerous and Disaffected Native"   62
5 Navosavakadua's Ritual Polity   98
6 Routinizing Articulating Systems: Jehovah and the People of the Land, 1891–1940   123
7 Narratives of Navosavakadua in the 1980s and 1990s   160
8 Navosavakadua among the Vatukaloko   178
9 Conclusion: Do Cults Exist? Do States Exist?   201

Bibliography   211
Index   219

LIST OF FIGURES

1. The Fiji Islands   xii
2. Viti Levu Island   xiii
3. Viti Levu Island: colonial boundaries mentioned in text   xiii
4. Northeastern Viti Levu: 1873 sketch by Swanston   20
5. Northeastern Viti Levu Island   21
6. Vatukaloko Inland Sites: author's sketch   21
7. Vatukaloko Chiefs   34
8. Chiefs of Rakiraki   35
9. Origins and Relations of the Vatukaloko   152
10. Relation of the Eastern Coastal Kingdoms to the Vatukaloko   152
11. Wives and Descendants of Degei   153
12. Descendants of Rokomoutu and His Son Vueti   154
13. Drauniivi Village in the 1980s: author's sketch   180

PREFACE

Neither Cargo nor Cult

It would be a classic anthropological story if I told you that I went to Fiji expecting to study a cargo cult or millenarian movement, and while there discovered that cults do not exist. My story is perhaps less classic. Studying the anthropology and history of the early 1980s, including Marshall Sahlins's work on indigenous history-making and Bernard Cohn's insights on colonial societies, I began my research in Drauniivi village in 1984. I began this research in the home of the descendants of a man called Navosavakadua of "Tuka Movement" fame (see Worsley 1968, Burridge 1969), already skeptical about the general category of cargo cult. Do cults exist? Over the course of my research I have come to understand how they both do and do not.

Colonial officials and missionaries in the nineteenth- and early-twentieth-century Pacific observed movements that came to be called "cargo cults." They wrote of Pacific people with millenarian (and sometimes anti-colonial) expectations who used magical means to get western things (hence the term "cargo" cult). Later, theorists of the cargo cult such as Peter Worsley and Kenelm Burridge were among the first anthropologists to grapple with issues of social change in a complex, connected decolonizing world. In defining or at least reinforcing the term as scholarly touchstone it is their contribution to have replaced earlier colonial and scholarly diagnoses of "native madness" with an

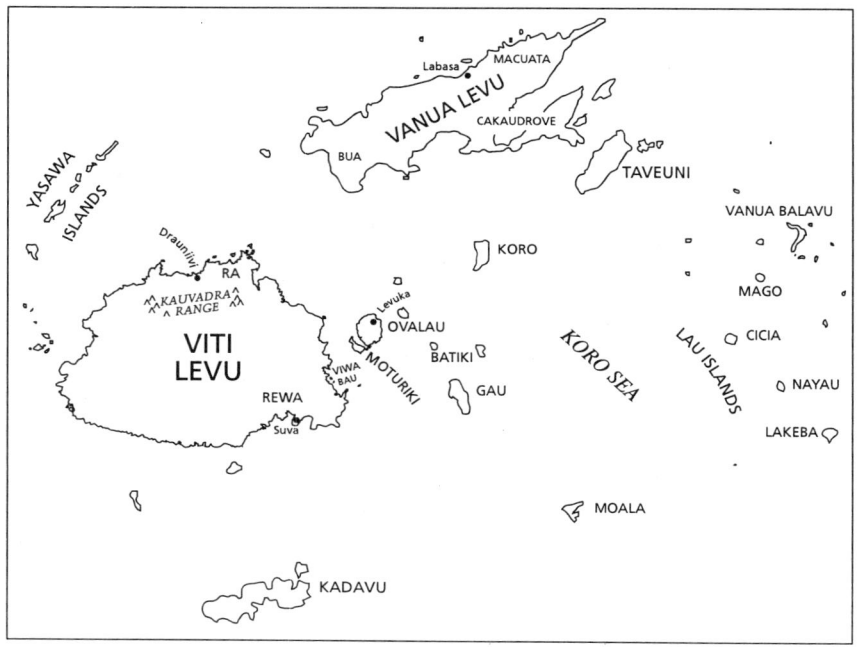

Figure 1. The Fiji Islands.

affirmative reading of the struggle of colonized people to make their histories. For Worsley the context of cults was political-economic, for Burridge a matter of access to moral redemption. Yet both theorists, and the cult literature more generally, accept unquestioned the notion that there *are* "cargo cults," or "millenarian movements," separate distinct phenomena, differing from mainstream social change. In the literature, the so-called cargo cults are often conceived to be moments of transition from one situation or stage to another (indigenous to western, magical to scientific, religious to political). Yet, before I went to Fiji I was skeptical, wondering why this should be so. Why was the political-religious history of Navosavakadua of Drauniivi marked as a "cargo cult" while the political-religious history of Fijian Christian conversion considered unremarkable? Why was Navosavakadua scrutinized as a political-religious "cargo cult" leader, while the ritual-political practice of Fiji's divine kings was taken for granted, even in their present-day transformations as parliamentary politicians? It seemed clear that the concept of cult itself, the bounded unnatural phenomenon, had its roots in colonial perceptions of the unexpected or unwelcome response to a trajectory of Christianization, "civil-

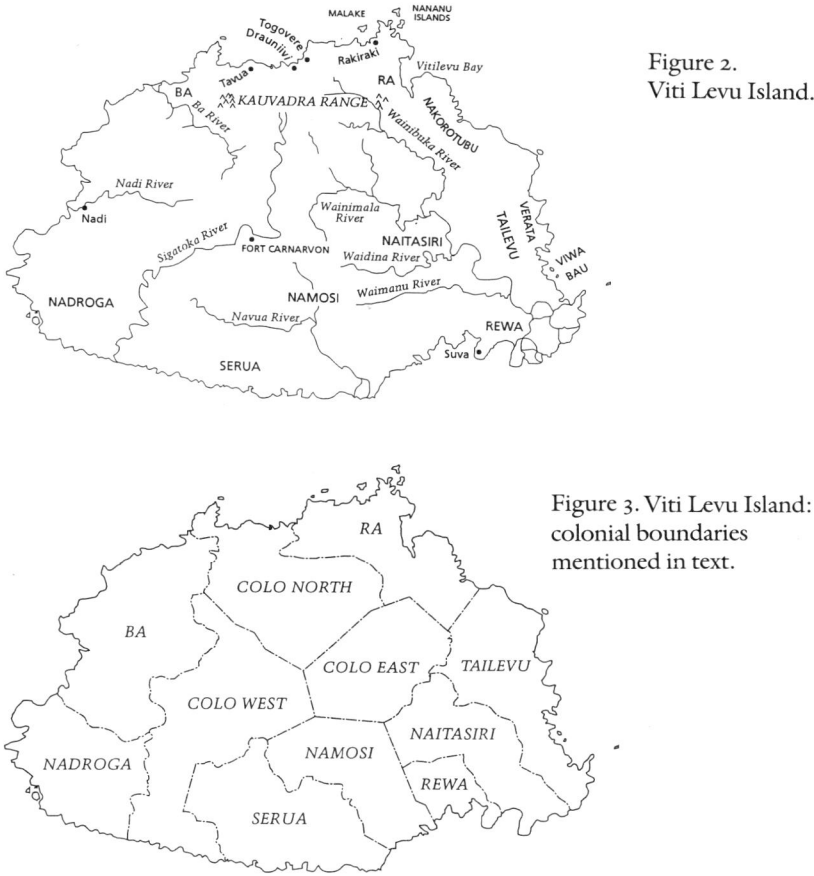

Figure 2. Viti Levu Island.

Figure 3. Viti Levu Island: colonial boundaries mentioned in text.

ization," or "westernization" that the colonizers conceived as natural and inevitable.

Other scholars have queried the concept of cargo cult in various ways. Most elegantly Nancy McDowell has suggested (paralleling Lévi-Strauss on totemism) that "cargo cults do not exist, or at least their symptoms vanish when we start to doubt that we can arbitrarily abstract a few features from context and label them an institution," and further that "as totemism did not exist, being merely an example of how people classify the world around them, cargo cults too do not exist, being merely an example of how people conceptualize and experience change in the world" (1988:121–22) (see also Counts and Counts 1976, Fabian 1979, Fields 1985).

But if, from the beginning, I intended to avoid the colonial reification, to dissolve the concept of cult, to reconsider Navosavakadua and Tuka within the fabric of ongoing Fijian history-making, then my research "epiphany" was also to learn the importance of the one sense in which cults do exist. They exist not necessarily as Pacific or nonwestern phenomena but instead as a category in western culture and colonial practice. In Fiji I found "cults" to be real — and feared — in the official correspondence in the colonial archives, and even in the language of present-day official power. Cults and movements were "things" to colonial officers and have come down to us as such in their records and in administrative practice. On the one hand, as I had expected, the reified colonial category has shaped the scholarly literature, even, paradoxically, in the work of those scholars who contradicted the colonial vision of the activities as sinister or irrational. (One result of the scholarly generalizing and typifying, incidentally, was the overestimation of "cargo," the focus on goods prominent in some New Guinea cases. The desire for "cargo" through ritual means may have struck a special cord in the imagination of capitalist, and even self-consciously anti-capitalist, European observers, both colonial and scholarly. In Fiji, however, Tuka was never primarily about goods; Navosavakadua's project focused on issues of leadership, authority, and autonomy.) On the other hand, I came to find that in Fiji "cults," first imagined and then made real in British colonial practice, have sometimes, though not always, become real in indigenous practice and self-definition, through the influence of powerful colonial projects of inquiry and regulation (see also Foucault 1977, Ginzburg 1983). This is our topic: the dialogical making of a cult and its consequences, out of what began as neither cargo nor cult.

Research Settings

This study was intended specifically as both a historical and an ethnographic project. In consequence, in research in Fiji (six weeks preliminary travel in 1982, a year and a half in 1984–1985, six weeks in 1986, and two months in 1991) I have moved between Drauniivi village in hinterland Ra province and Suva the colonial and post-colonial capital city, and between events in the present and accounts (oral, archival, inscribed on the landscape) of and from the past.

Writing of Drauniivi, I have made no attempt to disguise the name of the village, as it is situated already in a historical and scholarly record. (However, I have not used people's names except where they have specifically asked to be cited, or where they have made themselves publicly known, for example, in newspaper letters to the editor.) And this is no study of Fijian culture based on a village microcosm. Fijian villages themselves are highly heterogeneous — and Fijians themselves are currently at least 33 percent urban (1986 Fiji Census). But whether or not there is such a thing as a typical Fijian village, Drauniivi is certainly not one. Instead it is Drauniivi's unusual characteristics that should interest us. I believe much can be said about Fijian culture and history more generally, when approached from the hinterland perspective of "people of the land."

In the 1880s the name "Drauniivi" became notorious in the colonial record, associated with Navosavakadua and the Tuka movement. In the 1980s I learned to shift the analytic focus of my work from the colonially designated "Drauniivi people" to the history of the Vatukaloko people, the name by which the people currently resident in Drauniivi (and some nearby villages) call themselves. It is a *yavusa* name, a name that signifies common descent, ritual relationship, and a shared political history. It was the name that Navosavakadua and his kin used in the nineteenth century.

In 1984–1985 I lived in Drauniivi among the Vatukaloko people, for seven months spread out over a period of thirteen months. When I was not in the village, I was mainly in the capital city of Suva, sometimes with Vatukaloko relatives who were staying in the city, most often reading at the archives. In the village I lived with a family and participated in ongoing village activities: household tasks, village work, church services, a wide range of rituals, village meetings, preparations to receive visits to the village of local and national dignitaries. I accompanied members of my Fijian family on visits to relatives in other parts of Viti Levu island, to the annual Methodist Conference, to the Ra provincial fundraising festival, etc. I made special trips to meet and talk to knowledgeable custodians of local history in Ra. Throughout my time in Fiji I talked about Navosavakadua with his descendants and with others. In Drauniivi and environs, among the Vatukaloko people, I heard of and observed the ways in which Navosavakadua manifests himself in the lives of his Vatukaloko descendants today. I tape-recorded lengthy accounts of his genealogy, life, and miracles, told by generally acknowledged specialists in local history. I have learned much as well from a lively newspaper debate about Navosavakadua which appeared in 1984–1985 in the Fijian-language newspapers *Nailalakai* and *Siga Rarama*. The articles and letters, claims and rejoinders in this exchange were written by Fijians in debate with one another over their history and their present. In 1986 I visited several nineteenth-century village sites, one of which, Vale Lebo, was built by Navosavakadua. With Vatukaloko sponsors and an archaeologist colleague, I learned more about Navosavakadua's project in the course of surveying and mapping and long conversations about the cosmological landscape where Vale Lebo is situated. In 1991 I returned to Fiji — my first visit after the military coups of 1987 — to learn more about ritual and politics on the national political scene, and to learn more about how the Vatukaloko people continue to view their past and make their history in the hinterlands.

Equally important in the research is the work in Suva. There, in the capital, I attempted to see archives and the documents they house not simply as sources, but as sites and vehicles of the establishment and practice of official power. Of course when I read colonial minute papers about Navosavakadua and "the Tuka" I learned much about Fijian projects and categories. But I learned even more about colonial concepts of order and disorder, and the making of the Tuka cult in British colonial imagination. I also learned much about Fiji's colonial and post-colonial history by considering the archives as a field site, by considering the way the papers and artifacts were housed and organized in the National Archives of Fiji, at the archives of the Native Lands Trust Board, and at the archives of religious organizations, by charting the processes through which I and others were allowed or denied access to documents and following the current use of records in political practice in the post-colonial nation.

Finally, outside of Drauniivi and outside of the archives I learned of others in 1980s Fiji who sought to mobilize Navosavakadua's name and *mana*. In my research I also inquired into contesting narratives of Navosavakadua, interviewing and observing other Fiji citizens, including an Indo-Fijian visionary with his own version of Navosavakadua's significance in Fiji's past and present. There has been no single dominant truth about Navosavakadua and Tuka. Neither his descendants among the Vatukaloko people, nor colonial officials, nor scholars, have completely controlled the story of his life, though some among them have tried to do so. Thus I have come to think of this research and this book, at least in part, as a history of struggles to make and remake a sign.

ACKNOWLEDGMENTS

Above all I thank the people of *yavusa* Vatukaloko of Drauniivi village and their relatives in Ra and elsewhere in the islands for their *loloma* and for the opportunity to begin to learn from them about their remarkable ancestor and their special history. Most specially I warmly thank Epeli and Mere Nauwa and all the family at Kabukilagi for their kindly love. I warmly thank Jone Tuiwai, Turaga ni Koro retired, for sharing with me his extensive knowledge of history. I thank his family for their patience and kindness. I offer my gratitude to the Tui Vatu and the people of *mataqali* Nasi, Wakalou, Nakubuti, and Nasaro for all their hospitality and for teaching me so much. My warm thanks also to former Head Teacher at the Drauniivi Public School Aseri Waqa and the late Nani Waqa for introducing me into the village, and also to former manager at Yaqara John Fatiaki and Fane Fatiaki for guidance and hospitality. My thanks go as well to Vika Kidi Tagivuni for assistance in translation and especially to Vasiti Ritova for assistance in translation and for sharing her knowledge in so many other aspects of the research.

For hospitality while in Suva, I thank Shiu and Kamala Lal and family, and remember with affection the late Mrs. Phulbasi Singh. My thanks also to Bijan and Uttra Singh and family.

I thank the late Mr. Harigyan Samalia for talking with me and John Kelly in 1984.

For hospitality, scholarly collegiality, and friendship, I further thank Fergus Clunie, Ivan and Ateca Williams, Ratu Jone Madraiwiwi, Paul Geraghty, Pio and Salusalu Manoa and family, and Margaret Patel. Special thanks to Tevita Nawadra whose introduction provided my path to Drauniivi.

For initial language study while in Suva I thank Mere Vunibaka and Jone Cagi.

I thank the Fiji Government for permission to pursue research in Fiji in 1984–1985, 1986, and 1991. For access to archives and collections and for other scholarly assistance I gratefully thank Setariki Tuinaceva, Archivist, the National Archives of Fiji, and the staff at the Archives, especially Margaret Patel; I thank Fergus Clunie, then Director of the Fiji Museum, and all the staff at the museum; and I also thank Col. V. Navunisaravi, Commissioner of the Native Lands Commission, and the staff there. I also thank the Methodist Church of Fiji and the Roman Catholic Archdiocese, Suva, for the use of archival collections.

I further thank those institutions in New Zealand and Australia cited throughout the book for access to their various archives and collections. In particular I thank the Australian National University, Research School of Pacific Studies, and especially Dr. Deryck Scarr for his scholarly cordiality.

For funding to pursue research and writing I thank the National Science Foundation, the Department of Education Fulbright-Hays Fellowship Program, the Institute for Intercultural Studies, the Charlotte W. Newcombe Foundation, the Wenner Gren Foundation for Anthropological Research, and Vassar College. Additional thanks to Vassar College for funding for maps and indexing. Thanks to Jonah Shaw of Meredith Productions for preparing the maps.

Chapter 4 appeared in somewhat shorter form as "The Dangerous and Disaffected Native in Fiji: British Colonial Constructions of the Tuka Movement" in *Social Analysis Journal of Cultural and Social Practice* 26, published by the Department of Anthropology, University of Adelaide, South Australia.

This book began as a dissertation. I especially thank my teachers Marshall Sahlins and Bernard Cohn. Thanks also to Robert and Nancy Foster, Mark Francillon, Jane Fajans, and James Fernandez. For collegial assistance of many sorts I thank Don Brenneis and Henry Rutz. The dissertation would never have become a book without Ken Wissoker.

My husband John D. Kelly has been a part of the research and writing of this work from beginning to end as he pursued his own research in the Indo-Fijian community. Every page bears the improvement of his thoughtful comments.

To my teachers, relatives, friends and colleagues — and especially to the Vatukaloko people — I offer thanks for what I have learned, and I acknowledge my responsibility for misunderstandings, errors, and things I have yet to learn.

NEITHER CARGO NOR CULT

1

INTRODUCTION: CULTURE, HISTORY, AND COLONIALISM

Agency and Meaning in Colonial History

What shapes the lives of colonized people? Is their agency a product of indigenous cultural systematics, rejecting, encompassing, transforming external change? Or is colonial power the prevailing force in their lives; do they respond to, react to, resist incursion, in an agency already therefore shaped by colonial hegemonic structures? How are anthropologists to understand encounters, conjunctures, domination, asymmetries of power, beyond first contact moments into the complex societies of a connected colonial and postcolonial world? How, in particular, can we rethink a part of Fijian colonial history previously called a cargo cult?[1]

In establishing our rapprochement with history, it seems to me that anthropologists have used three analytic strategies to write about agency, meaning,

---

1. For readers unfamiliar with the very term "cargo cult," consider these quotations from a famous essay by F. E. Williams, an administrator-anthropologist in New Guinea in the 1920s and 30s.

> During the latter months of the year 1919 there began in the Gulf Division that singular and really important movement known as the Vailala Madness.
>
> Originating in the neighbourhood of Vailala, whence it spread rapidly through the coastal and certain of the inland villages, this movement involved, on the one hand, a set of preposterous beliefs among its victims—in particular the expectation of an early visit from their deceased relatives—and, on the other hand, collective nervous symptoms of a sometimes grotesque and idiotic nature. . . .

and colonial history. One strategy insists on the priority of cultural difference. Here the concept of culture and cultural difference, the preeminent contribution of anthropology to the social sciences, is invoked to shape accounts both of indigenous change and of indigenous apprehension of external incursion. One leading example is Marshall Sahlins's "structure and history" including his recent work on the multiple cosmologies driving the capitalist world system (1981, 1985, 1988, 1992). Another example is David Lan's (1985) account of the agency of spirit mediums in the guerilla war to liberate Zimbabwe. This approach produces narratives which insist upon local categories of meaning and local agency for an understanding of encounters with the world system or colonizing peoples.

In contrast, a second analytic strategy sees colonial power as the overwhelming tension-charged historical watershed forever changing the world of the colonized. Here colonial societies are understood to be products of the agency of external transformative dominators, and colonized people can emerge again as agents in their own right only as colonized, local, already transformed, resisters. Instances of this approach include world system scholars such as Eric Wolf (1982) who find transforming agency in capitalist penetration, and also studies which, influenced by Foucault or Gramsci, focus on discourse and particular (here colonial) systems of meaning and practice beyond the realm of political economy narrowly defined—law, literature, sexuality—that dominate and transform (see, e.g., Cohn 1987, Said 1978, Stoler 1989). For many such scholars the emphasis is on colonial constructions of others, especially those accounts which find any scholarship concerning "others" so intricately implicated in western categories or in the mechanisms of colonial domination that concepts of "culture" and "cultural difference" themselves become artifacts of colonial categorizing (Said 1978, and see, e.g., Clifford and Marcus 1986).

A third strategy finds a space in between insistence on cultural continuity and insistence on colonial transformation. As figured in Michael Taussig's (1987) recent work on terror, that space is chaotic: neither indigenous nor

---

> Perhaps one of the most fundamental ideas was that the ancestors, or more usually the deceased relatives, of the people were shortly to return to visit them. They were expected in a large steamer, which was to be loaded with cases of gifts—tobacco, calico, knives, axes, food-stuffs, and the like. (Williams 1977:331–41)

From such depictions came the general term "cargo cult." In this book it is my intention to challenge the very idea that this is a general phenomenon or a useful analytic concept (see preface, this volume).

colonial but an "epistemic murk" in between. The epistemic murk extends from participants to chroniclers. In Taussig's view such spaces almost defy portrayal, since even counterrepresentations and counterdiscourses risk replicating colonizer's discourses; montage and incompleteness are the techniques he uses to represent the chaotics he finds.

Establishing a strategy for writing a colonial history — as an anthropologist — is not a hypothetical question here. I want to begin with four narratives out of Fiji's past and present: a colonial official's essay, a present-day Fijian's recollection of an ancestor, a brief reconstruction of what I think Navosavakadua might have intended, and a cosmological history by an Indo-Fijian[2] visionary mystic. In their disjunctures and interrelations lie the problems I want to address.

Intersecting Narratives: Navosavakadua or the Tuka?

A Colonial Officer's Narrative of Tuka

In 1891 John Bates Thurston, British colonial governor of Fiji from 1888 to 1897, asked A. B. Joske,[3] irrepressible memoirist and commissioner and magistrate in the hill districts and Ra province, to summarize "the movement" in an article for *The Australasian*, a Sydney-based newspaper. I excerpt from this article:

> Superstition in Fiji
>
> In the country round about Kauvadra, the Mount Olympus of Fiji, there seems to have been always prevalent a superstition called by the natives the "Tuka," the priests of which professed to possess an elixir of life. . . .
>
> The first historical knowledge of it was about 30 years ago, when, owing to the spread of Christianity, the natives of different districts became able to have freer intercourse with one another [due to the cessation of warfare]. About then Saro Saro, a high priest of the "Tuka," gave a good deal of trouble to the late King Cakobau . . . [and was eventually] put to death by his tribal chief.

---

2. In different historical periods the people of Fiji descended from South Asian indentured laborers have been known as "Indians," "Fiji Indians," and "Indo-Fijians." I follow historian Brij Lal (e.g., 1992) in using "Indo-Fijian."

3. Adolph Brewster Joske later changed his name to A. B. Brewster, and as Brewster published *The Hill Tribes of Fiji* (1922) and other works on Fiji.

However, Saro Saro left a descendant, said to be his son — one Dugamoi — who, engrafting his native legends and superstitions on the Biblical narratives compounded a new Tuka. . . . [Dugamoi] established a great reputation among the followers of the "Tuka" as a high priest and prophet who gave him the title of "Na Vosa va Ka dua" [sic] literally, the man who speaks only once and must be obeyed. The Chief Justice of the colony . . . holds this title of honor amongst Fijians.

Dugamoi first came prominently into notice about the end of the year 1877. He then made a tour through the least civilized portions of Viti Levu [the main island of the Fiji group], predicting a millennium when all who died as faithful votaries of the faith would rise again, and aided by divine powers sweep all unbelievers from the face of the earth. . . .

The people of the eastern highlands of Fiji, partially conquered under King Cakobau's reign, closely related to those of the eastern highlands, who in 1876 had been in revolt against British authority, and who during that trying period had been with great difficulty kept steady, became very uneasy and excited, and to secure absolute peace Na Vosa va Ka dua had to be . . . deported to one of the eastern islands of the group, but after a short period of detention he was allowed to return to his home.

Again he started to preach his new and improved version of the "Tuka" supplementing native legends with what he found in the Bible. These doctrines have gradually spread over the northern coasts and eastern highlands of Fiji. . . . In the year 1885 Na Vosa va Ka dua began to have men drilled. Although the new reign of the "Tuka" was to be ushered in by the miraculous assistance of the gods, probably soldiers were thought to be a useful, if not necessary adjunct. No doubt Na Vosa va Ka dua aimed at the overthrow of the British Government in the group and the extinction of the Christian religion and of the white settlers. The drilling of troops speedily came under the notice of the authorities and warrants under the English statute prohibiting illegal drilling were issued. At first, these warrants were resisted, but after a brief period of anxiety to the authorities the ringleaders were secured without bloodshed. The chief prophet, Na Vosa va Ka dua, was exiled to Rotumah [a small island outside the Fiji group, which the British colonized and administered from Fiji] and others were sentenced to various terms of imprisonment.

With the removal of the leader and prime spirit of this movement it was thought that the fanaticism would die out a natural death, but there remained many priests of the "Tuka" who found that the steady spread of Christianity and progress of settled government interfered materially with the revenue they formerly derived from the simple credulity of their fellow countrymen. These men during the present year stirred up a vigorous revival of the "Tuka." They predicted the re-appearance of Na Vosa va Ka dua exalting him into a divine personage whom the foreign Government had in vain endeavored to kill. . . .

A village called Drau-ni-ivi and a few of its outlying hamlets have been the centre from which this disturbing movement has radiated. Whales teeth, answering to the Chupatties [sic] of the Indian Mutiny have been sent out from there calling upon the faithful to rally and be united for the overthrow of the Government.

It is a foolish, fantastic and fanatic movement. This is now its third outbreak, and it became absolutely necessary that it should be put down with a strong hand. The votaries of it mainly dwell in the glens and valleys of a rugged and almost inaccessible district. Knowing nothing of the power of the Government and seeing but little of the symbols of authority, they consider themselves all powerful and important. In time the delay of miraculous aid must have been explained by their priests, to whom but one explanation would have been possible unless they confessed themselves powerless impostors. This would have been the non-satisfactory propitiation of their tutelary gods and ancestral spirits. . . . To those cognisant of the traditions and inner thoughts of Fijians it is well known there could be only one satisfactory offering to Fijian gods, and that is human sacrifices, the burnt offering alike of Assyrian and Druidical superstitions.

The foregoing is a brief summary of the origin and progress of the "Tuka" superstition, which has been to the Government from the first a source of trouble and uneasiness. Its recent vigorous revival induced the Governor to personally investigate the matter, and for this purpose . . . he made a three weeks tour through the central mountainous districts of Viti Levu. . . . His Excellency deemed it the wisest and most merciful course to remove [the people of Drauniivi] at least for a while to a more civilised portion of the group where there would be little likelihood of their pernicious doctrines gaining credence . . . to prevent the spread of the "Tuka" superstition among the simple, yet wild, half-Christianized, half-civilized tribes living in the ranges at the back of Drau-ni-ivi. . . .

The Drau-ni-ivi people have therefore been removed, and are now located on good fertile Crown lands in the island of Kadavu. . . .

The Kadavu Islanders, possessing a large intermixture of Tongan blood, are perhaps the most advanced and intelligent . . . of our Fijian population. There is therefore no fear of the "Tuka" doctrines being received by them otherwise than with ridicule and it may reasonably be hoped that finding themselves among a strong but law-abiding and civilised community the Drau-ni-ivi people will profit by their association with them by qualifying themselves for what they will certainly long for — a permission to return to their own mountain district. (17 October 1891, attached to Colonial Secretary's Office minute paper 94/2036)[4]

4. References to minute papers in the Colonial Secretary's Office series, held at the National Archives of Fiji, will henceforth be by number only. The first two digits indicate the year, and the last digits the number in the series.

This narrative reveals central themes in the colonial imagination of "the Tuka." Joske finds no paradox in the topic: he presents an account tracing the origin, diffusion, alteration, and consequences of a doctrine of "Tuka." Joske's Tuka is either an autonomous phenomenon, a superstition which spreads like a disease in a receptive population, or an ideology perpetrated by its charlatan-priest author on a credulous faithful. By contrasting rebellious hill and interior people, prey to their charlatan leader, with the "advanced and intelligent" (and lighter-skinned) Kadavu islanders under "King" Cakobau, he constructs Tuka as marginal, deviant, and criminal, in the face of a developing colonial order on a British model. The article itself is a product of the colonial concern with self-presentation and legitimation of the colonial project, in the face of a wider, sometimes critical, audience of many factions in the larger Empire. It expresses as well much about colonial British concepts of society, order, religion, and legitimacy that I will explore in later chapters. Here, I want to note that in this British imagination of these Fijian events Tuka was construed to be a named doctrine leading to rebellion and disorder, and to note as well that this British imagination was no fanciful contemplation. Constructions of Tuka such as these would lead to arrests and deportation for Navosavakadua and the people of Drauniivi.

Narratives by Some of Navosavakadua's Present-Day Descendants

In contrast, when I sought to discuss the topic constructed in such colonial accounts with Fijian informants, a differently bounded narrative emerged.

Nowadays Fijians do not generally know the meaning of the word "Tuka." In Drauniivi village, among the people who call themselves Vatukaloko (a kin group and ritual name), those older people who do know it say, for example, "It was a thing of the devil, practiced by a heathen priest, who was not our relative. The people of Rakiraki knew it, we did not. Navosavakadua led the faction who rejected this thing of the devil which did not go in accordance with the ways of God, nonetheless we were blamed" (my summary and translation of a longer statement by a Nasi man). One informant added, "there is a law against it." This was all they had to say on the subject of Tuka, not, I believe, because they were afraid to tell me more, but because the word is not a focus of practice or concern to them. Moreover, the word is not used nowadays to describe any of the other practices (e.g., local healing, "witchcraft," and invocation of Fijian deities) which are sometimes classed as "things of the devil." Attempting to investigate "the Tuka movement" I drew a blank.[5] But Navosavakadua, his life, and deeds are a vast indigenously constructed topic, subject of discourse in at least two important indigenous genres: oral accounts (both formal narratives related by elders with specialized knowledge and gossip and anecdotes told by younger people and the less knowledgeable) and written accounts in Fijian-language newspapers. And then of course there is the role of Navosavakadua in the lives of his living descendants.

Here is a narrative of Navosavakadua by one of his descendants. In the 1980s this man was the elected headman *(Turaga ni Koro)* of Drauniivi village. (The administrative office of *Turaga ni Koro* originated in colonial indirect rule; the office is rarely held by Fijians of chiefly rank.) This gentleman is a historical and genealogical specialist. In particular he is heir to the knowledge of kin groups and relationships of the Vatukaloko people that was compiled by the village's representatives to the Natives Lands Commission in 1918, about which much more will be said in chapter 6.

> He [Navosavakadua] was a shy man who did not speak much. He didn't know evil paths. What happened to him was that he was given a task. He was a man of the *mataqali* (ritual kin group) Nakubuti, of the Makita subdivision. His hereditary standing *(itutu vakavanua)* was "*bulibulivanua*" [literally "maker of the land"; people of this standing install the Vatukaloko chief]. His father was Rareba Vunisa, whose third name was Tavakece. He was Navosavakadua's true father. His mother was Namasala, a lady from *yavusa* (ritual kin group) Navisama, from the village of Narara.
>
> His daily work was as a farmer. When our ancestors left the old village of Nakorowaiwai they lived at Waisai. In the mornings he used to go to bring his crops from the gardens at the old village.
>
> At the hill inland called Vatunisauka he went and met with the *mana* (miraculous or effective power) or the word which was given to him. He heard a voice, he didn't see any people. I don't know if it was a devil or God who spoke, he heard the voice say to him, "Mosese Dukumoi" (for that was his true name, the name given to him

---

5. Once while visiting in the interior district of Tokaimalo I asked an elderly gentleman about Tuka. Impatient and bewildered he turned to his son and the schoolteacher who was my escort. "She wants to know about dirt *(duka)*?" he asked. Any notion I might have had that embers of Tuka were smoldering in this community in the shadow of the Kauvadra range was considerably diminished as I was called upon to define Tuka. After I explained it as the British name for the beliefs and practices of Navosavakadua, I asked whether he knew any stories of Navosavakadua, or of the old days before the raising of the colonial flag. These topics he discussed without needing a gloss.

by his father and mother). . . . the echo of the voice said to him "Mosese, I want to take you, I anoint you to be my servant." And Mosese answered "what am I to do for you?" Then the voice said to him "I want you to spread the news that you can make people live [*vakabula na tamata,* literally make people live, sometimes also save people, in the Christian sense]. Do you want this power? If you want some other thing, wisdom, or to live peacefully, or anything you want, I will give it to you." Then Mosese Dukumoi said "I don't want anything, I only want you to give me the power to make people live." Then he heard the voice again, "If I give you the power to make life, will you achieve every task I set you?" He answered, "yes, I will try." Thus the task was given to him. . . .

And his religion, it was not Seventh Day Adventist, nor Wesleyan, nor Church of England, nor Catholic. Before they arrived, he had a religion, and it was the religion of God, he served God, he preached about God, before these other religions came. . . .

And when the power had been given to him, the people of the Twelve Tribes [Biblical twelve tribes, the term used now to name the indigenous confederation of peoples whom Navosavakadua led] then they called him Navosavakadua. He would speak once, then the command would be fulfilled. I don't know what kind of power it was, whether from devils or God, but I know that the God he served is the God we worship today.

There are many stories of the "miracles" of Navosavakadua, but the following one is probably the most important to Fijians, and, for different reasons, was important (in earlier versions) to European colonial officers as well.

A man died. He was baked with the food. His name was Atunaisa Sega, he is an ancestor of the people of the Wakalou kin group here in the village. Navosa told all the Twelve Tribes to assemble so that they might see the work he did. When the food (root crops) and the pig had been buried in the earth oven, then Atunaisa was brought. He didn't come in fear or refusing, he just came the way Jesus came, so that they could bury him in the earth oven. . . .

When the earth oven was ready it was dug open. It was steaming. The pig was cooked and the rootcrops were cooked, the man remained. He was bent over, there was no sign of a wound on him. Then Navosavakadua called three times "Atu, Atu, Atu, these people are here watching you. The pig is cooked, the food is cooked, the man is there. But how is the man?" He said to the people, "Now you will see the power I have been given, to make to live." Again he cried thrice, "Atu, Atu, Atu," and our ancestor stood up. "Brush the dirt off of your body so that you may see the ability of making to live that has been given to me." And he said, "You all can now tell the story. I don't know where the ability came from, whether from God or the Devil, but it is just the work given to me, to make men to live. See here. It is roasted, the food is cooked, the pig is cooked, but the man lives. All of you see it. Sit here and eat."

The food was brought. And no matter how many tens and twenties of them ate, and there was only one pig, and a set number of baskets of root crops, but however many ate there was still food left. And then he did another miracle following this. He told them, you put together all the bones of the pig, not leaving one aside. And they did this, then he called, and the pig got up and ran off.

But then there was trouble. The news of this was heard by the government. Then he was arrested. This occurred at the old village site here. The flag of the colonial government had been raised at the time. They said he did *"cakacaka vakatevoro"* (heathen works) or that he did *tuka*. Then he was taken away. There was not yet a road, he went overland. . . .

Then he arrived in Suva, where they imprisoned him in jail. They didn't give him food, yet he lived. They put him in a bag, weighted it, and put it in Beqa bay, in the middle of the water. Yet when the officer returned, he was standing on the wharf. This man and these works, they were not heathen works. If this was the work of the devil, he wouldn't have been able to do this kind of thing. He would just speak, and the thing would be done. I don't think a devil could do this. This is God's work.

Then they sent him to Lau island, and they tried to shoot him. This part of Navosa's work concerns Ratu Mara [a high chief of Lau and the prime minister of Fiji in 1984 when this story was told]. Ratu Mara's power is going strong now. Navosa was shot three times in Lau. When the King of Lau shot him twice, the third time he said "don't shoot me." But the government had made the decision. Then the King of Lau said "it is not possible for me to kill this man." Then Navosa said to the King of Lau, "Here is my present to you. One of your descendants will bring light to Fiji." This is Ratu Mara today.

All these things happened, then it was said that he be sent to Rotuma. He got married there to a lady named Mereseini Namoce. They had three children the oldest, a daughter, the second a boy named Timoci Nagata (Timothy the snake) because he was born twin with a snake. Their descendants live at Rabulu village and Vatusekiyasawa village, and in Drauniivi today.

That is the story concerning his life. If someone asks about your research, about Navosavakadua, you explain all this to them, and you tell them that "the explanation was given to me by the Turaga ni Koro (village headman) of Drauniivi village."

I have not heard any story of his competitiveness, or his giving a bad order. His possessions were left here, his *tanoa* (kava bowl) and his *kali* (wooden headrest). They are not weapons of fighting or destroying people or war. These are the goods of life. (Mr. Jone Tuiwai, Turaga ni Koro of Drauniivi village, 29 October 1984, my translation)

On the surface the Turaga ni Koro's account portrays his ancestor as a biblical martyr, utterly opposite to the "charlatan leader" portrayed by Mr. Joske. As we shall see, his insistence on Navosavakadua's devotion to Jehovah and his peaceful life affirms a current Vatukaloko-Christian cosmological system, which has taken shape over the last century in the dialogue between the nineteenth-century Navosavakadua's intents and actions, the Christian conversion of the coastal kingdoms, and the British interpretations and punitive reactions detailed in Mr. Joske's account.

Navosavakadua's Narrative?

Also revealed in this account, however, are continuants to a narrative that we can only begin to imagine: the narrative that Navosavakadua and his nineteenth-century followers might have told themselves about themselves as they carried out their history-making project. When the Turaga ni Koro tells us that Navosavakadua knew God before the European religions came to Fiji, he interprets what I take to be an aspect of the nineteenth-century Navosavakadua's insistence that Jehovah and Jesus were Fijian gods and that true power in Fiji was inherent in gods and people of the land. Further, when the Turaga ni Koro gives Navosavakadua's hereditary standing as *bulibulivanua* (literally "maker of the land" or installer of the chief) he avoids saying that Navosavakadua was a hereditary oracle-priest *(bete)*, but also suggests the important connection between Navosavakadua's hereditary standing and the notion of "making the land." (In this case Mr. Joske was right in calling Navosavakadua a hereditary priest, as older Fijian sources show, though he does not know their full meaning in a Fijian context.) For all that Navosavakadua's deeds may now be constructed as peaceful, in the context of nineteenth-century Fijian society the ability to raise a man alive from the cannibal oven would betoken a mastery over fertility and creativity in spheres of war, the ritual-politics of leadership, and the fruitfulness of the land. His *mana* (miraculous effective ability) here demonstrated as his ability to *veivakabulai* (save, or make to live) could be understood both in its nineteenth-century forms as an indigenous Fijian principle of effectiveness and power, and as it is now constructed and combined with a Christian concept of miracle-working.

We will return many times to these three narratives and their relations to each other. But we should also consider an example of the power Navosavakadua's memory has now for others as they frame new stories about Fiji's history. Navosavakadua's memory and reputation are powerful, and one new invocation of them gained particular notoriety in the 1980s.

Navosavakadua as Avatar

Not only "Fijians" live in the Fiji islands. There are two major groups in the post-colonial nation. "Fijians" or "ethnic Fijians" are considered to be descendants of the indigenous Pacific Islanders of the nineteenth century (about 48 percent of the population). "Fiji Indians" or "Indo-Fijians" are descendants of indentured laborers from South Asia who came to work British sugar plantations from 1879 to 1920, and other immigrants from South Asia (currently about 48 percent). Long kept separate by the British, since 1970 ethnic Fijians and Indo-Fijians have been faced with the task of together making a nation. The task has been complex and most recently tragic. In 1987 military coups replaced a "multiracial" Labour government with new thoroughly ethnic-Fijian chauvinist governments and constitution. Fijians are very close to 100 percent Christian, Indo-Fijians 80 percent Hindu with small Muslim and Christian groups. There is little history of intermarriage or explicit cultural syncretism. This fourth narrative, an explicit syncretist project, presents one of the very few exceptions.

Utterly atypical of most Indo-Fijians, and with little or no support from either Indo-Fijians or Fijians, an Indo-Fijian visionary mystic propounded his own vision and version of Navosavakadua. In 1984 this gentleman traveled to Drauniivi to raise Navosavakadua's flag and to prophesy in his name. He said of Navosavakadua's place in Fiji's cosmology and in world history:

> The King of Kings began as Krishna of the Mahabharata who when he had finished his work in India disappeared and changed his form. He sent a snake to Fiji, then went to Fiji himself and became incarnated as Navosavakadua, there he performed miracles and was deported. . . . Navosa said to the people of Drauniivi "Don't worry if I am gone for long. My flag will be raised." He pushed two stones into the ground, saying "When the stones rise it will be time." Those stones are now two feet above the ground. Then he went to Germany and became Hitler, he shaped the world, it was growing fast at that time. At another time he was incarnated as Jesus Christ. He returns each time in different forms. His next incarnation will be as a Fijian to found the new Kingdom on Maqo island in the Lau Group. The living God will arise from earth, flowers will sing, dogs will speak like humans. Fifteen

thousand flyers have been distributed prophesying this. (From my notes of a conversation with Mr. Harigyan Samalia in Suva, 1984)

We will return to this narrative, the late Mr. Samalia's visits to Drauniivi, and his vision of a unified nation of Fiji, in which all gods are one, in chapter 7.

Approaches to Culture, History, and Colonialism

So as not to be disingenuous, I must begin by saying that I have never considered these to be simply four narratives. There is a history already to the relation of these accounts (and the many other accounts from which I have selected these few), a history of interactions — of subjugation, incitement, construction, and powerful creativity, both official and hinterland — between these peoples, the Fijians, Europeans, and Indo-Fijians of the nineteenth century and the present. But how to narrate such a history? Is it one of cultural difference, indigenous transformation? Or of colonial hegemony and resistance? Of epistemic murk? Or is it a history that cannot be told, the very project itself misguided?

The Pacific has long been part of western scholarly proofs of plural "societies" and "cultures," at least since the days of Malinowski and Mead. One analytic strategy continues the theme of cultural difference as the defining force in anthropological and historical analysis. Insisting on cultural difference, the structure and history approach (Sahlins 1981, 1985, 1988, 1992, Hooper and Huntsman 1985) writes histories of Pacific people already with history, chronicling internally generated transformations in Pacific societies, and demonstrating the power of Pacific people to encompass novel agents and actions within existing categories and practices. Most radically, this approach makes the claim that not just structures (systems of categories) but also ways of making history are culturally different and irrevocably plural. These plural structures, histories, and agencies are seen as real, recoverable, and ongoing.

To adopt this analytic strategy to tell the story of Navosavakadua and Tuka would be to insist on the reality and the precedence of a non-western history, to write a narrative dominated by Fijian kingdoms, chiefs, warrior allies, and oracle-priests. Such a narrative would privilege Navosavakadua's own project, and its continuants and continuities into the lives of present-day Vatukaloko people of Drauniivi and environs. Considering British colonialism in Fiji it would stress the projects of Fijians as they shaped the system of "indirect rule" and the genealogical and structural continuities between pre-colonial, colonial, and post-colonial leaders. Its priority would be the reconstructive project, the search for Navosavakadua's own narrative. Here, the structure and history approach would be quite close to the otherwise dissimilar Subaltern Studies movement (see Guha et al. 1982 and subsequent volumes), seeking a hidden other's narrative, believed to have a superior reality and moral force.

To emphasize colonial power instead would create a narrative that replaces indigenous avoidance, encompassment of, or triumph over the novel, with the story of the brutal or subtle workings of external incursion. Such narratives find agency and the real in the transformations wrought by capitalism and colonizers. If the ground of analysis is the connected world system, then capitalist penetration with its global logic would be the key agent of change. In such a narrative Tuka, far from reflecting an "untouched" indigenous culture, an island of history, might owe its impetus and its form to Navosa's experience as a laborer on a copra plantation (cf. Keesing 1988). If hidden transcripts are still to be sought (as in Scott 1990) they are bound to speak to the colonially made world, even if ironic or resistant.

Another narrative strategy finds colonial power infiltrating the lives of "others" in realms beyond the political economic, but equally real. Meaning itself is the ground of manipulation, and of contest. Foucault, and Gramsci and Williams, from whom are drawn the current, almost omnipresent tropes of "hegemony" and "resistance," have laid the grounds for seeing in western polities and colonial societies the power of discourse and disciplinary practices to remake people's lives, to define the natural, and to constrain their very vision of the possible. Such a story would insist on following contact moments into routine colonialism (see Asad's (1973) use of the term) and the "post-colonial" nation itself. It would analyze the colonial apparatus—legal, economic, medical, educational, sexual—for the explicit and subtle transformations of meaning that created of Fijians a new and colonized sort of people. Most subtly we might find in Tuka, in the very resistance of a Navosavakadua, the terms and categories of the colonizers, indeed turned back upon them but operating nonetheless to expand a powerful and inescapable colonial discourse.

A third narrative strategy finds neither colonial hegemony nor indigenous encompassment, but rather a confused, disorderly space in between. Contemplating contradictions, chaos, and terror in the colonial terrain of the Columbian rubber plantations Taussig (1987) finds no coherent systems, old or new, but rather a jungle in which practices and images of terror (colonial and indigenous) reinforce each other. In such colonial spaces, the colonizers and the colonized seek meaning and agency, but their possibilities for agency are of the most brutal sort. Acting on the basis of fears, projections, fantasies, rumors, and fragments of information, they dwell in terror and make the most horrendous images real. To write such a narrative of Tuka we would look to the chaotics, the incomplete and unknowable aspects of both colonial and Fijian powers and practices, highlighting the cruelties and the colonial and Fijian images of the wild and powerful. But though some colonial places and times may indeed be terrains of epistemic murk (and Taussig is most convincing in the history he tells) not all are so chaotic. If we write of Tuka as neither indigenous nor colonial, but novel, must it be chaotic? Calling Tuka chaotic might even be complicit with colonial discourse, which relied on the trope of disorder to describe it. Could it not be systematic, in a novel way?

Most radical (at least in self-depiction) is that version of the narrative of colonial power that finds no reality beyond the contingency of narratives themselves. The epistemological argument that all narrative truths are partial, each limited by its narrator and context and genre of narration, comes from Said, from Marcus and Clifford, as well as from Taussig, and of course from Geertz (1973). The question is not what can we know of Tuka or Navosavakadua, but, why do we ask? Uncomfortable but important questions can be asked from this perspective about the genealogy of our curiosity leading us back to A. B. Joske. What is the relationship between his two personae as colonial official and amateur anthropologist? Are the theorists of cargo cults his scholarly inheritors? Am I? Is interest in "others" simply a vehicle for construction of the self? Is anthropological knowing, objectifying, codifying, describing simply a further exercise in colonial power-knowledge? Can we know anything of others past or present, and is our interest in knowing hopelessly, colonially compromised? Joske's own story is a fascinating tale of self-transformation, from suspect German-named merchant into Kipling-quoting official of the British Empire through the mechanisms of administration and publication. Would it be wiser to follow this narrative strategy and to write only of Mr. Joske? And of the nonexistence of cults? Wiser? Or safer?

In this book I want to argue for one possible resolution to the question of analytic and narrative strategy. First of all, I want to insist on, to privilege the premise that there is reality to this Fijian colonial history — a reality we cannot ever fully know or write that is nevertheless a ground irreducible to trope or audience for the estimation of truth. We do not need to seek a unitary true narrative of Navosavakadua and Tuka in order to acknowledge the existence of this reality. In fact, because audience and rhetorical tropes are also not reducible, there is no one "true" history of Tuka. Each of the narratives I have cited above must be understood as a construction, a partial truth if you will. And nothing I write is able or intended to reconcile or tidy up the ongoing revisions, contestations, forgettings, and multivalences, the unknowns and spaces and narratives with lives of their own that are the stuff of human history-making—indeed the stuff of the narrative I hope to write. But all is not contingent. There is more to be said of each account than the text itself, a contextualization that can move the uncommitted reader from incomprehension to awareness. (There is nothing new in this argument; it is the old cultural anthropological strategy. To my mind, the crucial break between Joske's "anthropology" and ours today is the Boasian insistence on respect, relativism, and the denaturalization of one's own culture through study of others.)

Perhaps more importantly, I would argue that there have never been simply four (or however many) "narratives" of Tuka. These narratives have been created and expressed, not simply in cultural contexts (to be explicated with reference to categories of meaning) but in ongoing projects—efforts to act, to engage, to contest, support, make, and change things and people. Narratives of Tuka have been expressed within indigenous, colonial, and post-colonial frameworks of discourse and cultural interaction. There have always been motives and consequences attached to the constructions of Tuka. We can know some of these motives and also some of these consequences: ritual spaces claimed and reclaimed, built and rebuilt; floggings and deportations; definitions fixed through documents and through prophecies; flags raised in extraordinarily contested redefinitions.

What I want to do, then, in my narrative, is to find a story of the making of narratives and a story of their fates as cultural systems are articulated, and some systems are routinized. It could be called narratography, this sort of effort to understand articulations, routinizations, and even routinizations of articulating systems. In framing my project in this way, I believe that real history is found both by the analytic strategy insisting on attention to indigenous history-making and that insisting on attention to colonial power. I am hoping to find "contestatory discourse" in Fijian history and "cultural categories" in colonial practice as well as vice versa. These are questions about the operation of cultural power. How do some narratives become official, others "hinterland"? What kinds of agency and practice—oracular, administrative, military, ritual—have given rise to what is real and important about Navosavakadua and Tuka? I hope to explain the importance of some Fijian rituals, and some British officializing disciplinary practices, but also to write of the officializing disciplinary practice among Fijians, and ritual among the British.

Under the perhaps cumbersome rubric of "routinization of articulating systems," I mean to address the consolidating, resolving processes that follow creative, forceful efforts to establish order by both colonizers and the colonized—the consolidating, resolving practices in which contests are definitively settled, new routines and agencies, meanings and arrangements established whereby people lead their lives. These processes often restrict, but sometimes new possibilities are opened including new spaces for resistance and contestation. From Sahlins's "structure of the conjuncture" I borrow the model of "the practical realization of the cultural categories in a specific historical context, as expressed in the interested action of the historic agents, including the microsociology of the event" (Sahlins 1985: xiv, also 1981). In the structure of the conjuncture of Hawaiians and Captain Cook, Hawaiians make history, in Hawaiian terms, as the British do in British terms. Cultural systems do not monolithically determine agency, for among the Hawaiians there are divisions and contests (as between chiefs and priests, and men and women) as among the British are divisions and contests (notably of class). Over time, in colonies, the structure of conjuncture is the object of multiple interested efforts to routinize or contest. From the analyses insistent on the force of colonial power I borrow Talal Asad's term and insistence on attention to "routine colonialism" (e.g., 1973:115) to focus not just on initial moments but on routinized colonial situations.[6] For in ongoing colonial societies, the distinction between that which is indigenous and that which is colonial is breached. Rather than indigenes and colonizers retaining separate systems of meaning, and rather than colonizers imposing their system and the colonized either becoming hegemonized or resisting (in indigenous terms or in the colonizers') over time in colonial societies such as Fiji, new articulations are made.[7] While novel, they are not necessarily chaotic. They are neither indigenous nor colonial, they are both and neither. Some flourish, some fall by the wayside. This book is the story of plural articulations, some defunct, some flourishing, some nascent, in a turbulent history of power, ritual, and history-making.

This narrative therefore moves chronologically to tell a story of a Fijian ritual and political history, the colonial making of a "cult," and the plural versions of past and present that are the consequences. Chapters 2–5 depict

---

6. As I will discuss in more detail in the conclusion, I am not following Weber's use of "routinization," at least in the sense in which he views it as the attenuation of authentic charisma.

7. Comaroff (1985:153) notes the evocative double meaning of articulation, both "to join together" and "to give expression to."

plural nineteenth-century Fijian and British cultural realities in complex conjuncture, leading to Navosavakadua's project: an articulation of a new ritual-politics for Fiji. Chapters 6–8 turn to the twentieth century, examining the routinization of articulations in the colonial society of Fiji. Focusing on narratives of Navosavakadua, these chapters depict creative articulations (official and private, forceful and quiescent), some of which fail and some of which have been made routinized, made real in peoples' lives.

More specifically, we begin chapters 2 and 3 with some Fijian history, focusing on the social landscape of the area called Ra, and the early life of Navosavakadua. These chapters consider contesting indigenous Fijian understandings of power, autonomy, and obligation, between eastern coastal kingdoms and interior hinterland peoples, between chiefs and "people of the land." The contests are expressed in myth, in the history of Navosa's people in the 1873 massacre at Nakorowaiwai, and at many points in Navosavakadua's own life. Into the ongoing conjuncture of opposing Fijian groups entered the British. In chapter 4 we begin to see the colonial creation of a cult. This chapter interprets the British colonial project, with its optimistic expectations of a natural trajectory of Fijian civilizability, its institutions meant, in various ways, to establish dominance and transformation, and the impact of Navosa's project on the British cultural imagination of themselves and Fijian others. Chapter 5 reconstructs Navosavakadua's 1880s mobilization of hinterland peoples through an articulation of Fijian and British gods, of Fijian and colonial forms of ritual-political power. His land-centered polity was novel, in Fijian and colonial terms, and dramatic though short-lived.

Chapter 6 traces consequences of Tuka in the lives of Navosavakadua's deported descendants and looks more broadly at the routinization of plural versions of power and truth in twentieth-century Fiji. Emphasizing processes of routinization chapter 6 contrasts the making of official and more private local versions of past and present, inscribed both in texts and on the very landscape. Chapters 7 and 8 trace these routinizations into the present, considering current versions of ritual-political power in post-colonial (and now post-coups) Fiji. Chapter 7 examines narratives of Navosavakadua in the 1980s, first his place in an unsuccessful post-colonial nationalist project of an Indo-Fijian visionary, and second in a public debate among Fijians in a national newspaper. Chapter 8 returns to the Vatukaloko and their current, relatively quiescent understanding of their ancestor, their colonial history, and their place today in Fiji and the world.

Finally chapter 9 returns to broader theoretical issues. If we can argue that "cults do not exist," should we not also ask "does the state exist"? I will argue that the creation of the very concept of cult is tied not only to the articulations of scholars and other observers, but also to the routinizing effects of official powers making states. If so, how are we to understand the different powers of center and hinterland, and of colonizers and colonized, to make history in a place like Fiji?

2

EMBATTLED PEOPLE OF THE LAND: THE RA SOCIAL LANDSCAPE, 1840–1875

Long before Navosavakadua was born, the Vatukaloko people made their history as "people of the land" in a complex ritual-political field. Here we begin with an event that took place when Navosa was young and then move back to consider earlier histories.

The Battle at Nakorowaiwai

In February 1873 a Fijian man called Koroi i Latikau set out to recruit men as laborers for European plantations in Fiji's eastward islands. He belonged to the Lasakau people of the kingdom of Bau, but he did not recruit for laborers among his own people along the southeast coast. Instead he came up to Ra in the northeast of Viti Levu island on a European-owned schooner and then went by foot up into the mountainous interior, into the lands behind coastal Drauniivi village (see figures 4, 5, and 6). He arranged to hire thirty men, offering muskets and trade goods for payment, and set out for the coast with the recruited men. But a whale's tooth had followed him into the interior. Within a few miles of the coast he was killed.

Here are two accounts of the killing. One is a letter written in February 1873 by the captain of the schooner which had brought Koroi i Latikau up to the Ra coast where he had joined the ship that would transport the hired men down the coast. The letter reports the killing to the Minister of Native Affairs.

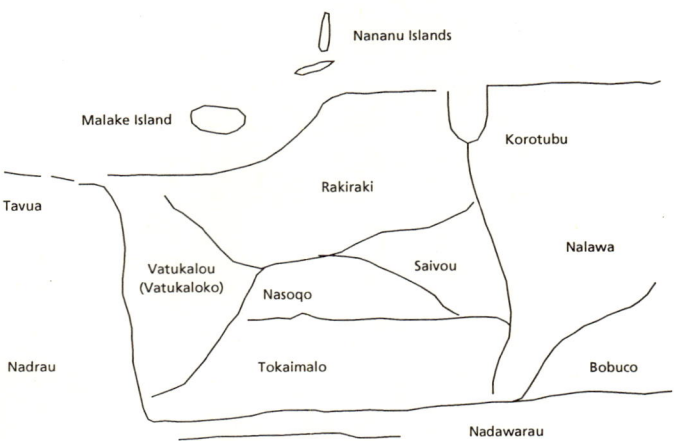

Figure 4. Northeastern Viti Levu: tracing of an 1873 sketch by Swanston.
Source: Cakobau Government Papers, Ministry of Native Affairs, inwards 89/74. Please note that I have inverted this tracing of Swanston's sketch to show north at the top. See also the more accurate map in Figure 5 (facing page).

Within a few miles of the coast he met a man called "Naloti" a Bua[1] man who had turned mountaineer, Naloti met him face to face on the peak and said You're a Bau man. — You Bau men are our pigs. — Yout fatten in Bau and you come here and we eat you. — And I'm going to eat you. — And he there and then clubbed Koroilatikau who had no weapon of any kind with him. — This rumour I heard at Viti Levu Bay from the mountaineers in that quarter. . . . I was told the story by Viti Levu men who were at Togavere at the time and were engaged by Koroilatikau to carry the trade up to the mountain town where he had engaged the labourers. (Punctuation as in original. The author is probably Thomas Morton, captain, from the Yasawa Islands; the letter is to Robert Swanston, Minister of Native Affairs. Ministry of Native Affairs 73/1120.)

The second account was told to me by Maciu Matana, an elder of Nasi kin group *(mataqali)* in Drauniivi village in 1984.

A man came from Bau. He led and a whale's tooth followed him. Koroikoya [Koroi i Latikau] led. In that time, Sadiri was sitting at the old village at Nako-

---

1. From the kingdom of Bua on the west coast of Fiji's second largest island, Vanua Levu. There was considerable movement between the coasts of Bua on Vanua Levu and Ra on Viti Levu, especially during times of warfare.

EMBATTLED PEOPLE OF THE LAND 21

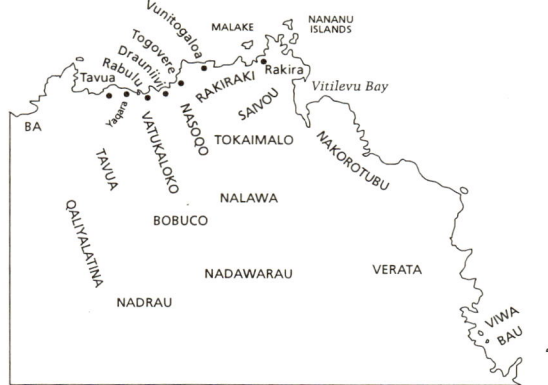

Figure 5.
Northeastern Viti Levu Island.

Figure 6. Vatukaloko Inland Sites: author's sketch (not to scale).

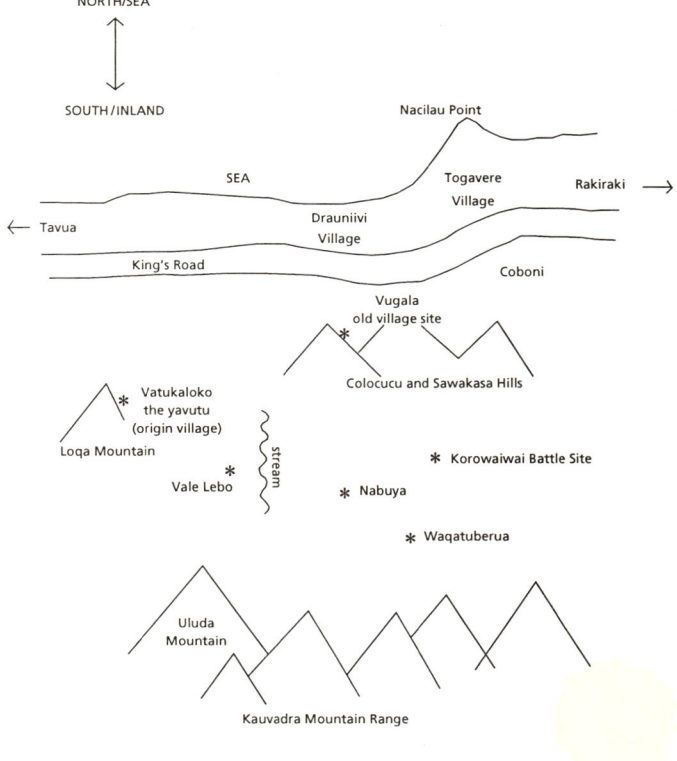

rowaiwai. The man from Bau, Koroikoya, arrived, following him was a whale's tooth in order that some village in the land might kill him. He arrived here and our ancestors said, "Yes, that's good, we will take the whale's tooth," and they clapped to claim it. Then they sent him into the interior, Vuda was the name of that man who sent him, . . . he said, "bring my axe, let us go into the interior." . . . Vuda carried the axe, until they arrived at a hill near Nananu. Then Vuda said, "O some people are having a *solevu* [ritual in which quantities of goods are presented]." It was at Yaqara, like when people bring together goods to install a chief, or like a wedding. Then Vuda saw it, and the Bauan saw it too. But they were standing before a big tooth of stone. And then Vuda took hold of him and hit him on his neck and destroyed him. He was dead. Koroikoya of Bau was dead. . . . He died, then the news arrived and Vuda was arrested, . . . because of Sadiri . . . he was arrested. It is not clear if he was put to cutting stone [road building], or if he was hung. Then there arrived the war, the war over religion, that took place at the old village, Nakorowaiwai, at the foot of the hills.

The killer of Koroi i Latikau took refuge at Nakorowaiwai, a village of the Vatukaloko people, Navosavakadua's people. Retribution was to be expected, from the powerful southeastern kingdom of Bau — and from white settlers. Koroi i Latikau was a Lasakau man, that is, a "dangerous man" in service to the chiefs of Bau, a hereditary procurer of cannibal victims for sacrifice. Here, in Ra, he had been procuring bodies, for his chief to hire out for labor on white plantations. His chief, Cakobau of Bau, was hereditary Vunivalu ("root of war") of the preeminent Fijian confederacy in the islands. He was also "King" of the "Kingdom of Cakobau," a new political organization for Fiji, uneasily joining Fijian high chiefs and white planters and settlers. Centered in Levuka where king and cabinet met, the kingdom claimed sovereignty throughout the islands, and had begun to routinize these claims, delineating provinces and designating Fijian governors and European wardens as authorities within them.

As chance — and colonial history — would have it, there was a government ship, the *Marie Louise,* near to the Ra coast. The *Marie Louise* was full of Fijian troops, mostly men from the island of Moturiki, a Bauan domain, and was commanded by a European man called Major Fitzgerald.[2] R. B. Leefe, planter and Warden of Ra, requested assistance from the major, and the *Marie Louise*

---

2. They were retreating from the Ba coast where a vigilante group of white settlers had defied Cakobau's government who had warned them not to take matters into their own hands following the killing of a settler family by Fijians from the interior. For an account of this complex conflict see, e.g., Routledge (1985:165–86).

anchored near Togavere, the village next to present-day Drauniivi. The troops on board waited at Togavere while the officers of the government, European and Fijian, observed the formalities of the form of warfare that Europeans practiced.

Local planters joined the forces, including Tom Burness from nearby Caboni and Georgius Wright who had bought land at Togavere. Wright later wrote an account of the events: "A messenger was dispatched requesting the villagers to give up the murderers, but the only reply was a challenge for the troops to visit them, where they would find some 'lovo's' (native ovens) ready heated to receive them" (Wright 1901:19). Informed of these events, Cakobau's cabinet met in Levuka, and proclaimed the Nakorowaiwai people "Rebels in Arms."

The Fijian troops, Major Fitzgerald, and the European planters marched five miles inland, accompanied by nearly five hundred "irregulars," as Wright called them, coastal Fijians from the area. They left in the afternoon, pitched a camp on the way, and on the next day, March 3, arrived at Nakorowaiwai. Wright described the town and the battle:

> As the top of the range was mounted, the enemy's position was seen below. The site of these villages about to be attacked was on a large flat and consisted of two large towns, surrounded by a deep and wide ditch full of water, the inner side of the ditch being surmounted by an embankment of about five feet in height. Crowds of savages could be seen rushing about in the nearest village and the lali (war drums) were beaten loudly as a challenge.

The people at Nakorowaiwai had readied themselves for war. *Tabua* (whales' teeth) had been sent throughout the polity to summon allies, and a number of fighting men had come to man the war fence. Women and children had left the fighting villages and had gone inland, but they had returned during the two weeks of deliberations by the government officials on the coast. When the forces were sighted, they moved from the fortified village to the village at its back. The men were dressed for war, painted and wearing white streamers trailing from the back of the neck, and were performing rituals of competitive boasting and demonstrating their strength.

As the Cakobau government forces advanced to within five hundred feet they sent a messenger to demand that the killer of the Lasakau man be given up. They were met with a defiant cry and challenged to come and meet the ovens. As Maciu Matana told the story, Sadiri, the war priest who had the power of invulnerability, spread his mats and cried out to his fellow warriors "Who is brave enough to sit on the mats to stop the guns? I am!" He spread the mats and sat on them, fanning himself, taunting the approaching troops. (Wright wrote "one of the cannibals who evidently considered himself bullet proof, an old superstition and heathen custom said to be brought about by charms and processes gone through by the Bete-ni-tevoro (devil priest), was seen running backwards and forwards past an opening in the outside wall or fighting fence" (Wright 1901:20).

The Ra coast men (the "irregulars") hung back, expecting to prepare a war fence themselves, and to fight for a number of days. But the European idea of war was different. Major Fitzgerald sent out a party of Europeans and Fijians from Moturiki with guns to attack the closer village of the two. Firing continuously, the men moved to within about 150 feet, and then charged over the stony ground down the hillside, through a muddy area up over the embankment, where they grappled with the Nakorowaiwai warriors.

But before considering the fate of Nakorowaiwai, let us ask about motives and meanings in this conflict.

Motives and Meanings

Who were the combatants in this military conjuncture and how are they connected to the history of Navosavakadua and Tuka? Who were the Fijians at Nakorowaiwai and why did they kill Koroi i Latikau, and defy Bauan and European forces? What claims to autonomy and power did they make and why? Who was Koroi i Latikau and what interest did Bau have in Ra? And who were the irregulars, the coastal Fijians who joined the troops? Who were the planters, and why were they allied with coastal and eastern Fijians? And why do present-day Vatukaloko people remember this battle, not simply as a battle, nor as the "Police Action" the Bauan-settler government termed it, but rather as "the war over religion?"

To begin, the people at Nakorowaiwai were Navosavakadua's kin. They were Vatukaloko people, ancestors of the people who live at Drauniivi village today. Although more recently "Vatukaloko" has been used to refer mainly to a single village community and the four kin groups who live there, older accounts show that in the nineteenth century the Vatukaloko were a very small and contestatory chiefdom *(vanua)* on the edge of the better known historically dynamic confederations *(matanitu)* and chiefdoms *(vanua)* of Viti Levu island.

Fijian social groups vary tremendously throughout the islands, and there is an important history to the reification of polity terms, categories, and practice in the colonial era (see France 1969, Clammer 1975). Here I will not reprise the arguments, but I will set out briefly some of the terms for Fijian groups that we will find in use in the accounts of Vatukaloko history. They are a hierarchy of complexity and size, from largest to smallest: *matanitu* (confederation), *vanua* (chiefdom), *koro* (village), *yavusa* (kin and ritual group), and *mataqali* (*yavusa* subdivision).

Nineteenth-century *vanua* ranged from tiny polities of a few hundred people, like the Vatukaloko, to those of thousands of people. In some parts of Fiji, chiefly-led *vanua* combined through alliance and conquest to form great *matanitu* which in the early nineteenth century may have numbered fifteen thousand people or more (Derrick 1950:48). Most broadly, the *matanitu* consisted of three types of people: the ruling chiefly *vanua (vanua turaga)*, its noble allies *(bati)* (who were often *vanua* in their own right), and conquered subject peoples *(qali)*.[3]

Bau was one ruling chiefly *vanua* that gave its name to the preeminent *matanitu* in the islands at the time of Cession to Britain in 1874. Other coastal and island chiefly *vanua* around which allies and subjects coalesced into kingdoms of greater and lesser degree in the nineteenth century were Viwa, Rewa, and Verata (like Bau, located along the coast of eastern Viti Levu), Bua,

---

3. Chiefdoms *(vanua)* were themselves composed of local level social-ritual-kin units, *yavusa*, which in turn were made up of *mataqali*. Hocart (1970 [1936]:104) called the *mataqali* a "temple group," a ritual congregation worshipping common paternal ancestors. They usually subdivided into smaller household or extended family groups (*tokatoka* has come to be a standard term; in Ra, *matanibure* was used in the nineteenth century). *Mataqali* also means a "kind" or "class" of people (Quain 1948:187) such as chiefs, warriors, priests, heralds, fisherfolk, or carpenters. *Mataqali* may be located spatially; nowadays several *mataqali*, of different kinds of people generally, constitute a village (Nayacakalou 1975:21). Members of *yavusa* too are people of like kind, replicating the statuses of more remote ancestor gods (Hocart 1950, 1970). They trace ancestry back to an origin site *(yavutu)* ("tumulus" as glossed by Hocart), a village, a burial, house, or temple platform mound, or sometimes a stone, generally in the Kauvadra range, from which the founding ancestor journeyed. Members of particular *yavusa* have a standing and function which derive from their respective relations to a chief and from the services they provide to a polity such as a chiefdom *(vanua)*. *Yavusa* sometimes is used to describe a group of *mataqali* of common descent which are not coresident but may be scattered across geographical and social boundaries. But nowadays in places such as Drauniivi, one finds a colonially imposed "one village to one *yavusa*" model.

Within a *yavusa* or a *vanua* or a *matanitu* the different "kinds" of people (chiefs, spokesmen, priests, warriors, servants, installing people, fisherfolk) or constituent units (chiefs, noble allies, conquered people) can be grouped into more fundamental oppositions—always contextual—between "chiefly" and "land" people.

Macuata, and Cakaudrove of Vanua Levu and Taveuni islands, and Lakeba, a large confederation in the eastern Lau group of islands, largely dominated by Tongans (Derrick 1950:53)[4] (see figures 1 and 2). In this study, though the projects of the chiefs of Bau and Viwa (and later Lau) will be of consequence, I will be focusing on history-making in the far smaller and less centralized northern and interior polities in Viti Levu—especially the Vatukaloko and their neighbors, the much larger *vanua* of Rakiraki—in areas where Viwa and Bau claimed or sought to extend their ritual-political sovereignty.

The Vatukaloko as People of the Land

My point is not just to outline a hierarchy of polity types in a static system, but to understand the kinds of arguments—including battles—that took place over authority and power. When the Vatukaloko claimed to be autonomous warrior allies *(bati)*, and when they acted as priests *(bete)* they invoked a particular standing relative to nearby groups in Ra, the northeast of Viti Levu island. And the whole Ra area, physically dominated by the interior Nakauvadra mountain range, had a particular relationship to eastern and coastal Viti Levu. In Fijian terms, they were *itaukei*, "people of the land."

A sometimes complementary opposition of two sources of power: that of dangerous chiefs *(turaga)* conceived of as relatively foreign or associated with the sea, and that of gods and *itaukei* conceived of as autochthonous and associated with the interior has inflected much of Fijian sociocosmological life in past and present. In these terms Fijians have made social, spatial, political, and ritual relations at levels from the household to great chiefly confederacies of nineteenth-century Fiji. These terms have also been used to articulate the relations between Fijians and other incoming groups including the British and the Indians.

Here is an example of a chiefly view of how chiefs make the sociocosmological world. In a description of the installation of the ruling chief of Rakiraki, nearest large-scale chiefly polity *(vanua)* to the Vatukaloko, it is claimed that the newly installed chief of a higher polity installs the chiefs of lower divisions, or of ostensibly subject peoples. In Rakiraki around 1912, anthropologist A. M. Hocart took notes of a description of this process.

---

4. For studies of these major coastal kingdoms and their relationships see works by Routledge (1985), Sahlins (1985), Sayes (1984), Thomas (1988), and the published works and unpublished field notes of A. M. Hocart.

The Rakiraki chief *(Tunavitilevu)* was installed by the hereditary *vu ni masi*, his land people, who place a turban on his head and thus give him the rule. Following the days of the ceremony, he embarks on a ship hung with flags, proceeding along the coast, stopping at places such as Tavua where members of a certain *mataqali* [ritual kin group] offer him rituals of respect *(vakasili vei koya)*, he then tells them to be chiefs at Tavua. Then at Navatunisala [a turn-of-the-century village of the Vatukaloko folk] he designates the Tui Vatu of the Vatukaloko people. Then returning from the lands of *qali* or *bati* [whether the Tavua and Vatukaloko were subjects or allies was a matter of perspective] he chose as well the head of his Kai Wai or fisherpeople at the island of Malake. (summarized from Hocart n.d.b: 4113)

In this version of the order of things in the chiefdom of Rakiraki, though the chief is installed by his own land people, he is then regarded as creating and authorizing the heads of the divisions (the noble allies *(bati)* and subject peoples *(qali)* of his chiefdom). Very specifically, in the point of view expressed in this narrative of the Rakiraki people, the Rakiraki chief has "made" the chief of the Vatukaloko people "from the top down."

From this perspective, chiefs embodied their polities and held the right to rule *(lewa)*, their projects "making the history" (Sahlins 1985:35–41) of the great polities of Fiji. The chief ordered not only social relations, but also the prosperity of the people, and the bounty of the land and seas. This is because the chief was a living instantiation of the founding god of the people. For a chief was (and is) made *(veibuli)* in a ritual process that conceives him first as a dangerous outsider who marries into a line of autochthonous people. He is ritually murdered in the installation ritual, and is reborn as their god. The chiefly line is therefore a synthesis of outsider and autochthon, or chief and people of the land. The chief is called child chief *(gone turaga)*. In succeeding generations as sister's son to the people of the land, he has a claim upon them, that of *vasu* (sister's son) which allows him to seize what he wishes. His mother's brother's children are his *qali*, tributary people, or his *bati*, uneasy allies, a superseded line (see Hocart [1969], Brewster [n.d.a], and Sahlins [1985]).

From such a chiefly perspective, held by the confederation of Bau (and the dominant view of Fijians—and Fiji scholarship) Koroi i Latikau's quest was an exercise in chiefly hierarchical prerogative (not his own, but on behalf of the chiefs in Bau he served). Certainly in the great kingdoms, and their subdivisions, the chief or leader at each level is the focal point, the central organizing figure who stands for the whole of the people, and the kingdom of Bau claimed rights of sovereignty over the entire coast of Ra. But, even given the centrality of chiefship to an understanding of Fijian history-making there is still more to be considered about the perspective of "people of the land."[5]

The *itaukei* ("people of the land" or "owners of the land") authorized and controlled chiefly rule with their own complementary authority, an "ownership" connoting autochthony and a special relationship to the gods of the land. As land people, installing people "made" the chief in installation rituals, oracle priests read the omens in the course of chiefly projects, other ritual experts created cadres of invulnerable warriors or performed the sacrifices necessary to chiefly projects, and warriors and allies fought for—and sometimes betrayed—their chiefs. In some cases and some places, ostensible allies or subjects denied the rights chiefs and chiefly kingdoms claimed over them. In such terms did the Vatukaloko people at Nakorowaiwai kill Koroi i Latikau.

In the origin stories of land people, chiefs do not necessarily come from the sea, or even if they do, the agency of the autochthonous original or subject people is different and greater than in the Rakiraki version. Certainly the chiefly version from eastern coastal kingdoms has come to be widespread and is taken as authoritative particularly since the colonial era, when coastal chiefs and colonial officers joined to authorize myths of voyages from Africa or waves of migration ending in light-skinned conquering strangers.[6] But there stubbornly remains a genre of tales—and practice—insisting on autochthonous origin and power.

In some of these land peoples' versions, the original Fijians sprang from the soil itself (Brewster n.d.a). A stranger chief may arrive among them and marry a local woman, but the emphasis in the story is on how the local people meet and choose to install the stranger as chief. Carrying this land perspective further, in other versions origin is fully autochthonous, without foreign combination. (As a Vatukaloko man said to me in 1985, "I hold to Fiji only, I do not come from South America, Egypt, or Tanganyika. I have always been here, not arrived from there.")

The Vatukaloko people in particular have told "land-centered" accounts of

---

5. See Hocart on Fijian chiefship, the ritual-polity, and "land" and "sea" as principles organizing multiple domains of Fijian life (concerning land and sea, see especially Hocart 1969 and 1929:8ff.); see also Thompson (1940:32ff.), and Quain (1948:3ff.) and Brewster (1922). On "land" and "sea" and the making of history in Fiji, focusing on chiefship, ritual, war, and sacrifice see Sahlins (1985:73–103).

6. For a paradigmatic example of a chiefly-perspective origin myth see the colonial Fijian-language newspaper *Na Mata (The Herald)* 1892 and Hocart's summary and comments (n.d.a:318–23). For a discussion of "authenticity" and origin myths in Fiji see France (1966), and, contra France, e.g., Routledge (1985:40–41).

their origins, of the making of chiefs, and of the ongoing power of the land in a Fijian polity. They have been telling, writing, and inscribing these stories on the landscape, most recently since 1909 when they returned from deportation to rebuild Drauniivi village. This version especially explains the origin of the four *mataqali* making up the present-day village of Drauniivi, and why one provides the chiefs of the Vatukaloko. (How this scheme may have come into being to rebuild Drauniivi in 1909 will be discussed in chapter 6.)

> First Jehovah created the heavens and the earth, and then he made a stone. . . . Then God said to the stone "Let two people appear, a woman and a man." The name of the man was Rasarilevu, the name of the woman Naikanivatu. Then God told them to marry. Then they had three boys: Lekaninabuya, Qisoya, Degei. They lived in different places in the Kauvadra range. . . . Then Lekaninabuya, the eldest of them, got married, taking a young woman from her place in the land called Vatukaloko. They had three boys: first Bulibulivanua, second Saumaimuri. They were born together, they were twins. Then their brother was born following them, and he was called Lewanavanua. They lived in the land called Vatukaloko. . . . Then the two twin brothers gave their younger brother the rule of the land, that he might lead their land. He was the younger brother, the twins were the elders. Thus were the kin groups [*mataqali*] begun. (1984 account by two Vatukaloko gentlemen, one of Nakubuti kin group, one of Wakalou kin group, my translation)

This then is a story which privileges the role of installing land people in the creation of sociocosmological order. The standings and relationships of the three[7] main *mataqali* of the Vatukaloko people in present-day Drauniivi village are expressed in a history in which the twins Bulibulivanua ("maker of the land," ancestor to Nakubuti kin group, the installing people) and Saumaimuri ("the chief (or prosperity) to follow," ancestor of Wakalou kin group, the chief's warriors)[8] gave up their initial standing as leaders (by right as they

---

7. The fourth group is said to be of more recent origin and was explained to me as a genealogical offshoot of Wakalou *mataqali,* one of the original three.

8. Ideally, the Wakalou people should be the warriors to the chiefly line, and this ideal model was one presented to me when I began to ask about the different ritual-political identities *(itutu vakavanua)* of these groups. Historically, as I will describe in this chapter, and in chapter 6, the relationships are more complex. The chiefly line of Nasi also have another line of warriors, the Nasoqo people farther inland. Once a Nakubuti gentleman told me that Wakalou were (he said "are") Nakubuti's warriors, which I think suggests how recent Nasi's rule over Nakubuti may be. In the 1993 installation of the Tui Vatu, both Nakubuti and Wakalou have been called "king-makers" (Ritova 1993), but it was members of Nakubuti (subdivision *tokatoka* Lotio) who formally installed him. For more on some of these complexities, see Kaplan (1988 ch. 3), and below.

were elder) to their *younger* brother Lewanavanua ("rule the land," ancestor of Nasi, the chiefly kin group).

Thus when the current chief of the Vatukaloko, the Tui Vatu, was installed in 1993, the entire sequence of events was initiated by the people of the land, and it was the installing people of Nakubuti who ritually authorized the new chief. In the course of the ritual, the new chief (son and grandson of previous chiefs) took the role of a stranger, to be transformed and installed as the chief of the whole. In this installation, the chiefly narrative and that of the powers of people of the land both jostled and coincided. The father of the new Vatukaloko chief, who died around 1980, was never formally, ritually installed. His grandfather had been, in 1908. When I asked about this history, I was told that due to some conflict with a Rakiraki chief and colonial administrator early in this century, the Vatukaloko had been forbidden to install their leader, but that the current Tui Navitilevu had agreed to allow them to go ahead. But the decision as to if and when he would actually be installed then rested with the Vatukaloko installing people, who waited about a decade. In Navosavakadua's era and perhaps since, as I will discuss in chapter 5, power has been wielded by installing people, sometimes in contest with chiefly rule, and in such periods of chiefly hiatus.

In 1985 I had spent a year hearing, reading, and thinking about Vatukaloko narratives of their origin, including both intricate local detail and accounts that had world cosmological scope, detailing how all Fijians, and indeed all the peoples of the world, are also descended from the man and woman Jehovah made and set to live at the place in the Kauvadra range called Vatukaloko. Tracing out one set of genealogies, I was startled to find Degei, famous ancestor of Rakiraki, and Vueti, the ancestor of Bauans (both of whom are chronicled nowadays even in schoolbooks and tourist literature), appearing in minor roles as younger brothers to the Vatukaloko ancestors.

I once asked Mr. Jone Tuiwai, in Drauniivi, "But what about Degei? What about the story of the ancestor who voyaged to and then from the Kauvadra range, and married many times, whose descendants founded the eastern coastal kingdoms?" He laughed with delight at my question, and said "That is what the officials [British and Eastern Fijian] asked my father at the 1917 Lands Commission Hearings."

> Savenaca Komaisavai [one of the Fijian members of the Lands Commission] said "Jovesa, there's just one question we have for you." They asked him the thing I've made clear to you. . . . "What about Degei?" Jovesa Bavou said "He is the third man after me." This means "I am the oldest." If you listen to people throughout Tailevu

[eastern Fiji, in the domains of Bau and Rewa] they will call "Hey, older brother *[tuakaqu]*." Ratu George Cakobau, the former Governor General [descendant of Cakobau] calls us "the elders" *[na qase]* or "my older brother." Because we are the oldest, they are the younger.

From the coastal chiefdom of Rakiraki and from the hinterland perspective of Drauniivi, we have two versions of the way power in the world is ordered, an argument in shared terms. Many different histories can and have emerged from such differing constructions of the powers and relations of chiefs and people of the land. To suggest only a few: as in Rakiraki chiefs may be seen as synthetic figures, who embody the ancestor god and themselves initiate and create the polity. Or they may be viewed as dangerous strangers to be defeated. People of the land may act toward the chief as mother's brother to a favored sister's son, or as elder brothers who have yielded the rule willingly, as when, among the Vatukaloko, it is said that the Nakubuti and Wakalou ancestors gave the rule to the ancestor of the Nasi chiefs. But it is equally possible for elder brothers to invoke their position as the superseded autochthonous line in order to assert their own autonomy and authority in relation to chiefs and their projects, as did the Vatukaloko at Nakorowaiwai.

These plural possibilities are the ground of Vatukaloko history-making throughout the nineteenth century. We will get a more nuanced sense of the contending forces at Nakorowaiwai if we consider several episodes in earlier Vatukaloko history, as set down in an uneven but richly detailed array of recollections, written and oral, by Fijians in both private accounts and officially solicited testimonies, and by local Europeans. The power of chiefs and of people of the land was invoked in struggles among the Vatukaloko themselves, between the Vatukaloko and their Rakiraki neighbors, and ultimately between the Vatukaloko, white settlers, and the preeminent kingdom of Bau.

The Rise of the Vatukaloko Polity

Nowadays, Vatukaloko is frequently used to refer to the people who live at Drauniivi village, and they are called a *yavusa* (kin group). Historically, in the 1870s the Cakobau government and local white settlers used "Vatukaloko" to refer to a small hinterland polity, which was a very small chiefdom. This Vatukaloko polity stretched in territory from the mythic origin village in the Kauvadra mountain to the coast where the present-day Drauniivi village stands (see figures 4, 5, and 6). In addition to people of the Nasi, Wakalou, and Nakubuti kin groups the polity included a number of other peoples, who "listened to" the Vatukaloko and had come to help defend Nakorowaiwai. The Vatukaloko chiefdom was located on the fringe of the northernmost of the larger coastal chiefdoms of Viti Levu island, the kingdom of Cakova now better known as Rakiraki.[9]

The three groups, Nasi, Wakalou, and Nakubuti, were probably of distinct origin, and their relationship as the "Vatukaloko" was forged in a series of alliances and enmities over the early and middle nineteenth century. In the 1840s, like the other hill people of the time, they were most probably small groups, of around thirty to fifty members, living in highly fortified villages on mountain sides, with planting grounds nearby (Fergus Clunie, personal communication). By the 1860s they had moved down to villages along the flats near the tributaries to the Yaqara river (in lands the people of Nasi, Wakalou, and Nakubuti would later, when whites asked the question, call their "own"). In the 1860s they still inhabited easily defensible inland mountain villages such as Vugala, and had settlements in the marshy wet lands called Nakorowaiwai, but they had also spread out farther down to the coast to the villages called Drauniivi and Vatunisala. It was probably in the years following the battle at Nakorowaiwai that Navosavakadua, of the *bete* (oracle-priest) line of the Nakubuti people, first came to his powers and founded a small settlement, called Vale Lebo, close to ancestral grounds of the Nakubuti people. Vale Lebo was a pilgrimage place, to which those who sought to consult Navosavakadua came with offerings.

As "Vatukaloko" all three groups stood in the relation of dominant strangers to the land-owning peoples of the coast. They had intermarried with people on the coast[10] and Vatukaloko influence stretched from the villages of

---

9. For a much fuller reconstructive account of this local history, see Kaplan (1988, ch. 3). This narrative is based on five types of sources: missionary and *beche de mer* trader accounts of the peoples of Ra (usually garnered from coastal people rather than inland groups during brief visits); the records of the Claims to Land by Europeans (ELC) Commissions held in 1880 (in which Fijians and local planters testified to the alienation of Fijian land beginning in 1860); the records of the Native Lands Commission (NLC) inquiries held in Ra in 1918 (at which Fijians including the Vatukaloko people testified in order to be allotted land); texts by Vatukaloko people written from 1918 to 1993; and oral histories from informants in 1984–1985, 1986, and 1991. These accounts are texts, told in historical contexts, which I use for multiple purposes in constructing this book. In particular the interrogating colonial project of the Lands Commission and some self-definitions of the Vatukaloko people since 1909 are discussed later.

10. The people of the coast were the Namacuku people (now primarily in Togavere village), the Wailevu, and the Nasaro.

Togavere, Drauniivi, and Vatunisala on the coast inland to the interior lands of the Nasoqo people, special allies *(bati)* to the Tui Vatu. Oral historical accounts tell of gifts of salt and fish that were sent up from the coast to inland towns, and yams and kava plants sent in return down to the coast. Nowadays the Vatukaloko people call their old polity the "Tini ka Rua na Yavusa" (found in the Bible, the phrase means the Twelve Tribes of Israel) and tell of old relationships of kinship, alliance, and sometimes enmity with its members[11] (see figures 4, 5, and 6). Some, but not all, of these ties may have been made later, in the 1880s by Navosavakadua. Not all of these groups currently acknowledge any past allegiance to the Tui Vatu, though some still acknowledge *(vakarorogo)* the Tui Vatu, and some members of each of the "Twelve Tribes" have attended ritual events at Drauniivi village connected with Navosavakadua. As I will explain in the next two chapters, colonial districting over the past century and the reification of boundaries by the Lands Commission records belittled the autonomy of the inland groups and do not preserve a record of the relationships and influence of groups such as the Vatukaloko. Only in 1991 did the Vatukaloko achieve some recognition of their former standing from the state, when they became part of a district called Naiyalaya.

Originally descended from brothers or not, a key preoccupation in Vatukaloko accounts of their history from 1918 was the question of how the groups came together, and how Nasi became the line of the chiefs (see figure 7). Claims and counterclaims concerning the power of installing land people versus that of chiefs demanding fealty recur in these narratives. In self-characterizations from 1918, spokesmen for the Nakubuti people, Navosavakadua's kin, presented themselves as powerful installers. These elders told of Nakubuti and Wakalou freely giving Nasi the rule, some seventy years before. "I have heard," said Taivesi Mamaqa, "that the Kai Lomolilevu [Nasi people] came to stay with us in the old days at Vatukaloko. I have also heard that we gave them their standing as chiefs. They led us thereby" (Taivesi Mamaqa (Nakubuti) 1918 NLC). I think it is also possible that the Nasi people conquered the others by force. Other accounts from 1918 suggest that there were struggles over whether Nasi or Nakubuti was the ruling line.[12] As I look with

11. In 1986 I was told that the Twelve Tribes included the peoples of *yavusa* Mali, Nadokana, Namacuku, Navatu, and Wailevu (now mainly all on the coast), the Nakorosogo and Nacolo people (inland people), the Nadurakuma, Naliwani, and various Tokaimalo groups (also inland), the Wacakena (inland on the Kauvadra slopes, close to Uluda mountain), and the Nasoqo, Bobuco, Korosavoulevu, Nadrau, and Nubu people (deep inland) (see figures 4 and 5).

12. In the 1830s and 1840s these internal differences were played out when the Vatukaloko participated in a dynastic dispute in the nearby kingdom of Rakiraki. The basic division was Nasi

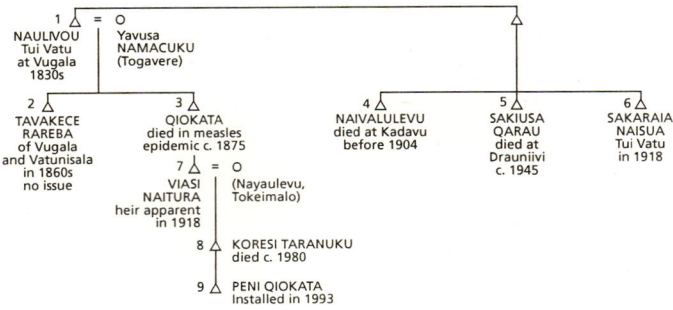

Figure 7. Vatukaloko Chiefs.

hindsight at Vatukaloko history, it seems to me that these tensions between chiefly and installing lines presaged the ambiguities and creativity of Navosavakadua's leadership to come.

If internally contesting, the Vatukaloko were also capable of uniting in the face of other, encroaching chiefly polities. Long before Koroi i Latikau the Bauan came to recruit among them, the Vatukaloko had fought other powerful polities to proclaim that they were independent allies, rather than subjects.

The Vatukaloko and the Kingdom of Rakiraki

The history of the Vatukaloko in the early nineteenth century was crucially bound with that of the nearest major chiefdom, Rakiraki. While the nineteenth-century history of all the various kingdoms of Fiji, as chronicled in the colonial era, is in general a history of chiefly strife and war between polities great and small, European observers considered the Rakiraki kingdom to be unusually factionalized. This was explained as a mark of a poorly devel-

---

people (the Tui Vatu chiefly line) against the Wakalou and Nakubuti people, a division already seen in the myth of the relations of Lewanavanua the younger brother (ancestor of Nasi kin group) and his twin elder brothers Saumaimuri and Bulibulivanua (ancestors of Wakalou and Nakubuti kin groups). Although the details are not clear, it would seem that it was the Wakalou people, allies (*bati*) who move ambiguously between support of Nasi and Nakubuti, who instigated this particular feud, by appealing to the Rakiraki people for aid against Nasi. Most significantly, years later it was the leader of Nakubuti who was considered to have reconstituted the polity, by sending to ask to have the Nasi people return. As a Nakubuti spokesman records it, the Nasi people apologized ritually to Nakubuti, and the Nakubuti people then built a house for the Tui Vatu as an act of fealty.

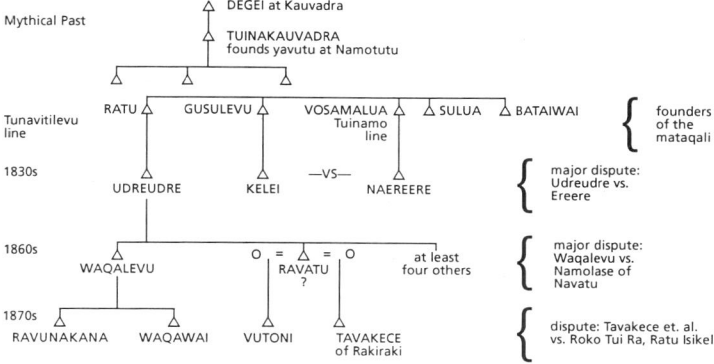

Figure 8. Chiefs of Rakiraki. Sources: NLC, ELC, Fison (1867), Lyth (n.d.).

oped polity, in comparison to the centralized eastern Fijian kingdoms.[13] In the 1830s the contest was between two closely related chiefs: Naereere and Udreudre (see figure 8). Udreudre was the eventual victor (he has come to be the subject of tales for tourists as a notorious cannibal). Recollections and histories of the late 1830s and early 1840s by people of and near the Rakiraki polity described their flight or their fate as the two chiefly forces swept around the land, sending whales' teeth *(tabua)* to secure allies, and pursuing old enemies (see also Lawry 1850, Lyth n.d. BV 112 reel 3, Sukuna NR volumes 44 and 45).[14]

The Vatukaloko, or at least some among them, began on Udreudre's side. When at first Naereere triumphed and seized the Rakiraki chiefs' origin village, Udreudre and his allies fled and took shelter among the Vatukaloko. It is

---

13. Here I cannot provide a systematic or historical explanation of these constant dynastic struggles, but they must be noted as we talk about the nineteenth-century Ra social landscape. The Rakiraki disputes themselves took place in the context of frequent conflict with the other major Ra polities of Nalawa, Saivou, and Nakorotubu (see figure 5), and conflict among inland groups, such as the Nadawarau and Bobuco peoples. Involvement in these disputes by the major kingdom of Bau, through their allies and agents, especially the chiefs of Viwa, was common throughout the nineteenth century, particularly during the reign of Namosimalua, chief of Viwa, who established paths of enmity and alliance throughout Ra and the areas of the interior close to his tiny island seat of power.

14. References to the volumes of Rakiraki and Raviravi polity histories, boundaries, and landholding compiled by Ratu Sukuna in 1926 in the course of the establishment of Native Reserves of Land, held at the Native Lands Commission, will henceforth take the form Sukuna NR (abbreviation for Native Reserves) and volume number.

said that Udreudre himself went to Vugala, the mountain fortress of the Nasi people of Vatukaloko.

But the Vatukaloko people at Vugala turned, as border villages so often did, to support Naereere's faction and betrayed Udreudre. Unfortunately for the Vatukaloko folk, Naereere's victory did not last.[15] The final victor Udreudre celebrated his victory by founding a new chiefly village in the heartland of Rakiraki. Then he took revenge. He began to attack village after village, all those who had fought him in the family struggle for power. He left alone those Vatukaloko villages that had loyally sheltered his allies, but went farther west to punish the people who had betrayed him at Vugala. Many of them were taken as prisoner to his new village. After five years of exile the Vatukaloko were permitted to return. Some had fled westward and then returned to Vugala, and they were there when the prisoners returned from Rakiraki (Sukuna NR 34, 35).

Vatukaloko recollections from the 1918 Land Commissions seem to confirm the betrayal of Udreudre, and they were largely concerned with detailing the different loyalties of the Nasi, Wakalou, and Nakubuti people during this Rakiraki dynastic struggle. But they also challenged a Rakiraki narrative of the Vatukaloko as disobedient subjects. A Nasi man said, "When Rakiraki was at war, Naudreudre [*sic*] fled to Vugala to our elders [among the Nasi people] and presented the offering of a visitor *(matamata ni vulagi)* to Naulivou the Tui Vatu. He gave ten whale's teeth and two women, named Degei and Raiyagayaga" (Epeli Nauwa (Nasi) 1918 NLC). Describing this "gift of women" Epeli Naua was making a political claim that the Vatukaloko were *bati*, noble allies with ties of marriage to the chiefly line, not subject *qali*. The fact that Udreudre of Rakiraki actually sheltered with the Nasi people at Vugala also supports this claim about the ritual-political tie. But after the Nasi people turned against Udreudre they were treated as conquered *qali*, carried away as prisoners. Despite their claims to have been noble allies, this history of the Vatukaloko—or the Nasi people at least—as treacherous *bati* affected their relations locally in ensuing warfare up through the 1860s, and their interactions later with encroaching Bauans, and influenced the perceptions later colonial Europeans would have of them.

15. Summarizing the history in 1926, chronicler Ratu Sukuna reports without comment accounts stating that following his victory Naereere went to Bua in Vanua Levu where he was presented with many ceremonial goods, which he brought back and presented to Udreudre along with the title and standing of Tuinavitilevu, chief of Rakiraki (Sukuna NR 45). Perhaps, instead, Naereere was actually defeated and fled to Bua, returning later to present tribute *(soro)* to Udreudre, the victor.

A final note on the Vatukaloko's ambiguous role as *bati* to the Rakiraki chiefs, and the warfare that their insistence on autonomy incited. In 1849 when the missionary R. B. Lyth journeyed along the northern coast of Viti Levu his Fijian companions pointed out to him the mountain town of Vugala (the Nasi peoples' stronghold) which had recently been taken by the Rakiraki people. They told him that the bodies of fifty people had been taken for cannibal sacrifice to the chiefs at Rakiraki's center. Lyth wrote: "The reason of this bloody massacre was that the Thokova [Rakiraki] chiefs were not satisfied with the quantity of fish the Vugala people had of late taken to them. For although partly independent yet they had been wont to take occasional supplies of fish and food to Rakiraki. The two parties are still at war" (Lyth n.d.). To bring fish and food was the mark of a conquered subject *(qali)* not a noble and autonomous ally *(bati)*, and clearly the Vatukaloko were disputing the characterization of them as subjects. Waqalevu (Udreudre's successor) and his successors would claim and sometimes receive offerings of food and coconuts from the Vatukaloko, but the Vatukaloko would continue to protest that the Tui Vatu "stood alone" without "listening to" higher authority (e.g., at the 1918 Native Land Commission). Nowadays the Vatukaloko acknowledge *(vakarorogo)* the chiefs of Rakiraki, but there are forms in which they continue to relate a history of autonomy. Certainly in the 1860s, as the first white settlers moved into the lands ruled by the Vatukaloko, the Tui Vatu transacted land without reference to the Rakiraki chiefs — or to the local landholders *(itaukei)*, either.

White Settlers and the Alienation of Land

In the 1860s Bauan-European influence, and white settlers themselves, began to move up into this area of the Ra coast. Several settlers moved northwest, up from Viti Levu bay into Rakiraki territories and then along the coast toward Tavua. Leaving the larger polities, they met with new groups and sought to come to know the ruling chiefs (not necessarily the *itaukei* [owners]) in order to buy or lease land. Initially they were not the focus of hostility in the lands of the Vatukaloko. In the 1860s much of northern Ra and the interior was involved in the wars between Waqalevu of Rakiraki (Udreudre's successor) and his neighbor Namulase of Navatu (Smythe 1864; see Epeli Nauwa 1918 NLC). To the west of the Vatukaloko, Bauan chiefs were demanding goods from the Tavua people, and skirmishes developed there that may have involved the Vatukaloko as well. At this time the Vatukaloko and many other Ra and interior groups sold land, for guns and trade goods.

In 1861 Samuel Avery St. John had bought lands from the Vunitogaloa people at the edge of the Rakiraki polity, and he introduced another settler, Clough, a Canadian to Tavakece, the Tui Vatu (Vatukaloko chief) and his people. Tavakece and others[16] sold Clough lands of which they were not the *itaukei*. In 1880 one of the signatories described the sale:

> Naisoro is my land. I knew [Clough]. I sold Naisoro to him. . . . I remember thirty guns. Can't remember the small trade. Some of the original owners of the land were at Vunitogaloa and at Drauna ivi [*sic*] and I went down and consulted with Tavakece and sold the land. We did so as we were in difficulties owing to war. We sold to get guns as war was coming down on us. Tavua and Colo and Rakiraki were coming down on us. Tavakece did not take this land by conquest. He lived at Vatukaloko [probably Vugala] inland. They left their land and came down to us and became our ally. Tavakece signed first as he was chief. He and I were equal, were related. We signed Cluffe's [*sic*] deed at Vatunisala. We were all there together as it was war time. (Donu 1880 ELC 778)

St. John, Clough, and their visitors and associates were the only Europeans in the area in the early sixties. But as the Fiji cotton boom developed in the middle of that decade[17] a succession of planters came into the area, buying land from each other or the owning peoples, paying guns and trade, involving the local people and each other in complicated transactions. George Woods, a minister in the Kingdom of Cakobau, bought the land at Coboni near Togavere in 1873, and Togavere became a much used port. In 1871 William Isaac Thomas and his father settled on the Nasoro lands that Tavakece had sold to Clough, and Tavakece demanded a new payment (see ELC 778) of guns and trade. The Fijian landholding system did not coincide with the European notion of fee simple, and Tavakece did not believe that he had alienated the land when he made his contract with Clough. The Thomases grew cotton and ran cattle. In 1874 the cantankerous Thomas Frederick Burness arranged to rent the same land that Thomas had leased from the new Tui Vatu Naivalulevu and others who claimed the right to negotiate with Europeans. Burness claimed that he leased the land at the plea of the local Fijians, as Thomas had threatened to burn their villages.[18] However, there is nothing to show

---

16. The sellers were Tavakece and five other Vatukaloko men, two Wailevu men and a Nasoro man, the *itaukei* Wailevu, Nasaro, Namacuku, and Veivatu people, according to later ELC testimony.

17. A consequence of the embargo on cotton from the American South.

18. Later assessors would note that "this whole lease was adopted by Burness as a means of annoying, if not of ousting, Thomas with whom he is on as bad terms as he is with every other

that Thomas or the other settlers were on bad terms with the Vatukaloko people, especially compared to the aggression and hostility between planters and "mountaineers" nearby to the west in Ba.

Bau, Viwa, and European Encroachment: Christianity, Labor, and Vatukaloko Interpretations

The encroachment of Europeans into the Vatukaloko domains had only just begun. More importantly, the plans and projects of Cakobau of Bau and his ally in Ra, Ratu Isikeli of Viwa, would soon reach into the northern area of Ra in new ways. The chiefs of Viwa had long been influential in Ra since the days of Ratu Isikeli's father, Namosimalua, who involved himself in local conflicts in the more eastern and southern parts of Ra, managing on occasion to indebt both sides to himself (General Report on Lands in the Ra District ELC; see also Smythe 1864:226).

Bauan and Viwan interests and the interests of traders, settlers, and other Europeans were sometimes compatible. As early as the 1830s Namosimalua had used his paths to the various Ra groups to facilitate *beche de mer* gathering by New England sea captains along the Ra coast.[19] Later Bauan and Viwan expansion and extraction along the Ra coast served to fuel the great struggle between the eastern polities of Bau and Rewa, and the other eastern kingdoms. In the 1850s too the Viwans provided a path by which other Europeans, including missionaries, established their projects in Ra, but again these paths were often opened primarily to suit their own rather than European purposes.

Religious conversion and labor recruiting were the two European projects that would most affect Ra, and they came to the north and interior largely through Bauan and Viwan intermediaries. In 1839 Wesleyan Methodist missionaries had established a station on the island of Viwa, where by 1845 the Viwa chief Namosimalua and his wife had converted; their son was given the biblical name "Isikeli." Though the missionaries were concentrating on converting Cakobau and the other great eastern chiefs and no European mission-

---

person with whom—so far as our experience as Land Commissioners goes—he has ever had anything to do" (1880 ELC 777).

19. *Beche de mer* (sea cucumber) was valued as a delicacy in China, and hence, like sandalwood, was procured by Americans and Europeans who moved through the Pacific with China as their ultimate destination.

aries were stationed in Ra, from Viwa some mission-trained Fijian teachers did go out to eastern coastal Ra, especially to the Nakorotubu people, whose ties to Viwa were strongest. In 1847 Nakorotubu, Rakiraki, and Ba were established as circuits, each with several resident Fijian teachers though no sooner had they been sent, than the teachers in Rakiraki fled in 1849 due to warfare between coastal and interior groups (Viwa/A/1 Reports and Accounts of the Circuit 1840–1858).[20]

The white missionaries at Viwa were interested in tales from Rakiraki, home of the Fijian god Degei, and sought to interview Rakiraki people when they came down to Nakorotubu and Viwa (see Lyth n.d.). By 1850 the sons and grandsons of Udreudre of Rakiraki had converted to Christianity, including Waqalevu, who succeeded him. (As we shall see, Udreudre's grandson, Ravunakana, joked with missionary Lorimer Fison in 1865 about an old priest who professed to have found a *"wai ni tuka"* or "elixir of life" (Fison 1867).)

As mission-trained teachers were established in towns on the fringes of the Rakiraki domain, at Navatu and Vunitogaloa, rumors of the new religion spread inland and to polities further west including the Vatukaloko, but it was not until the late 1860s that Fijian catechists were assigned to Togavere and Vatunisala, coastal towns of the Vatukaloko polity (Viwa/A/3).

Although coastal Fijians and European missionaries were afraid to go up into the hill areas, Ra and interior people frequently came down the coast to work on plantations. The 1860s saw a flood of European immigrants to Fiji, men seeking to make their fortunes in cotton, while the Americans fought their war. The new plantations were in need of laborers, and through his many networks in the area Ratu Isikeli, the chief of Viwa, supplied them from Ra.[21] He did so initially through exercising his prerogatives and relationships as a ruling chief, and, beginning in 1870 added to this a new authority as governor of Ra, in the newly formed Kingdom of Cakobau. Thus, both Wesleyanism and labor recruiting came on paths mediated by the plans of Bau and Viwa, in the context of the long-term relations and strategies established by the Viwa chiefs.

The Vatukaloko people, fitful border people to Rakiraki, had no relation-

20. References to documents of the Methodist Mission in Fiji, held at the National Archives of Fiji, will henceforth contain the archival classification number and some indication of the nature of the document (report, baptismal record, etc.) when relevant.

21. In 1871 planters living in the Rakiraki area protested that they could not hire laborers, as so many men were being recruited for plantations in the eastward islands.

ship, and certainly no obligation to Viwa, let alone Bau. Yet, whether summoned by Ratu Isikeli, through the Rakiraki people, or by some other chief of Viwa or Ra, Vatukaloko men too had joined the ranks of indentured laborers. Fijian recollections and European records (Brewster 1922, Sutherland 1910) relate that Vatukaloko men, including the young Navosavakadua and his father, worked on Selia Levu plantation in Taveuni in the 1860s or 1870s. (These accounts do not say whether they went willingly to the plantations, or were sold as defeated prisoners of one or another of the wars that still racked Ra and the interior). When young men went down from the hills to work in plantations, they returned with goods and guns to support local ritual and political endeavors. By 1870 some of the Vatukaloko had encountered the European plantations of the coast, and there were resident white planters, mission-trained Fijian catechists, and labor recruiters among the Vatukaloko people.

"Mountaineers" and Chiefs, Heathens and Labor Recruiters: Prelude to the Battle at Nakorowaiwai

As plantations increased and made use of the labor of Ra men, and as more settlers flooded Ra and the north, white settlers began to distinguish between good natives and "mountaineers," Christians and heathens, peaceful and warring tribes. The opposition had roots in part in the coastal Fijian distinction between themselves and the *kai colo* (hill people). In their dealings with Europeans, chiefs such as Isikeli of Viwa constituted themselves as different from the Ra people, as recruiters rather than workers, Christians rather than heathens, and chiefs rather than low-ranking mountaineers.

By 1870, the Bauan domains were nominally Christian, and most coastal Fijians, including those of the Rakiraki kingdom, had followed their chiefs in cutting their hair and putting on the clothes of Wesleyanism. There was a Christian teacher at Togavere, the coast of the Vatukaloko territory, and another nearby at Vunitogaloa (though the missionaries wrote that continuous warfare in the area "very much interfered" with the mission (Viwa/A/3, Minutes of Circuit Quarterly and Local Preachers Meetings)). While news of the new god of the coastal kingdoms may have been of interest to the Vatukaloko (who lived, they believed, at the source of the world's divine power), in the early 1870s the Vatukaloko and inland groups had yet to convert. Many depended on leaders like Sadiri whose warrior strength was derived from a powerful autochthonous relation to the ancestor deities of the Kauvadra mountains. Local warfare required the rituals associated with battle, the leadership of war priests who also created invulnerability in warriors, the visions of oracle priests to guide battle plans, and other ritual experts to sacrifice cannibal victims. Moreover, the Wesleyan religion, or the rumor of it, came mixed with the tidings of Bauan incursion into the hills. In July of 1867 the Reverend Thomas Baker, who ventured into the hill country in Navosa, in western Viti Levu on the upper Sigatoka river, was clubbed and eaten. In the following year Cakobau sent an armed force led by young Bauan chiefs inland to avenge Baker's murder. They were routed by the inland people (see Macnaught 1971). Reverberations of this proof of the ineffectiveness of Cakobau's god spread through the hills. No respect was gained for the new Kingdom of Cakobau, established in 1870 by coastal chiefs and a group of Europeans.

In 1871 in Ba, hostilities solidified between planters and "mountaineers," and a climate of apprehension developed among white settlers along the entire coast, including those near to the Vatukaloko. In 1871 Thomas, from his plantation, wrote to George Woods, Cakobau's Minister of Native Affairs, with news of attacks on the families of planters by men from the nearby village of Vakatabadua, ten miles inland from Navatu, and asked that some of the forces at Ba be sent over to the Rakiraki side (Ministry of Native Affairs 71/8).[22] In 1872 St. John was in conflict with the new chief and the people on the land at Vunitogaloa, at the border of Rakiraki and Vatukaloko lands. He complained that "since the death of the old chief Burebalavu the natives were stealing." Moreover, the new chief, Ratu Meli ("Donu"), demanded their land back: "My boundaries are well known [St. John protested,] they were registered by Pritchard, the British Consul. . . . I wish these people to remove their plantations and the chief Meli his house off of my land at once" (Ministry of Native Affairs 72/406).

In January 1872, Thomas wrote to the Minister of Native Affairs of the Cakobau government to tell him that he had received word that "the *kai colo*" (hill people) had burned six coastal towns, and that the coastal town of Vatunisala, on his plantation, had "revolted and joined the mountaineers." He asked the government to act "to ascertain how far the lives and property of White settlers along this part of the Coast of Viti Levu are jeopardized by this movement" (Ministry of Native Affairs 72/406).

---

22. References to papers in the Cakobau Government and Ad-Interim Government series, held at the National Archives of Fiji, will henceforth be by name of ministry or series and by number. The first two digits indicate the year, and the last digits the number in the series.

The people at Vatunisala were Vatukaloko folk, joining "mountaineers" who were simply their relatives, members of the Vatukaloko polity which spanned the geography and stereotypes of coast and hills. Perhaps it was local dispute that provoked the incursion that so worried Thomas. But perhaps the Vatukaloko were beginning to take a stand against the burgeoning institutions of the Cakobau government. By 1872 Cakobau was designating local chiefs as magistrates and administrative officers and had chosen Ratu Isikeli of Viwa as governor of Ra. Europeans were calling for the appointment of Bauan chiefs at all levels of administration in Ra, arguing that the factionalism of the Rakiraki chiefs made it impossible to appoint an officer who could carry out his position. Fijian Christian teachers were distributing copies of a law code, "*Na Lawa E So.*" A system of taxation had been proposed, and a census to determine taxable people was underway. The Vatukaloko people were counted in the Rakiraki district, where Ratu Isikeli and G. B. Evans, his European secretary for Ra, were to oversee the census work and to deal with tax defaulters, while Tavakece of Rakiraki (heir of Udreudre and Waqalevu and newly appointed "lieutenant governor" of Ra) was instructed, in conjunction with R. B. Leefe, European warden of Ra, to gather the taxes in the Rakiraki district (see Ministry of Native Affairs series, especially 1871–1873).

It is unlikely that the census takers went inland to Vugala (Tavakece's [the Vatukaloko Tavakece] town) or to Nakorowaiwai. But the Vatukaloko were probably well aware of the increasing incursions into their lands. In 1873 at least one white observer attributed "unrest" in the area near Togavere to the detention of Namulasi the Navatu chief and two Rakiraki chiefs in Levuka under sentence from the Ra Warden's Court, and the resentment of Ra towns at the interference (Executive Council Kings Cabinet 73/134). While "unrest" may have been warfare, continuous with the warfare in Ra throughout the whole nineteenth century, it may also have been the beginning of the straightforward division between people such as the Vatukaloko and the new "Cakobau government." Having roots both in the Fijian land-sea distinction as well as the "heathen mountaineer" versus "Christian coastal" opposition that the planters made much of, this enmity was built on old experiences, for Bauans and their Viwan allies had been encroaching on Ra for half a century. However, two new factors, the concept of government brought to Cakobau's kingdom by its European members, and the new foreign God, Jehovah, would bring novel conclusions to a conflict conceived in older terms. In 1873 Bauan-European projects and Vatukaloko autonomy came into collision in the Battle of Nakorowaiwai.

Epilogue: Massacre and Lotu

To return to the battle at Nakorowaiwai.

As Sadiri the invulnerable priest showed himself in an opening in the fighting fence, he was shot by two Europeans. The fence and the village were taken. People were found in their houses and killed. The village was set afire, and as the thatched houses began to burn, those within them tried to flee. But by then the coastal warriors had rushed in and killed all the people they could capture. Those who fled from the first village to the second were caught and killed as well. A few escaped into the bush, and a few women and children were saved to be taken captive by the Europeans. The *Fiji Times* report at the time stated that 157 persons were killed, while years later in 1901 Georgius Wright, who had been an eyewitness, gave the number as three hundred. "*Sa samu ko Nakorowaiwai*" (Korowaiwai is destroyed utterly) is a local Fijian proverb meaning utter annihilation.

The destruction of Nakorowaiwai was a shock to the Vatukaloko people. As Tom Burness returned to his plantation on their land, as Warden Leefe and Ratu Isikeli sent out search parties to apprehend the villagers who had fled and send them down to Levuka, the other members of the Vatukaloko polity assessed the implications of the success of the Bauan-European forces. In July of 1873 several mountain chiefs came down to Togavere to *soro* (ritually apologize and concede defeat) for their participation as allies of the Vatukaloko people at Nakorowaiwai. They signed a handwritten document, which I reproduce below as best as I can transcribe it:

Meeting at Toga-vere of chiefs from the Mountain Towns

Bolabola — Chief Ratumasia [?]
Koronivatu [?] — Rakanaci, Kubu

The above named chiefs except [*sic*] of Lotu of their own wish and obey the government and now desire to take the oath of allegiance.

Koro [name of a chief or elder] of Drau ni Ivi
Draunikova [?] — [?oe]
Dakunisava — Vuanivesevi

The above named Chiefs wish for a [Christian] Teacher to be stationed in their town.

(Executive Council / King's Cabinet 73/73)

In January 1875 Amineasa Tora was appointed by the Viwa circuit to the post of Fijian teacher in Drauniivi village (Viwa/A/3, Local Preachers Meeting).

The destruction of Nakorowaiwai heralds the beginning of lost Vatukaloko political autonomy, "political" in the sense that colonizers would use the term, in a new field of Fijian-colonial relations and meanings. If the killing of Koroi i Latikau was motivated by longstanding Fijian arguments about autonomy, it led to a European deus ex machina, the ship the *Marie Louise*. And, to the Fijians, *deus* was irreducibly connected to the political agencies and issues. The *Marie Louise* had been near Ra only by chance, but the battle had permanent consequences. For in 1874, Cakobau and other eastern high chiefs signed a Deed of Cession, and Fiji became a British colony. If the battle of Nakorowaiwai helped confirm the British construction of rebellious inland peoples, this war over religion (as the Vatukaloko remember it) informed Vatukaloko perceptions of the threat to their autonomy posed by the alliance of coastal enemies with the white men and their god. The measles epidemic of 1874, spread at meetings of major chiefs in which the new colonial government was announced, signified to many Fijians the anger of Fijian gods toward those of their descendants who allowed the cession of their land. But much was still to be resolved about divinity in the new colony, especially for the Vatukaloko. It might seem that when the Vatukaloko (or at least some of their chiefs) requested a Christian teacher, they surrendered not just political autonomy but also the ritual authority on which that autonomy was built. What could it mean when the people closest to the Kauvadra range, heritors of Sadiri the invulnerable warrior priest, "accepted the *lotu*"? Change and challenge were coming to an already dynamic terrain.

3

NAVOSAVAKADUA AS PRIEST OF THE LAND

Out of the ashes of Nakorowaiwai Navosavakadua would forge a new polity and a new project, mobilized against enemies old and new. By the mid-1870s he had built a pilgrimage place called Vale Lebo in the foothills of the Kauvadra range. By 1878 he had "come to colonial attention" as an oracle-priest, a practitioner of a kind of ritual called *kalou rere* who prophesied the return of the Twin Gods Nacirikaumoli and Nakausabaria and the expulsion of foreigners Bauan and British.

Let us imagine Navosavakadua at Vale Lebo. Nowadays what remains at this place close to Nakorowaiwai is a group of at least twenty mounds, once foundations of buildings.[1] Probably there was a large thatched building with a heavy ridge pole, set high on the largest, rectangular stone-faced mound that remains. Was it a "Tuka *bure*" like the ones colonial authors Joske and Thurston described? And on another high, round stone-faced mound I picture the god house *(bure kalou)* where Navosavakadua may have sat, drinking kava and listening to the Twins and other Kauvadra gods.

---

1. I first visited Vale Lebo in 1985; I would like to thank John Fatiaki for taking me there. In 1986 I worked with an archaeologist colleague to survey and map the site, including the high circular stone-faced foundation of a temple and a large central building, also with a stone-edged foundation. Individual *yavu* (foundations) were identified and associated with Navosavakadua by some of his descendants from Drauniivi and Rabulu villages. I am very grateful to all who participated in this study. For more on the sites of Nakorowaiwai and Vale Lebo, see Kaplan and Rosenthal (1993).

Descendants of Navosavakadua have told me that it was here at Vale Lebo that Vatukaloko people, and others, came to bring him offerings and to hear him pray, to see him do miracles and prophesy the future. One called Vale Lebo a "religious center" *(koro ni lotu)*. From these narratives, and colonial accounts, I picture the arrival of people, walking inland from the coast over the hills, or coming down from interior hill villages (see figures 5 and 6), bringing whales' teeth, food, mats, tapa cloth, and roots of kava *(piper methysticum)* and receiving in return some form of *wai ni tuka*, water of life or immortality, perhaps as mixed *yaqona* (pounded and infused kava root), perhaps as water from a spring, miraculously flowing from Kauvadra rocks. From a colonial account I picture the arrival in 1877 of messengers carrying whales' teeth sent by certain Rakiraki chiefs to Navosavakadua, seeking the power of Kauvadra gods to begin a war against Bauans and the new colonial British.

In this chapter I want to begin a narrative of the young Navosavakadua named Dukumoi commencing his powers in the spirit of Sadiri, the invulnerable war priest of Nakorowaiwai. And I want to try to understand as well how he came to call himself, or be called, "Mosese" and also "Navosavakadua" (he who speaks once and is effective). To begin, in this chapter we can think about him as a moving force among the Vatukaloko people, as an oracle priest to gods of the Kauvadra, involved in a local historical set of relations. Farther on, in chapter 4 we will have to consider him as a twice deported "dangerous and disaffected native" in the context of a British colonizing project. Do we have an alternative to seeing him either in "purely indigenous" terms, or as a man already shaped by the powerful terms of the colonizers? In chapter 5, when I discuss his ritual-political endeavors from the 1880s on, we will see that he was neither and both, and we will try to devise a better way to characterize his agency. Here, I want to begin by considering his Fijian antecedents: What were his powers as an oracle priest? And how, initially, did he seek to use them in the *"kalou rere"* ritual against British-appointed provincial officials in 1878?

Navosavakadua as *Bete* (Priest)

Navosavakadua, or Dukumoi as he was known as a child, grew up in warring Ra. He was one of the Nakubuti people, the superseded rulers who by the late nineteenth century had become the installing people to the Tui Vatu of Nasi, the chief of the Vatukaloko. Within Nakubuti, Dukumoi's subdivision was Makita, the priests *(bete)* of Nakubuti. Within the other Vatukaloko kin groups *(mataqali)* too there were priest subdivisions. Today at least, and perhaps in the past, the priests of Nasi (subdivision Vale Levu) can act as executive assistants to the chief as well as oracles, likely a continuant of a former role as war leaders. But Dukumoi and the Makita priests of Nakubuti seem to have served a different role, not in service of the Tui Vatu, but rather more directly in service to the gods of the Kauvadra. Navosavakadua himself is remembered among the present-day Vatukaloko people primarily as an oracle and as a worker of miracles.[2]

In 1873 during the battle at Nakorowaiwai, Dukumoi may have been working on a plantation in Taveuni, an eastward island (some of his descendants, and at least one colonial account, say so). But he probably knew or knew of Sadiri the invulnerable war priest, and he probably had contact with or at least knowledge of another famous priest, Sarosaro, as well, just as he probably knew of the mission-trained Fijian teacher stationed at Togavere, the village next to Drauniivi, in the 1870s and heard of other emissaries of the white men's god. Like all of the Vatukaloko people, he had a special relationship with the ritual center of Fiji, the Kauvadra mountain range. The Vatukaloko polity stretched from the villages in the mountains themselves, with their many origin sites, to villages that are on the coast, but are never out of sight of the mountain range, green and golden when sunlit, dark and brooding when shadowy. Site of the most powerful versions of the power of people of the land, stressing the rootedness and autochthony of Fijian gods, Kauvadra was no historical, remembered origin spot to the Vatukaloko, as it was to far-flung eastern and coastal people. Instead, Navosa and his kin—like the present-day Vatukaloko and their inland neighbors—could daily tread the ground of their history.

The Vatukaloko were not unusual in Fiji in the centrality of gods in all aspects of life. Throughout the islands a range of ritual experts mediated between deities and people, re-creating the relation of gods, origins, and people that is manifest at the Kauvadra range. And it is the great chiefly kingdoms that Hocart and Sahlins have described as "ritual polities" headed

---

2. It is nowadays hard to reconstruct details of Navosavakadua's relations with the people of Nakubuti, Wakalou, and Nasi, as a member of the Vatukaloko polity. It is possible that his powers and renown brought him into conflict with others among the Vatukaloko. For example, his renown and resources may have assisted the Nakubuti people in their powerful role in the Vatukaloko polity, diminishing the power of the Nasi chiefs. This seems likely because executive power among the Vatukaloko was held by Nakubuti people, right after Navosavakadua was taken from them, for several decades at the turn of the century. But Navosavakadua is only rarely remembered in terms of internal factions among the Vatukaloko and is, instead, discussed as the focal point of communication between the Vatukaloko and divine power.

by divine kings, incarnate gods. In addition, in the great chiefly polities of eastern Fiji there were important priests *(bete)* who served the chiefs as well as the great war gods and the ancestor gods *(kalou vu)* of chiefly families. These gods were the original ancestors, who founded the lines that became the heads of chiefdoms or confederations. Access to these deities was possible through their particular priests, who were often selected hereditarily. Ranked according to the rank of the deities they served, these priests presided over large temples *(bure kalou)*. Seated within them, beneath strips of white bark cloth, the conduit of the god, they would drink kava *(yaqona)*, become possessed by the deity, and deliver predictions and pronouncements on matters such as battle plans, impending chiefly marriages, or the cause of drought in the land. Whales' teeth and other offerings were made to major deities, conveyed by their priests. Sacrifices in war were cannibal sacrifices, but the gods also received the harvest offerings of first fruits and kava *(yaqona)*, "the water of the land."

Lesser matters were also ordered by the will of the gods, and lesser gods too had their mediums. Lesser gods might be ancestor gods of junior or non-chiefly lines, or gods less connected to particular groups but well known to have particular attributes or interests in particular aspects of human activity; for example, war, agriculture, or sexuality. Priests who did not command great temples might nonetheless be sought after as effective diviners or seers, using clubs, coconuts, and other devices to signal outcomes of problems posed to them. Seers *(dau rai)* and dreamers *(dau tadra)* could predict the future, communicating with deities either in trance or in dreams. Other experts invoked deities for sorcery and for curing. Although the hereditary standing *(itutu vakavanua)* of priest is one of the standard social divisions (all defined by service to a chief) that make up Fijian ritual polities, not all those born into the standing become active conduits of the gods. Moreover, the gods may possess individuals not born to the standing. Circumstances, such as warfare, often determined the need to communicate with the gods, and their vehicles. Nonetheless, hereditary *bete* are predisposed to the ritual role (see Williams 1852 [1982]:215–36, Rokowaqa 1935:30ff., Hocart 1950; see Quain 1948 for an example of a non-hereditary *bete*).

But even given the centrality of gods and their priests throughout Fiji, among Fijian priests, Sadiri the war priest at Korowaiwai was one of a special kind of ritual expert, identified with war, the interior hill people, and invulnerability. Priests such as Sadiri conducted rituals that conferred invulnerability on young men and warriors, and they led their warriors in battle (see Clunie 1977). Across the islands invulnerability rituals had a variety of names, including *kalou rere* (literally "fearsome god"), *kalou vatu* ("stone god") or *luve ni wai* ("spirits of remedy" or "children of water"), and *domidomi*.

Here is a description of a stone god *(kalou vatu)* ritual written by Pere de Marzan, a Marist missionary who worked among hill people at the turn of the century.

> The rites were called "*kalou vatu*," literally "stone gods" "because the adherent once possessed by the spirit becomes physically insensitive like stone; neither spears nor bullets can do any harm to his body." The *kalou vatu* rites were normally practiced to prepare for war, but were also done "simply for pleasure." The central men's house was enclosed by a fence of bamboo and vine, and special food *tabu* were observed. In the central houses a leader, known as the Vunikalou (root of the god) invoked the gods in a chant or meke, while participants drummed. *Yaqona* (kava) was drunk, and the chant repeated, and one by one initiates became possessed by the *kalou vatu* (stone god). When possessed the Vunikalou would spear or strike the possessed men, proving their invulnerability. (De Marzan 1907–1913:9–10)[3]

The *kalou vatu* deities were "gods of the mountain." De Marzan lists some by name but does not say whether they were ancestral deities who entered into descendants, or unrelated deities more fluidly invoked by the leader of the rites. Throughout the islands young men of warrior age participated in such rituals, but the great invulnerable warrior-priests and specially powerful cadres of invulnerable warriors came from the interior hill peoples. The warrior-priests and their special cadres of invulnerables served in the wars of the coastal chiefs as noble allies, and also fought in more local conflicts. In Ra and the hills the constant state of warfare required a constant state of ritual preparation, including the consultation of deities through oracles, and the invocation of the strength of deities, both in polity rituals and in such invulnerability rites, well into the 1870s.

The earliest colonial comments on Navosavakadua and his followers (by both Fijian and European officials) called his activities *kalou rere* rituals (78/550). Colonial accounts also linked Dukumoi to a Rakiraki priest of invulnerability called Sarosaro (see Brewster [Joske] 1891, writing of events thirty years past). (Joske claimed that Sarosaro was Navosavakadua's father, though this is contradicted by present-day Fijians who trace his genealogy in the Nakubuti kin group.) In the 1860s, missionary Lorimer Fison wrote (from

---

3. I read the De Marzan papers at the Catholic Archives, Suva. This condensation in English is based on Nicholas Thomas's translation from French to English of some of De Marzan's published works (De Marzan 1907–1913).

Viwa) of an old priest in Rakiraki who dispensed "*wai ni tuka* [water of tuka] an elixir of immortality."[4] I think that this may well have been Sarosaro, who figures in Joske's and other's recollections. In an extract from his journal that was published in the *Wesleyan Missionary Notices*, the missionary retold a story told to him by Ravunakana, son of Waqalevu, the Rakiraki chief. In the story, Waqalevu heaped ridicule on the old priest for his claims of invulnerability:

> "Well," says Waqalevu, "is all this true about your Wai ni Tuka [water of tuka]?"
> "It is true, sir," answered the priest.
> "Indeed," said Waqalevu. "Then *you* have drunk it yourself, eh?"
> "Yes," returned the priest, "I have drunk it."
> "Very well then," said the chief, "if you're clubbed it can't hurt you now, I suppose?"
> "It cannot hurt me, sir — nothing can hurt me," said the priest, quite boldly.
> "Good," cried Waqalevu "Now to-day shall we prove the truth of your words. Hi! you there! Bring me a club!"
> So a club was brought, at which the old priest began to cast uneasy glances.
> "Now then," continued Ravunakana's father, "if your words are true the club won't hurt you; and if they are false it will serve you right to have your head cracked for your lies and cheating. Are you ready? Are you willing to be put to the proof?"
> When he got thus far in his tale Ravunakana broke forth again into a roar of laughter.
> "Well," said I, "well! what did the priest say?"
> "Say!" cried my friend with another roar. "What did he say? What *could* he say? Why he was dumb! Not a word could we get out of him. And so we all know that he is a liar and a cheat." (Fison 1867:599)

This encounter between the Rakiraki chief and the invulnerable priest may or may not have happened. In 1870 Fison wrote to a colleague: "By the way, I have since found out that the tale about 'How the Cheating Priest was found out,' is if possible a bigger lie than that wh. the priest himself told about his Wai ni tuka. That miserable Ravunakana! But the poor wretch is dead now, & it were useless to reproach him" (Fison to George Stringer Rowe 3 March 1870).[5]

Did Ravunakana build his story on an already extant tension between coastal

---

4. I thank Dr. Deryck Scarr for this reference and Dr. Alan Tippett for identifying the author as Fison.

5. This quote is from Fison's Letterbook 2:619 (Fison Papers, National Library of Australia MS 7080). I thank Mark Francillon for bringing this note to my attention.

chiefs and invulnerable priests? Between chiefly authority and other readings of power? Or did he tell a story of charlatanry that the missionary hoped to hear? While the latter is an intriguing possibility that could perhaps quite literally locate Tuka's origins in the longings of the British imagination, I do not think that Ravunakana had invented the priest and his *wai ni tuka* as well as the encounter with Waqalevu. Fison's 1867 *Missionary Notices* journal extract and later colonial texts make clear that Fison and others knew of the priest from sources aside from the young chief. But it is interesting to consider the possibilities in this early moment in the articulation of coastal chiefly and Christian attitudes toward priests of the land. On the one hand, coastal chiefs soon came to condemn priests of invulnerability. Within two decades high Fijian chiefs (convened yearly by the British as part of the system of indirect rule) would liken Navosavakadua to Sarosaro of Rakiraki, condemning both as practitioners of *luve ni wai* or *kalou rere* (Great Council of Chiefs Meeting 1886). On the other hand, as we shall see, in the 1870s certain among the Rakiraki chiefs turned to Navosavakadua for access to divine power.

Whether or not the events ever took place, Ravunakana's anecdote suggests that *wai ni tuka* was intended to create invulnerability, as were the *kalou rere* rituals of warrior priests such as Sadiri. But while ritual invocations of invulnerability by young men and in warfare were known throughout Fiji from early accounts of the 1830s, I do not know the historical depth and spread of "*wai ni tuka*" and its specific content prior to its development by Navosavakadua. One way of thinking about Sarosaro's *wai ni tuka* immortality in 1867 is to suppose that he mimicked and contested salvation through baptism or communion promised by the missionaries of Jehovah. This might be so, but it is also clear that a range of remedies prescribed by priests, and the invocation of invulnerability for Fijian purposes in the *kalou rere* rites, long predate the coming of the Christian god to Fiji.

It must have been at some time in the late 1860s or 1870s that Dukumoi became Navosavakadua. He was a young man, and it may have been in the course of rites such as the *kalou vatu* or *kalou rere* that he gained his special powers. His descendants say that he heard a voice, when he was alone on a hill. He became a channel to Kauvadra gods, and most particularly he began to speak for the Twin Gods, Nacirikaumoli and Nakausabaria, the rebellious grandsons of Degei.[6] Like other priests before him he communicated with the

---

6. Degei is perhaps the best known of Fijian ancestor gods, said to have taken on the form of a great snake who lives in a cave in the Kauvadra range (see accounts by Brewster (1922) of the cave) or lies wrapped around a great stone (in 1982 I saw one such stone, at Uluda mountain in the Kauvadra, ringed with sea shells.) In an account from 1834, Degei and his family survived a great

gods to predict and shape the activities of the other members of his polity. He was believed to be invulnerable and could convey invulnerability. Moreover, as the appellation Navosavakadua signifies, through his communication with deities he was able to perform "miracles," simply by speaking. He "spoke but once and was effective."[7] In the 1870s, he established his spatial center of power at Vale Lebo, regrouping the Vatukaloko survivors of the battle of Nakorowaiwai and mobilizing the power of the Kauvadra gods against invading Bauans, white men, and Jehovah.

Vale Lebo was built on land close to the Kauvadra range at a place called Nabuya, near the stones where Leka of Nabuya, an ancestor of the Nakubuti people, was installed after he came down from Kauvadra. But by 1875 this land was also part of the range that Tom Burness called his own, and also on the border of two new colonially designated administrative units. The requests that were brought to Navosavakadua, and brought by him to Kauvadra gods, seem to have involved polity struggles, quarrels, and plans for war, as well as illnesses and requests for healing. The struggle that we know something about is the request from certain of the Rakiraki chiefs, great-grandsons of Udreudre (whom the Nasi people had betrayed), sons or grandsons of the skeptical Waqalevu, who came to consult Navosavakadua, and to involve him in invoking Kauvadra deities in opposition to colonial-Bauan authority. In the spirit of Sadiri, Navosavakadua mounted a *kalou rere,* but it was a mobilization of the gods of the land of unprecedented scale and impact, in a new context.

Navosavakadua, the Twins, and the Rakiraki Chiefs

Like the ill-fated incursion of Koroi i Latikau into the hills, it was the encroachment of Bauans—through their subordinates—into Ra that initiated

---

flood at Kauvadra and voyaged down the coast, his descendants founding many of the polities of Eastern Fiji (Routledge 1985:41). In other accounts, Degei quarrelled with his sons or grandsons (the Twin Gods) and caused a great flood to send them away. As they voyaged, they created the physical and social landscape of eastern Viti Levu and the islands (see Derrick 1950:11 for a typical account). (From the 1880s come colonially solicited accounts of Degei's own arrival in Fiji as part of a great migration in a canoe called Kaunitoni, captained by Lutunasobasoba; see France 1966.) More particularly, he is the ancestor god of the Rakiraki people. There are multiple constructions of the story of Degei, emphasizing chiefly or land perspectives (see chapter 5).

7. Waterhouse (1868) lists Vosavakadua as the name of a god of fishermen, but does not specify his attributes. The term *"vosamana"* also applies to chiefs: from a chiefly-centered perspective it is their power alone to speak and constitute the world.

Navosavakadua's first encounter with the new British colonizers in 1878. In Ra the British attempt to establish indirect rule immediately crystallized long-standing conflicts over ritual-political autonomy and subjugation. The Vatukaloko, and even the Rakiraki people, confronted and sought to reject the new rulers and boundaries of the Bauan and British colonial alliance.

In 1874 the British colonial administration reconfirmed Cakobau's governor of Ra, Ratu Isikeli of Viwa, as the Roko (highest provincial official) of the newly designated Ra province. Other provincial offices and local-level offices were to be filled by local chiefs. But no Vatukaloko people gained posts in the new hierarchy. The Vatukaloko polity was never recognized as a *vanua* by the colonial British, in part because of their earlier alienation of land, claimed under colonial procedures by Burness, Thomas, and others in the 1880s, in part because more powerful polities claimed to rule in Vatukaloko lands. The old *vanua* was not incorporated or adapted as an administrative district in the new system of indirect rule. Instead, it was disaggregated and divided. Initially many of the Vatukaloko towns on the coast were included in a district called "Vunitogaloa" named for the Rakiraki fisherfolk whose lands on the coast abut the Vatukaloko. A Rakiraki man was designated as their Buli (administrative officer).[8] Although Vunitogaloa was later redesignated as part of Raviravi *tikina* (provincial subdivision or district), the new boundaries still separated the coastal Vatukaloko from their inland relatives and allies, and it was assumed from early on that these were Rakiraki dominions.[9] The inland Vatukaloko people (including their allies the Nasoqo people, and the related

---

8. The Vatukaloko lands were still largely claimed by the contentious Thomas Frederick Burness, who in 1878 directed the people to withhold coconuts from the Roko Tui Ra when he came to collect them. On the one hand the people complained about Burness to the Roko, on the other hand they refused to obey the orders of the Roko and took orders from Burness.

9. See Native Reserves records concerning Raviravi and Rakiraki *tikina* (NR 44 and 45). Concerning Burness's tyrannical role in the area, see Great Council of Chiefs Meeting minutes (1877) and Wilkinson 78/550. Wilkinson, musing about the basis of Burness's influence over the people of "Togavere," thought that the planter offered to shield them from taxes or governmental interference. Burness may have also been threatening the Fijians with retribution for their involvement in the Battle of Nakorowaiwai. Throughout Ra, Wilkinson identified conflicts between the aims of local white traders and labor recruiters and the new government. Government officials (and local planters) found towns emptied of able-bodied young men who went off to other island plantations, thus hindering the cultivation of tax gardens. Local traders bought up yams, including seed yams, leaving the people hungry. Wilkinson believed that the influence of white settlers was causing an improvident *"veiqati"* (competition among Fijians) to sell off produce; he argued that the traders encouraged improvidence by telling Fijians that this was the way to gain money and enjoy the benefits of the *"vakaberetania"* (British) way of life.

Lamisa and Bobuco people) were included in Tokaimalo and other *tikina*'s (districts) that were then placed in the entirely separate administrative province of Colo North.

The boundary divisions challenged the autonomy of Ra ritual polities. And so did the leaders appointed by the colonial government. The Vatukaloko had fought among themselves and against the Rakiraki chiefs to protest outside claims of sovereignty, just as the Rakiraki people had fought against encroachments from Viwa and Bau. In 1878, in collaboration with the Rakiraki chiefs, Navosavakadua began to mobilize gods and people. He had moved down to the coast to the Vatukaloko town of Drauniivi, and Drauniivi became the center of the elaborate ritual preparation that the colonial Native Commissioner called a *kalou rere* (Wilkinson 78/550).

What I write here of Navosavakadua's *kalou rere* comes especially from a reading of David Wilkinson's 1878 Report to colonial Governor Sir Arthur Gordon. Wilkinson (the Native Commissioner), Alexander Eastgate (European Stipendiary Magistrate in Ra), and Ratu Vuki (Roko Tui Ba) were assigned to investigate charges by the Rakiraki chiefs against Ratu Isikeli the Viwa chief (and Bauan ally) who was appointed Roko Tui of Ra province. Wilkinson, an Australian, had come to Fiji in the 1860s and settled on Vanua Levu island, where he became friendly with the pro-missionary chief of Bua and acted as his secretary. He spoke Fijian and was the official interpreter and translator of the Deed of Cession in 1874.

Reconstructing Navosavakadua's acts looking over Wilkinson's shoulder has its limits. On the one hand, it would be possible to dismiss this, and all colonial accounts, as colonial constructions, or on the other hand to cherish them only as such, and in either case to deny the possibility of knowing anything of Navosavakadua's project. But I read Wilkinson mindful of the histories told by Vatukaloko people today, with some conviction that a reconstructive narrative, always partial, of a Fijian history and mobilization that was real, is both desirable and possible. Concerning Wilkinson in particular, there are aspects of his narrative that make it particularly unclear. They may owe less to the colonial context than to Wilkinson's personal characteristics. As others have noted, his spelling is terrible and his train of thought is often muddled (see France 1969:139ff.). However, his knowledge of Fijian language was considered to be excellent: he based his report on his own interviews with various Fijians who were arrested, and apparently also on eavesdropping on Fijians talking to one another; for example, he quotes a conversation between a man from Ba and one from Tavua.

According to Wilkinson, in 1876 or 1877 Navosavakadua, at Drauniivi, was told by the gods that the land was to be visited again by the Twins, Nacirikaumoli and Nakausabaria, grandsons of Kauvadra god Degei, who had "fled in disgust on the people adopting Christianity and other modern ideas." (Most other accounts, both earlier and later, attribute the flight of the Twins to a pre-Christian version of the story of Degei, in which the Twins fought with Degei at Kauvadra, and then fled, founding the various Fijian polities. Twentieth-century accounts by Vatukaloko informants see Europeans as descendants of the Twins, who married women in other lands during their exile.) A large temple was built for Navosavakadua (perhaps at Vale Lebo or at Drauniivi, or perhaps it was a mythical structure); it was a four-sided house constructed with four enormous *vesi* wood poles. Two "personages" preceded the Twins to *butuvanua* (tread the land), as divine chiefs would do, and to prepare the way. (This too strikes me as odd. Sometimes nowadays the Twins are called "the two" *(ko irau),* and it may actually be that it was simply that the Twins themselves came to prepare the way for the events to follow. Or indeed there may have been a double set of visits.) According to Wilkinson, the "personages" appeared in various shapes and forms, working miracles and dispensing their power to others, sometimes showing themselves in the shape of a dead warrior. They communicated the doings of the spirit world. The spirits were congregating at Kauvadra in preparation for Siganilewa, "judgment day," for which there were to be four years of preparation.

Nacirikaumoli and Nakausabaria arrived in a square-rigged ship called the *Ndrundru.* They approached the coast and landed at Drauniivi under cover of a thick mist or heavy shower of rain. They were welcomed on the coast with elaborate ceremonies of welcome, and went on inland to the Kauvadra range, where the gods were congregating. From the Kauvadra they went out to inspect the doings in the land, to assess the number of true men *(tamata dina)* who had been informed by Navosavakadua and his followers that the gods were in the land and who had begun to prepare themselves for the endeavors to come. Assuming varied forms they went down the east coast of Viti Levu to attend the colonially convened meeting of the Great Council of Chiefs at Rewa. As they trod the path to Laselase (the meeting house where the chiefs were convened) the earth trembled, and as each Twin entered one side of the house it collapsed. (Wilkinson writes that he remonstrated with his informant, saying that he himself was there at the meeting and saw no such thing, the man answered that only the true men *(tamata dina,* "those in the know" Wilkinson translates) could see it.)

The coming of the Twins began a ritual period in which the gods were present in the land, what I would see as a *kalou rere* on a grand scale. Wilkinson heard that the air was full of the spirits of the ancestors. Messages were sent to the true men from Kauvadra by clouds which assumed certain meaningful shapes and forms. All sorts of miracles were or would be possible, and Wilkinson's informant listed them: *tuka* (immortality), *vakatavovoka* (changing the old body for a new one), *vakatuvuri na bula* (causing water to spring up from the ground), and *ka mana* (miracles generally). All were taking place at Drauniivi, proof that the age of gods had come. The true men perceived the miracles, could see the gods, and were to gain powers from them to enact an eventual triumph over the new government.

Moreover, the Kauvadra gods whom Navosavakadua invoked spoke to the specific interests of their descendants who consulted them. Immediate enemies were present to be fought and "plotted against" (Wilkinson's terms) by the true men. Thus the chiefs of Rakiraki enlisted Navosavakadua in their plan against Ratu Isikeli of Viwa.[10] The appointment of Ratu Isikeli as Roko Tui of Ra province reprised the insult of Cakobau's appointment of him as Ra's governor, and evoked at least two generations of the encroachment of Viwa chiefs along the Viti Levu coast. But the "plotters" had more immediate grievances. Vutoni of Rakiraki, then senior living heir of the Rakiraki chiefly line, had been appointed Native Stipendiary Magistrate for Ra, and Tavakece, another Rakiraki chief,[11] had been appointed Buli Rakiraki. But both chiefs were removed from their positions not long after, Vutoni for adultery. Ratu Semi of Viwa, brother of Ratu Isikeli, was then appointed to hold both offices. In 1878 the chiefs of Rakiraki gathered together to petition the Governor to remove Ratu Isikeli and his brother.

More generally throughout Rakiraki and the hill polities inland, organization against the Roko Tui Ra proceeded in a ritual and warlike context. The gods of the land were consulted by the Rakiraki chiefs. Wilkinson tells us that Tavakece and followers took advantage of a mortuary exchange ritual *(reguregu)* at nearby Ba to organize further participants, also "true men," and

10. This account is based on 78/550, Scarr (1970), and Governor Gordon's Despatch to Colonial Office 83/16, 23 May 1878. References to Despatches to Colonial Office will henceforth be by Despatch and number, or by abbreviation CO and number. Governor's despatches are found in Governor's Letterbooks, National Archives of Fiji. Colonial Office records (now held at Public Record Office, London) were examined on microfilm in Canberra. The National Archives of Fiji was unable to provide me with "'Translation of Evidence taken at Navolau in the Province of Ra January–February 1878 during the enquiry into certain charges preferred by the RakiRaki Chiefs against Roko Tui Ra and Ratu Semi Native Stipendiary Magistrate' Provincial Office and Armed Native Constabulary Correspondence (Suva, Central Archives)" cited by Scarr (1970:12).

11. Not to be confused with Tavakece Rareba of the Vatukaloko people.

promised the Rokoship to Tevita Rasuaki, the Buli of Vunidawa district, who betrayed them. They later made overtures through traditional channels to the high chiefs of Korotubu to the east and south in Ra, who accepted their whales' teeth but also informed the Roko Tui Ra of the incident. As the plan proceeded they met more openly at Rakiraki to compose a letter of complaint against the Roko. Wilkinson later reported what he was told were Tavakece's words at Rakiraki:

> The things we have written are very well but that's *vakapapalagi* (in the way of foreigners) the charges are nothing they will answer them all and turn some of them upon us, if we are to be successful we must proceed *vakaviti* (in the Fijian way) we hate the Roko we hate the Magistrate and we want our land back. Let us stick to that and when they see what we are able to do they will hear us, let every man woman and child say we hate the Roko and his brother and will endure them no longer. And when we go to meet them let no man come empty handed let it be seen we are earnest and let no man that is true to us remain at home if he does he is no true man. (Wilkinson 78/550)

The true men went armed with clubs, spears, and axes to the Ra Provincial Council meeting at Navolau in early 1878, perhaps planning to kill the Roko and his brother. Their opportunity was lost, in part (Wilkinson speculated) because he himself unexpectedly accompanied the Roko to the meeting. The subsequent colonial inquiry into "the Charges preferred against the Roko Tui Ra" resulted in the arrest of Tavakece and Vutoni of Rakiraki and a number of other Ra and interior men, including Navosavakadua. Wilkinson tells us that the Fijian police who marched Navosavakadua overland to Navolau, where the inquiry was held, were careful to observe prohibitions *(tabu)* against touching his body, because they knew of his dangerous power as a vessel of the Kauvadra gods. Following the inquiry, a number of the principle figures, including the Rakiraki chiefs — and Navosavakadua — were deported to other provinces by order of the Governor.

Navosavakadua's role in the conflict was in the tradition of the oracle priests, combining "political" activity and direction from Kauvadra deities that was to continue to perplex Europeans. He was the central oracle in "the *kalou rere* business at Drauniivi," yet apparently he was not considered to have been a leader or instigator of the revolt against the Roko Tui Ra.[12] Here is my sense of

---

12. I can only be tentative here, because the archival record of Navosavakadua's 1878 arrest and deportation is not fully available. In 1886 James Cocks, Assistant Native Commissioner, searched the records concerning Navosavakadua for then Governor Thurston. He says that Navosavakadua,

the situation: to the Ra and interior peoples, the Viwan, Bauan, and European claims to sovereignty were challenges to authority rooted in ritual-politics in relation to the gods of the land. And although at some levels the Rakiraki chiefs' agitation would lead to colonial attention to finding locally suitable chiefs, in the main the colonial project would by definition create further challenges to their autonomy. Navosavakadua's role as a warrior priest was as the necessary communicative channel to and from the gods to enable warfare and strategy. His deportation experience would not alter this role. Rather, in 1883 he would return to Ra to continue his career as medium and leader.

Looking over Wilkinson's shoulder, we begin to see the formation of a narrative that will develop in the British imagination. We begin to see the invention of "Tuka." But we can also see, in this and later British narratives, names, events, and motives that were not simply a mirror to British expectations. What Navosavakadua intended and what the British saw are two sides to a complicated project. I will say more about this in chapter 5.

Navosavakadua and the People of the Land

If Navosavakadua summoned Fijian gods, in an extended *kalou rere* rite, he did so on behalf of the *"itaukei,"* or people of the land. Navosa's mobilization continued the history of the Vatukaloko as *bati*. The ambiguous potential of the land people/foreign chiefs relationship was an indigenous ground for contest and new articulations of political and ritual power.

---

together with fourteen others, was deported from his district in 1878 for conspiracy against Roko Tui Ra. However, Navosavakadua is not listed by that name, nor as Dukumoi (or any spelling variants), in the section of Wilkinson's report that recommends removal of certain men and lists them by name. (Unless he is one of the six, "fast young men" noted by the Governor's commissioners, since there is a name there (in Wilkinson's handwriting) that might be "Navosa," but there is a later printed reference to "Namara," so I think it must have been someone else). It is curious that a large section of the Commissioners' report and the papers from 1878 deal with Navosavakadua, but that there is no specific mention of steps taken against him. However, Cocks, writing in 1883, cites an 1883 report of the Great Council of Chiefs resolving that Navosavakadua ("who is there called Navosa") who was deported to Lau be permitted to return to Ra. In the absence of the Armed Native Constabulary records, which may contain statements by or about Navosavakadua and his participation in the 1878 revolt against the Roko Tui Ra, I can only write tentatively about the link between Navosavakadua and the Rakiraki chiefs and British conceptions of it. However, there are extensive colonial records concerning Navosavakadua's ritual-polity which he established between his return to Ra in 1883 and his second arrest in 1886, which I will discuss in later chapters.

In the account of *wai ni tuka* in Rakiraki, it was not just the missionary Fison who was skeptical of the claims of Sarosaro the *bete*. The Rakiraki chiefs themselves mockingly proposed to test his invulnerability. Later, coastal chiefs disparagingly linked Sarosaro and Navosavakadua and other Ra peoples as perpetrators of *luve ni wai,* or *kalou rere,* contrary to good order, and it was reported that Sarosaro was clubbed in the late 1860s at the behest of his "tribal chief." In 1883 Buli Tavua and the older married men in Tavua turned in to the colonial authorities a group of young men, who they said were carrying on Navosavakadua's work while he was in Lau. Yet it is also the case that in their action against the Roko Tui Ra, the Rakiraki chiefs were allied with and inspired by Navosavakadua and his communications from the Kauvadra gods. Invulnerables, like *bati* more generally, fought in chiefly wars, but they were never completely controllable by chiefs, having always the option of "turning." It is possible that in the emerging Fijian-colonial field, the mobilization of the Vatukaloko people and in Ra and the hills more generally could simultaneously invigorate the strategies of the Rakiraki chiefs, and at the same time serve as a much broader mobilization of *"itaukei,"* potentially as much in opposition to the Rakiraki chiefs as to Viwa, Bau, and the colonial government.[13]

People of the Land and the New White Men

If Navosavakadua and the Vatukaloko people were people of the land, they were also "dangerous and disaffected natives" born of "rebels in arms" (Cakobau's designation of the people at Nakorowaiwai in 1873) in the colonial imagination. Navosavakadua was different from Sadiri or Sarosaro. His transformation from the young Dukumoi to Navosavakadua the oracle-priest was comparable to the biographies of other nineteenth-century priests. But his adoption of the name Moses, and the biblical allusions that entwine with the return of the Twins and the gathering of the gods at Kauvadra, mark a differ-

---

13. It has been argued that *"tuka"* and *"luve ni wai"* appear always in the context of challenge to authority, whether against Fijian or colonial authority (see Scarr 1984:93). Perhaps so, if we specify challenge to authority in a Fijian rather than colonial sense, that is, as a relation intrinsic to the Fijian polity, based in the contradictions possible in the relation of land people and chiefs. Such challenge to authority is found in the "rebellious" potential of *bati* (allies) in relation to chiefs, where the challenge is in fact an aspect of the principles that constitute Fijian polities. A comparison might be made to the politics of usurpation seen in other Pacific polities such as Hawaii. This potential was further strengthened in Fiji because it is not the *turaga* chiefly line but the land *bete* who communicate with the gods and fight with their inspiration.

ence. Indeed, as I shall argue later, it was in seeking to encompass Jehovah and Jesus that Navosavakadua would come to establish a new land-centric ritual polity, of a form radically different from the Fijian chiefly polity. So too the Rakiraki chief Tavakece differed from his grandfather Udreudre, writing a letter of protest against the Roko Tui Ra, though he did not believe in its efficacy; soon after, though surrounded by his own armed men, he would not raise the signal to kill the unarmed Roko and the Native Commissioner at the Provincial meeting. These differences arise in the context of the white settler and British colonial presence. What was the experience of "people of the land" in the colonial encounter?

We will see that certain aspects of British colonial practice articulated differently with "land" and "chiefly" people. The rule and reorganization of the peoples of Fiji by the British, from the top down, and their colonizing projects of codification and centralization created an asymmetry, not necessarily so regarded by the coastal peoples, but utterly manifest to the inland and Ra land people. This is not to say that the British purposely set out to deny the autonomy of the people of the land. Indeed they considered themselves to be "preserving native custom." But in fact, they were to fracture the reciprocal roles of *itaukei* and *turaga,* largely misunderstanding "land" claims of autonomy as "heathen superstition" and exaggerating the "political" authority of chiefs. It was in this context that Navosavakadua was to be constructed as a "dangerous and disaffected native."

4

COLONIAL CONSTRUCTIONS OF DISORDER: NAVOSAVAKADUA AS "DANGEROUS AND DISAFFECTED NATIVE"

How did "The Tuka" become a thing in the British imagination? Who were Navosavakadua and his relatives to the British who colonized Fiji? From 1878 well into this century colonial records capture, characterize, and create them, as a cult.

The Colonial Narrative

Wilkinson's report on the *kalou rere* in Ra led to colonial action. In 1879, Sir Arthur Gordon, the colonial Governor, ordered the deportation of the originators of the "charges against Roko Tui Ra and the plot to overthrow the Government," among them Navosavakadua. Of the events in Ra he wrote to the Colonial Office in London:

> it was shown that consultations held avowedly for the purpose of framing complaints against the Roko and Native Stipendiary Magistrate were really intended by certain chiefs . . . to prepare their way to open revolt against the authority of the Government and the overthrow of Christianity in favour of a superstition of mingled elements somewhat resembling that of the Maori Hauhau. This religion was designed [? word unclear] as a common bond of union among those whom the leaders wished to make use of for the accomplishment of political ends: those objects being — according to their own admission, the resumption of powers over the peo-

ple of the district, of which they deemed themselves unjustly deprived, and the reimposition of various oppressive privileges which had fallen into disuse, among them, that of selling the services of men of their tribe in consideration of a payment to themselves. . . .

I . . . summoned those who had been most active in the spread of the new superstition and had taken the chief part in the movement against the Government to appear before me. . . .

I met these persons in number about 20, and made a further enquiry from them into the origin and ramifications of the conspiracy. Those less seriously implicated being about half the number were sent back with a caution to their own province. The remainder, whose immediate return it seemed important to prevent were "prohibited" from doing so for a certain time and different places of abode temporarily assigned to them.

As they were all willing voluntarily to repair to the localities pointed out to them, I did not think it necessary to take formal measures under the "Peace and Good Order" Ordinance of 1875 for their deportation. (CO 78/16)

Among the deportees was Navosavakadua, who was sent to Lakeba in the Lau group, where he remained until 1883.

In 1885 John Bates Thurston, Colonial Secretary and acting Administrator in Gordon's absence, reported to the Colonial Office that "events of an unusual character were transpiring in the mountainous parts of Colo East [province, in the northern interior of Viti Levu island]."

The information first communicated to me was to the effect that a party of strange men numbering some 60 or 70 in all had appeared at the towns of Udu and Savudoi near the junction of the Wailoa and the Wainimala [rivers].

The party had blackened faces, a habit usually adopted in war time, were attired in flowing robes of Masi or native cloth, carried guns with them, and performed certain evolutions resembling drill under command of persons whom they termed "sartini" or sergeants. (CO 83/43)

Thurston enclosed with his despatch reports from W. S. Carew, Resident Commissioner in Colo East, and from A. B. Joske (later Brewster), Assistant Commissioner. Carew reported that: "I lost no time informing Roko Tui Ra . . . asking him to bring in . . . [the] men accused of disturbing the peace by practicing military drill and in other ways . . . under the leadership of one of their number named Bete, who was styled the sergeant of "Navosavakadua's" soldiers. Navosavakadua himself being a heathen priest hereditarily living at "Drau-ni-ivi," "Rakiraki," district of Ra province who has for some time been stirring up sedition in all the surrounding districts."

Always sensitive to local Fijian polity relations in the interior, Carew's reports, like Wilkinson's report on Ra province after the charges against Roko Tui Ra in 1878, move back and forth between explanations of local "political" relations, and assessments of Navosavakadua's project and influence in the area. A series of incidents were reported, all signs of unrest in the highlands: A local Buli (district official) had been found guilty of adultery in a Provincial court held by Joske and the Native Stipendiary Magistrate, and Carew named his successor. A group of Nasoqo people (allies to the Vatukaloko in the old Vatukaloko *vanua*) whom Carew had resettled on their "ancestral lands" had built a new village in an unauthorized and isolated spot, and had constructed several temples *(bure kalou)*, while another division of Nasoqo people were also reported by a Fijian Wesleyan teacher to have built a temple instead of the leper's house they had been told to build.

Of one of these Nasoqo villages, Carew reported: "[It is] styled a "Koro ni vunivuni" or place for the concocting of schemes or conspiracies, and was a short time back visited by Navosavakadua who was received with great welcome and feasted. This man has there a white pig which the people are feeding; this would be killed and eaten at some future occasion upon the occurrence of some predetermined event, and there may be significance according to Native ideas in its colour which I have been careful to mention here" (CO 83/43).

As to the men who had marched and drilled (they were of an inland group called Togavere, not to be confused with the village of Togavere on the coast next to Drauniivi) Carew described the "condition of affairs" among them, noting that during Cakobau's government several Togavere men had been "court martialled" for betraying an expedition sent by Cakobau to take part in a local conflict between people of Bobuco and Muaira. The Togavere people were dispersed, and in the colonial period found themselves divided between the districts of Buli Nalawa and Buli Muaira. They were dissatisfied with this leadership and with their boundaries, Carew concluded, and thus ripe for the interference of Navosavakadua.

> Perceiving the condition of affairs amongst the Kai Togavere, the priest Navosavakadua has stirred up a movement, aided by two other heathen priests of Togavere named Naceva and Taumoli, based upon a very ingenious and dangerous compounding of Fijian mythology and belief with the teachings of Old and New Testaments.
>
> He has given out that the return of the Degei's two sons, Nacirikau Moli and Nakausambaria, lost at the time of the legendary Fijian deluge, is at hand when the world is to be upset (vukica) and the Lotu and Matanitu [Christianity and Govern-

ment] driven out. He also pretends that the teachings of the Christian Bible are altogether compatible with Fijian mythology and heathen practices but that the people have been shamefully deceived by the substitution of the names of Jehovah and Jesus for those of Degei's sons already mentioned.

In anticipation of the return of these two he has required the constitution both of a force of "soldiers" and of female attendants, not that I know of, so far as regards these last, for sensual enjoyment but in order to the procuring of a fitting establishment in accordance with his assumed importance. The text preached by this person is "O cei ena cakacakataki kemudou? Dou buita na ka kece, ka muri au" which means, "Who shall ransom you? Leave all and follow me." (CO 83/43)

Thurston had Carew and the Roko Tui Ra (the Fijian official heading the province) arrest and try the marching men, and those who resisted arrest, for unauthorized drilling and "disturbing the peace." He required as well greater attention to the highland area, writing to Carew: "What do you think of the future of the 'Holy Land' as I understand the region of Degei is called. Should not this move in which you have been very successful be followed up by the close inspection of all the villages in that quarter. By the general disarming of the people and by the general waking up of those wretched turaga ni koro [village headmen] at large, including some of the Buli [district officials]" (Carew Papers, Thurston to Carew, 11 December 1885).[1]

As for Navosavakadua, he was arrested and tried separately. Years later then Assistant Commissioner Joske wrote a description of Navosavakadua, who was initially brought to Vunidawa, Carew's station, after his "lieutenants" and "marching men" had been sentenced in their various provinces.

It was quite a thrilling moment when he arrived under the escort of a picturesque guard, armed with club and spear. A retinue came with him, including a number of female attendants who were known as *Alewa ni Lemba* or *Lemba* women [*leba* is a fruit]. . . . The girls told us that they were sick of the Prophet and were tired of continually preparing *kava* for him. He was certainly not much to look at, being very black and of a decidedly Melanesian type. He looked bilious and overfed, and had a dazed far-away look as if he was continually under the influence of narcotics. Undoubtedly he was always more or less stupid with the unlimited drinking of *yangona* [kava] and smoking of coarse rank native tobacco.

Navosavakandua not having committed any actual overt offence in Tholo [Colo East province], was sent down to Suva, and from thence was relegated to his own province of Ra. There he was charged on two informations with conduct calculated

---

1. The Carew Papers are held at the University of Otago, Dunedin, New Zealand.

to create a breach of the peace, and tried before the Stipendiary Magistrate. I went over to attend the Court, not as a judicial officer, but to watch the case from my special knowledge of *Tuka*. The Prophet was brought round from Suva in the twelve-oared barge of the Commissioner of Native Affairs, and landed at Rukuruku at the head of Viti Levu Bay. . . . The Prophet was found guilty and sentenced to six months hard labour on each charge. If ever I saw a change come over a man's face I did so in Navosavakandua's. The coxswain of the barge in which he had come round was a minor Mbauan chief, Ratu Rusiate, and he and the rest of the crew had thoroughly rubbed it into their prisoner that I was sure to get him hanged. Therefore when he heard that he was only to have a year in jail he took fresh courage and hope, and life was once more worth living. Immediately sentence had been pronounced H. L. Tripp, my brother magistrate ordered the prisoner's hair to be cropped, and this was promptly done and I was an eye witness of the fact. Yet when I got back to Vunidawa rumour had preceded me, and I was told that we failed to accomplish that impious crime as when the scissors were applied to that sacred head they refused to perform their office, and bent backwards rather than commit such a sacrilege. (Brewster 1922:244–45)

In 1887 colonial officials enacted a new ordinance "To provide for confining Disaffected or Dangerous Natives to particular localities" (Ordinance 20 of 1887) as legal grounds to deport Navosavakadua to Rotuma. When the new Governor, Sir Charles Mitchell, minuted the Colonial Office to tell them that the "dangerous fanatic" was being sent to the remote island, an enclosed report explained that "it was found that all the followers of this man became disobedient, dissatisfied, disaffected. Wherever Dugumoi went symptoms appeared it was proved to be cause and effect" (Blyth Memorandum, enclosed in CO 83/46).

Navosavakadua was deported to the small island of Rotuma, far north of the Fiji group. The Resident Commissioner there sent monthly reports on him to the Governor, they portray a quiescent prisoner. The Commissioner noted, for example, that Navosa had married a Rotuman woman, but his reports gave little discussion of his reception by Rotumans, or his influence in that community. He remained in Rotuma until his death in 1897 (97/2036).

Yet despite the deportation of the "Prophet," in 1891, Joske, Carew, and the new Roko Tui Ra (Ratu Jone Madraiwiwi) variously reported "a revival of *tuka*" in the Ra and Colo provinces. Now regarded as "endemic with occasional periods of epidemic activity" (Joske 91/1133), in some places Tuka practices concerned the return of Navosavakadua, in others, a wide variety of activities took place, including distribution of *wai ni tuka* ("water of immortality") and attempts to raise the dead (Joske and Roko Tui Ra 91/1133). In the same year Thurston, now Governor, personally undertook a trip through the hill areas, having practitioners of Tuka arrested, overseeing public floggings, lecturing the people, and ordering the resettlement of offending villages. After reaching the coast, he assembled the people of the villages of Drauniivi, and adjacent little settlements called Vale Lebo[2] and Vatunisala.

> I caused the natives of the towns just mentioned, the Bulis of Ra, and indeed all the people present to be assembled in the Rara or public square. Silence having been proclaimed by the Chiefs I addressed the people upon the subject of my journey across the island and entered into sufficient minuteness into what had occurred and what I intended to do as regards the inland people.
>
> I then recited the history of the district since the days of my earlier acquaintance with it and dwelt upon the unruly and turbulent disposition of the people. I then referred to the history and proceedings of Navosavakadua, his false teachings and the evils which he had originated both in his own district and in those forming that part of the mountains with which it was connected by friendship and old associations. I adverted to the fact that as they all well knew, Navosavakadua and many of his followers had been punished and removed by the first Governor of the Colony: that upon their subsequent return home under promise of amended behaviour, they had again promoted and preached the worship of false gods and brought about a recurrence of evils; that being again removed they were, after warning and caution allowed with the exception of Navosavakadua himself, to return again to their homes and now, after a certain lapse of time I found them once more recurring to evil and forbidden practices.
>
> The Tuka, or worship of their ancestral spirits, the building of Bure Kalou [temples], and the assumption of authority by the old priests or the sons of the old priests of cannibal and heathen days was, I explained inconsistent with the worship of the true God and also inconsistent with the order and good Government of the country established by the Queen. I could therefore as Governor bear with them no longer. Patience and forbearance had been extended to them in an unusual degree and I must now take steps both to prevent their occasioning further mischief as well as to make them a warning and example to others. It was therefore my intention to remove the whole of the people of Drauniivi . . . I should destroy their towns and prohibit their sites ever being occupied again unless the Government in time to come was satisfied that they had thrown off their present evil practices and had become loyal and obedient people. (Thurston to Secretary of State, Despatch 53, 12 August 1891)

2. Probably named after the inland pilgrimage place called Vale Lebo.

The "people of Drauniivi" were therefore deported to the "fertile island of Kadavu," with the aim of "completely cutting off their communication with the mountain people, and . . . of ameliorating their condition morally," in association with the more civilized and fairer-skinned people of Kadavu (CO 83/54).[3]

In 1914 it was again necessary, urged the Resident Commissioner and District Commissioner of Colo North, on behalf of himself and "his" Fijian district officials, to deport practitioners of Tuka, this time Boubuco people of Qaliyalatina district (14/6625). Navosavakadua had died in Rotuma, in 1897 (97/2036), and the people of Drauniivi had been allowed to return from Kadavu to Ra, first to the Roko Tui Ra's town, Nanukuloa, and later back to a new "Drauniivi" on the coast. A new generation of administrators sought out the previous minute papers and despatches for "authority on Fijian matters." Native Commissioner K. L. Allardyce cited Thurston, and Carew, but decided that "while it is clear that certain of the people in the interior of Vitilevu are still 'seeking after strange Gods' there is not the same danger to be apprehended from the practice of 'tuka' now as there was 23 years ago." After consulting with Russell, the Resident Commissioner of Colo North, he determined to deport only twenty-three "leaders" and "secondary rank" Boubuco people, rather than the entire eighty-four persons "implicated in the outbreak."

From Russell the Native Commissioner received "a brief description of Tuka and allied practices," along with copies of descriptions and despatches from the earlier administrators.

> "Luveniwai," "Kalourere" and similar practices to these are penal by Native Regulation. The following definitions are in accordance with the ideas of the present generation living near the home of Fijian mythology, the Kauvadra range.
>
> (a) "Luveniwai" is intercourse with the water-spirits.
>
> (b) "Kalourere" is intercourse with the "domidomi" or spirits of the forest.
>
> (c) "Similar practices." Under this comes the practice of "sika" and "kudru" in which a god speaks through a priest, and also the practice of procuring (or pretending to procure) the materialization of a god.
>
> (d) "Tuka" A return to heathenism, with all its attendant practices (of which

---

3. In 1894 Thurston again faced what he called "disorder" and "old evil customs such as Kalou Vu and Kalou Rere" in the hills of Vanua Levu, during the so-called Seaqaqa War (for some details see Deering 1962). He made a trip to the site of the conflict and lectured the people on loyalty and morality, seeking to suppress what he saw as an incipient outbreak of Tuka.

cannibalism is an essential feature), the destruction of foreigners, and the reign on earth of the twin Gods who will confer immortality on their votaries.

Tuka, first known to Europeans in 1885, is founded on the prophesied return to Fiji of the twin gods, Nacirikaumoli and Nakausabaria, who were banished, by the supreme god, Degei, for rebellion. In 1885 and 1892 [*sic;* should be 1891] preparations for the programme of Tuka was in full progress, but on both occasions was, at some expense, suppressed. After the expedition of 1892 Nadarivatu was founded, with a force of 50 Armed Constabulary, to keep Tuka in check in the interior and on the coast. From time to time, since then, symptoms of the practice were noticed and suppressed by Mr. Joske, the then Commissioner, . . . I am in hopes that measures will now be taken which will check it for many years at least. (14/6625)

Through time and the reification of colonial documents like those above in the creation of a "historical record," unexamined British categories have set the terms of the discussion of Navosavakadua and his people. Even scholars sympathetic to anticolonial movements have couched their arguments within categories constructed in the nineteenth century. In Tuka the British believed that they were encountering "events of an unusual character" which marred the natural and inevitable trajectory of their colonizing project, in which Fijians, already Christian, were to become fully "civilized." They called these "unusual" events "superstition," "movement," "rebellion," and later even "cult." Offended by Tuka and seeking to control it, they labeled and reified it as a manifestation of Fijian disorder and irrationality, and tried to exorcise it from the body politic through deportations. In a scholarly narrative, we have come to see Tuka as a cult.

In Fijian terms, Navosavakadua's project was neither disorderly nor irrational. It was a movement of "people of the land" in the context of the colonial encounter. But in the colonial encounter the British preferred chiefly authority and forged relationships with chiefs in an elaborate system of indirect rule. They did not recognize or institutionalize the ritual-political authority of people of the land. This is not to argue that the British simply imagined that Navosavakadua and his followers planned warfare against them. Rather, I want to think about the ways in which British administrators apprehended (and provoked) challenge to their rule, and thus to examine the assumptions of their colonial project. I will argue that the British constructed Tuka and its prophet even as they sought to control them.

So, here I want to reconsider the narrative with which this chapter begins. The point will be to trace a British imagination of disorder in Fiji through three stages of colonial expectation and experience: initial optimism, acknowledgment of awkward moments, and finally the reification of a "rebellious" or "disaffected" substratum in Fijian life, typified by Tuka. In so doing, British administrators projected categories of order and disorder onto different Fijians and different Fijian projects, thus inventing both positive and negative Fijian tradition.

In this discussion I run the risk of presenting Fiji Europeans, or even all colonial Europeans, as a homogeneous group. Of course they were not. Planters, missionaries, and colonial officials differed, sometimes to the point of European antiadministrative "disaffection."[4] Here we will touch upon Governor Gordon's thwarting of early planter aims, and in later chapters we will see administrative anti-Catholicism, and how alternative possibilities for Fijian articulations were made possible by the presence of non-Wesleyan missionary groups. The official colonial minute papers reveal constant debates between officials: in chapter 6 we will see a later colonial governor challenging Gordon's orthodoxies. Even so, more could be said than I do here about differences between aristocratic, political-economic, and evangelical discourses, about national differences, gender differences, and so forth. But there were also real similarities, especially in the fundamental imaging of European order and Fijian disorder. If in this chapter I stress commonalities, arguments in shared terms, and resolutions of internal contradictions in the colonizing project, it is especially to show the building of a powerful colonial orthodoxy of practice and terms that had real consequences for Navosavakadua and the Vatukaloko, and for the ways in which Tuka became a thing and a cult.

British Hierarchy and the Colonial Project in Fiji

European presence in the islands began with explorers and beachcombers, but the first sustained European settlement was that of the Wesleyan missionaries beginning in the 1830s. A different wave of European settlement intensified in the 1860s, as New Zealanders and Australians—settlers such as Tom Burness and the Thomas family—set up cotton plantations on the strength of the world cotton boom. The origin myth of colonial Fiji is "Cession," in which an increasing troubled land was offered to the Crown by Fijian chiefs unable to

---

4. In the 1880s white settlers proposed to federate Fiji with New Zealand, hoping thereby for settler government in place of Gordon's elaborate Native Administration and Native lands policies (see Scarr 1984:104–6).

rule white settlers as they had controlled their own people, and accepted reluctantly by Queen Victoria and the Colonial Office in 1874.

Among Fiji scholars the early history of colonial Fiji has been written largely as a conflict of humanitarian missionaries and colonial administrators versus rapacious settlers. It is true that when Sir Arthur Gordon established the Native Administration (a system of indirect rule) and land reservation system in the 1870s he explicitly intended to benefit Fijians rather than white settlers. The "Native Administration" constituted colonially enforced structures of Fijian authority through Rokos and Bulis (Fijian provincial and district officials) who were ostensibly "hereditary chiefs." It followed provincial boundaries reflecting indigenous groupings that had been set up in the Cakobau governments and by Sir Hercules Robinson (who had negotiated Cession on behalf of the Crown). The new land system mandated the reservation of Fiji's lands for Fijians (currently 83 percent is so reserved) through the establishment of the Lands Commissions. Fijians were not forced to work for money, since government revenue was obtained through a communal tax garden system. In scholarly literature, Gordon's claim to rule through preservation of authentic custom has had both unquestioning admirers (Legge 1958) and critics. The critics have argued that colonial codifications of Fijian leadership, social groups, land tenure, and even origin myths were false orthodoxy, based on ignorance, arrogance, and nineteenth-century social evolutionary theory, in contrast to diverse Fijian reality (France 1969). More recently in the study of colonial societies the debunking of colonial constructions has given way to an interest in the relation of colonial constructions and colonial power (for Fiji see Clammer 1975, Kaplan 1989a, 1989b, Kelly 1991, Kaplan and Kelly 1994, Thomas 1990; on colonial Africa, Fields 1985 is particularly relevant). The issue is no longer Fijian reality versus colonial supposition, but rather how colonial knowing (the colonial imagination or gaze) remade the colonized. This turns our attention back to the discourse of the colonizers, problematizing tropes found in their narratives that might otherwise seem natural.

If we scrutinize the colonial project as itself a basic problem, then the focus of study shifts from the "invention of tradition" to a larger and more complex field of colonial motivation, perception, and regulation. Here we can consider the origin of these "inventions" in certain powerful and very real British principles concerning hierarchy, order, and disorder.

Sir Arthur Gordon's aristocratic "humanitarianism," Thurston's invocation of "good government and good order," and British constructions of "danger and disaffection" are linked to an English model of the proper, moral polity.

The English polity is hierarchical, but it is a top-down hierarchy, different in crucial ways from the Fijian polity based on the complementary chiefs–land people opposition. The English ruling class constituted themselves as society, simultaneously the personification of, and the arbiters of, the proper, the good, and the orderly. It is the "English peculiarity," write Corrigan and Sayer in their powerful analysis of enduring features of the English "state," that

> dominant images of national identity and tradition—of, in that significant phrase, national character—are closely bound up with both the culture of the English ruling classes and the (claimed) history of the state forms through which their power is organized. We mean this to apply to those celebrated elements of "national character," the supposed reasonableness, moderation, pragmatism, hostility to ideology, "muddling through," quirkiness, eccentricity and so on of "the English," every bit as much as to the more evident patriotic symbols of the rule of law, the "Mother of Parliaments," and the Royal Family. This very particular set of cultural images was fundamental to the construction of English capitalist civilization, in a number of ways. (1985:192)

In such images the English ruling class identified itself with the nation as a whole and saw their own interests as that of the polity. These images provided as well the "moral energy for English imperialism" including both ruling class dominance in relation to such groups as women and working classes within England, and English imperialism in places ranging from Wales, Scotland, and Ireland to far-away colonies such as Fiji (see Corrigan and Sayer 1985:193–95). That is to say, that both the English polity and the relation of England to the colonies were conceived in these terms of relation between a core society (the ruling class) and the larger society it was seen to support and order. In colonies such as Fiji, the relation of ruling class core to "others" was replicated contextually, even though planters, missionaries, and many colonial administrators were not themselves initially "aristocratic."

In general, the European purpose in Fiji was to impose order from above, on a field which though differently conceived by missionaries, planters, and administrators was in all cases conceived to be inherently inferior and disorderly. Planters sought to put wild nature to economic use, missionaries to lead the heathen to God, and colonial administrators to raise savages to civilization and the local Europeans to the rule of law, through the creation of a polity in the British mode. This is not to say that Fiji Europeans saw themselves and their projects as similar. A consistent opposition between planters and missionaries parallels a contradiction described for English history by Corrigan and Sayer, that the English ruling class manifests a double "projection of its needs onto the majority of the population. Insofar as the latter constituted labour power they were property to be used and improved like any other instruments or factors of production, but insofar as they were also potentially civic beings they were to be morally regulated and civilized into understanding their society and their place within it" (n.d.:13). In Fiji in the 1870s, Governor Gordon made a choice between two such projections (which I read as two facets of the shared trope of ordering of disorder for colonial purposes). In so doing, he also chose between the settlers on the one hand and the missionaries on the other, authorizing claims of the latter through official policy.

Fiji was a late colony, and Gordon interpreted the planter and missionary constructions of Fijians in terms of other colonial experiences and imperial possibilities. Settlers as planters sought to exploit Fijian labor, but Fijians had come to be considered inefficient and difficult plantation laborers. On most of Fiji's plantations, the laborers were taken from other Pacific islands, and this "blackbirding" labor trade had already provoked outcry. Gordon resolved the contradiction of the need for exploitable labor and the desire to civilize the Fijians, on the basis of his experience of indentured South Asian Indian labor when he served as Governor in Trinidad and Mauritius. A more "advanced" society, India, would supply workers, while the Fijians progressed. To aid the Fijians in their progress, all further alienation of their land to Europeans was prohibited. Thus Gordon's government confounded the planter expectation that they would become the ruling elite, and define the aims of a colony through the settlement and exploitation of the land of Fiji. A more "authentic" representative of Britain's elite (Gordon was the fourth son of a British prime minister, the Earl of Aberdeen) became the arbiter of policy and project.

Gordon's vision of the Fijians and their place in the social evolutionary hierarchy — and his vision of Indian society as well — are revealed in an address to the Royal Colonial Institute in 1879:

> No one would dream of placing on one level the acute and cultivated Hindoo or Cingalese and the wandering and naked savage of the Australian bush. The Fijian resembles neither; but he has more affinity with the former than the latter. . . .
>
> The people are not nomadic; they live a settled life in towns of good and comfortable houses; they respect and follow agriculture; their social and political organization is complex; they amass property and have laws for its descent; their land tenures are elaborate; they read, they write and cypher. Women are respected, hold a high social position and are exempt from agricultural labour. There is a school in almost every village. The chiefs possess accounts at the bank, conduct correspondence, and

generally exhibit capacities for a higher grade of civilization. On the whole I class them in this present condition with the Horas of Madagascar . . . Like them the Fijians all profess an at least nominal allegiance to Christianity, and that it has largely influenced the life and character of the great masses of the population, not the most incredulous can, I think, deny. Like them too they have shown a gradual progress, which is, in my estimation of far more hopeful augury than a rapid imitativeness of unfamiliar habits. . . .

It should always be borne in mind that the state of society for which they are intended is not that of England in the present day, but more nearly resembles that of the Highlands of Scotland some three or four hundred years ago, or that of remote parts of Ireland in the days of Queen Elizabeth. (1879b:12–14)

Gordon approved of the settled and ordered aspects of Fijian life, as he perceived them, though his vision of Fijian society was a partial and constricted one. Gordon and fellow colonial administrators took for granted as "Fijian" many practices and institutions formed in the nineteenth-century relations between certain Fijian groups and European settlers and missionaries, including some from the "Cakobau governments" of the early 1870s, most notably Cakobau's extensive claim to sovereignty. Gordon's image of Fijians as civilizable rested on a twofold foundation: the apparent successes of the forty years of missionization in the islands prior to the establishment of the colonial polity, and the complexity and hierarchy of Fijian society, especially the leadership of Fijian chiefs. Ironically, "Hindoos" of a "more advanced civilization" (as Gordon saw it) would be found, later on in the colony, to be less deserving of administrative affection than the incipient-Christian Fijians. Equally, Indian "coolies," advanced enough for exploitation, as the Fijians were not, would be denied (in Fiji) their social complexity, indeed would be forced into casteless low-ranking "equality" in the service of economic exploitation, while Fijian hierarchy was idealized, reified, and codified, and Fijians protected from the iniquities of the plantation system.[5]

---

5. There are further ironies in the history of planter and missionary endeavors among Fijians, and Gordon's policy-making. In the history of England, and in many colonial societies, it can be argued that Methodism and labor discipline went hand in hand to "make a working class," in E. P. Thompson's terms, in a complex refashioning of moral, temporal, and political-economic categories and practices (Thompson 1963; Comaroff 1985). But in early colonial Fiji Methodist Fijians were not to be the laborers. Nonetheless, Methodism did evoke profound changes in Fijian society. Ultimately, in British policy, it resonated with a different form of hierarchy. In Fiji, Methodism did not create a proletariat, but helped instead to define a new class of "commoners," thereby redefining the people of the land.

Christianity and the Civilization of the Fijians

The mission presence in the islands was important to Gordon because in the British administrative imagination missionary success had shown that Fijians were civilizable. From 1830 on, the Wesleyans had created a religious polity, of which Gordon wrote:

> But that for which I was most unprepared, for I had heard least about it and do not think its political significance had been hitherto fully appreciated is the really wonderful organization of the Wesleyan body here. I know nothing equal to it except the Jesuits. In every village there is a "lotu" teacher. The different links of superior administration are admirably fitted on to one another and finally the Head at Navuloa has at his command a perfect machinery which enables him to know down to the minutest detail all that is doing in every part of the islands. His statistics and information are far grander than those which the government can obtain and his power is real, absolute and in constant exercise. (Gordon to Carnarvon 21 August 1875, Carnarvon Papers, quoted in Legge 1958:25)

At the inception of the colonial polity the missionaries and their institutional framework of circuits and teachers were routinized. Following the conversion of Cakobau of Bau in 1854, the islands were ostensibly largely Christian, notably excepting the interior, northern, and western peoples of Viti Levu island. Jehovah had triumphed in the islands, imposed—it would seem—from the top down, by white men and chiefs. To Gordon and other colonial officers, Methodism seemed to be the religious component of Fijian tradition, the "established church" (Brewster 1922).

For colonial administrators and missionaries alike the categories of conversion were straightforward, in Fiji and among the peoples of the world more generally. Knowledge of the true God was held by Europeans, and preached by them to heathen others. The process of individual or local conversion might be subject to interpretation (was chiefly conversion sometimes opportunistic and "political"?), but the categories were fixed. By the 1850s the terms "Christians," "heathens," and "backsliders" were regularly used to distinguish different categories of Fijians, used by Europeans and Fijians as well. As we have seen in the story of the battle at Nakorowaiwai, settler, missionary, and administrative narratives of battles, enmities, and strife among Fijians well into the 1870s used *"tevoro"* (devil) and *"lotu"* (Christian) as the denotations for various opposing Fijian groups. Indigenous histories and motivations, though often known, were equally often subsumed in the implications of these categories of conversion.

Fijians were called upon to assert or acknowledge conversion as a defining characteristic in appearance as well as behavior. "Putting on clothes" was to both Fijians and Europeans the outward sign of inward conversion (see, e.g., Wright 1901:55). Wearing *sulu* (wrapped garments) of imported cloth and cutting the hair were social indicators implying, Europeans believed, the acceptance of European God and rule, and the putting away of nakedness and unruly warlike display. In the missionary rhetoric, and that of early colonial usage more generally, conversion implied the movement from nakedness to decorum, from warfare and cannibalism to warfare for the sake of the conversion of others, and thus, ostensibly to a state of "peace and good order," and ultimately from savagery to civilization.

Colonial administrators of the 1870s were based in the domains already converted (the majority of the coastal kingdoms following Cakobau's conversion in 1854). This transition to Christianity and all it implied was the status quo, an accepted part of Fijian social nature, and tautologically verified the colonial goal of further civilizing the Fijians. In 1874, as Governor Gordon began the colonial codifications of Fijian custom for the purpose of indirect rule, Christianity was conceived, not as deviant but as standard, in the Fijian way of life.[6]

Hierarchy and the Civilization of the Fijians

Fijian chiefly hierarchy was the other basis for the colonial assessment of the "civilizability" of the Fijians. The legal legitimacy of British rule was itself defined by the Deed of Cession in which thirteen Fijian chiefs ceded the island to Queen Victoria. Gordon knew little of the ritual relations that made and empowered indigenous Fijian rulers as divine chiefs, relations based on installation by the ritual authority of people of the land. His Colonial Secretary (later Governor) Thurston, though more knowledgeable about Fijians, saw them as well from the vantage of a European planter and politician. Both, as Europeans were wont to do from earliest contact, saw "pragmatic" power,

---

6. This was despite the fact that Fijians were legally entitled to freedom of religion. On the one hand, Gordon explicitly cited the rights of Fijians to maintain practices that were customary, including "religion." On the other hand such practices could not include cannibal sacrifice ("murder") or warfare (1879a vol. 1:vi–vii). Ultimately no non-Christian "religion" was ever found acceptable.

from the top down, as the basis of Fijian political leadership, unconnected with ritual authority, or in their terms, "religion," since it was not "true religion."[7] Thurston clarified the relationship of legitimate authority and Christianity when, haranguing Navosavakadua's relatives in Drauniivi in 1891 he said, "The Tuka or worship of ancestral spirits, the building of Bure Kalou, and the assumption of authority by the old priests or the sons of the old priests of cannibal and heathen days was, I explained, inconsistent with the worship of the true God and also inconsistent with the order and good government of the country established by the Queen" (14/6625). There was no question of a Fijian religion in any way consistent with the true God and good political order. The assumption of authority by Fijian priests was now illegitimate. In the context of a project of indirect rule, what Fijians might legitimately assume authority?

Gordon wrote of Fijian chiefs that they "generally exhibit capacities for a higher grade of civilization" (1879b:12). It was at root a projection of British hierarchical principles rather than an understanding of, or endorsement of, Fijian principles of divine kingship that informed this construction of chiefly legitimacy. In preferring the chiefs Gordon and Thurston followed traders and planters, who had already constituted chiefs as economic and political agents,[8] and missionaries (e.g., Williams 1858:36) who early on had found that access to Fijians, and indeed the conversion of Fijians, had to be accomplished from the top down. But it was Gordon, and Thurston, especially who fixed the Fijian chiefs as an aristocracy.

Like Christianity, chiefship was taken by Gordon, and by later colonial administrators as a baseline, as natural and proper order. It was an aspect of Fijian culture which was to be "preserved" and utilized in the colonial process of legislative and institutional ordering and civilizing. Fijian chiefs, conceived as British aristocracy, endeared the Fijians to administrators, and presented the aspect of "civility" that Gordon so often remarked upon. When it suited

---

7. For example, Gordon and Thurston both knew Cakobau after 1854 when he had become "Ebenezer."

8. *Beche de mer* and sandalwood traders had first enabled chiefs to have bank accounts, as the whites made relationships with chiefs in order to gain access to fishing grounds, sandalwood stands, and the labor to process these resources. In interaction with settlers and planters in the 1860s, chiefs were further constituted as a separate class when they were sought out to alienate land, and to act as brokers for Fijian labor for plantations. In such cases settlers construed chiefs as petty dictators, operating from the top down, possessing people and land, like property, rather than as ritually authorized by their people.

them, colonial administrators were to join in putative "chiefly rituals," legitimizing and creating chiefly apparatus through their own participation.

The colonial projection of an aristocratic model of rule made Fijian chiefs into a class. Certainly Fijian chiefs made use of European guns, goods, God, and the Native Administration to their own ends. A working understanding of this new version of chiefship was made between the British and the Fijian chiefs they favored: the core (though not the whole) of this new class was connected genealogically and in cultural aims to pre-colonial chiefly figures and long-standing projects. But once colonial administrators had constituted themselves as the arbiters of tradition, with a vision of Fijians as increasingly Christian in spirit and hierarchically organized in polity, the administrators found their authority threatened by aspects of Fijian life that did not fit the colonial model.

The Colonial Project and People of the Land

There was no place in the British top-down polity for ritually and politically autonomous "people of the land." Contradictions arose when authority was claimed by Fijians who were not the colonially empowered. War in the mountainous interior of Viti Levu island in the 1870s, protests in Rakiraki against the Roko Tui Ra in 1878, and the rise of Navosavakadua were all assertions of various aspects of unrecognized Fijian interest. Such claims were not conceived by the British as projects of people of the land, since no such category was identified or legitimized as part of Fijian tradition in the official view. Rather, they became what I call "negative tradition," imagined as different from proper custom.

The invention of tradition literature (see Linnekin 1983 and Hobsbawm and Ranger 1983 for founding uses) has tended to focus on the use of the concept of "tradition" to positively authorize and valorize. In Fiji a curious two-sided colonial invention took place: some institutions were constructed, labeled customary, and made official, with great approbation. Others were constructed, and found inherent in Fijian nature, but despised. These were legislated against. In this process, of course, they too gained a new and different reality (on this sort of inquisitional creativity see Ginzburg 1983). Onto Fijian practices outside of and in conflict with those selected for inclusion in the civilizing process, the British projected images of disorder, and later of disaffection and danger, the unsavory residue of colonial orthodoxy in the making.

British Optimism and the Hill Tribes

The first challenge to Sir Arthur Gordon's early optimism was the problem of the northern and hill people of Viti Levu. Years earlier missionary Richard Lyth recorded his impression of the Ra (northern) coastline of Viti Levu during a voyage in 1848: "We glided along the coast almost imperceptibly till we found ourselves opposite the lofty Kauvadra mountains the supposed abode of the serpent god Degei, who lies in the sacred cave which I suppose no living person ever saw. . . . His name will soon be forgotten" (Voyaging Journal, microfilm BV 112 reel 3 232).[9] The missionaries came from the east, through the Tongan connection with Lau, and thence to the most powerful coastal kingdoms of Viti Levu and Vanua Levu. Ra and the Viti Levu highlands were one of their last heathen frontiers, but this was not anticipated in the early missionary accounts. Writing in the 1840s, when Bau too was yet to be converted, Thomas Williams did not prefigure the marked "heathen" classification of the hill people that would develop in the 1860s, writing instead that "Native tales about the great size and ferocity of the mountaineers and of their going naked, deserve no credit; the chief difference being that they bestow less care on their persons and are more rustic in manner. On visiting these highlanders, I always found them friendly, nor do I remember that they ever used me unkindly" (1858:103). Stereotypes of "mountaineers" based on the Scottish highlanders inflected colonial perceptions, but the missionary Williams, far from bringing to Fiji a predisposition to find particular savagery among mountaineers, ascribed to a coastal kingdom (Somosomo) a particular and superior depravity, as "the vilest of the vile" (1858:40).

It was in the 1860s that the indigenous Fijian coast-interior opposition (a spatial version of the chiefs — land people opposition) became paradigmatic in the European vision of the variation within Fiji, paradigmatic when overlaid with religious categorization. The "heathenism" of the interior people was decisively set for the Europeans of Fiji when missionary Thomas Baker was killed in the interior in 1867. Planters along the northern coast, on the Ba river and in Ra both before and after the missionary's death, called the mountain people who raided their plantations "bigheads" or "devils." The planters at the battle of Nakorowaiwai called the Vatukaloko "bigheads" and Sadiri a "devil priest." Within this framework of relations, the northern and interior peoples of Viti Levu island came to be considered, treated, and legislated as different in the colonial body politic.

9. Lyth Papers, Mitchell Library, Sydney. Microfilm in Regenstein Library, University of Chicago.

In 1876 Governor Gordon oversaw the "Little War" (as he called it) in which the interior people were subjugated to the new colonial polity (see Macnaught 1971). In an elaborate correspondence he later published (in two volumes as *Letters and Notes Written during the Disturbances In the Highlands (Known as the "Devil Country") of Viti Levu, Fiji 1876*) he chronicled a shifting colonial construction of the hill people from "natural heathens" to "willful rebels." Initially, in the administrative view the hill people ("Kai Colo")[10] were differentiated as those peoples who remained to be persuaded to join the colonial polity, under the authority of the Queen. Cession, and their nonparticipation in it, marked them as a social and political category in the British administrative project. More broadly, it was the "heathen tribes" who eschewed both Christianity *(lotu)* and Government *(matanitu)*. Administrators sought to replicate Cession, first at a meeting in 1875 at Navuso, where they were told by Cakobau's eldest son, "Now under the Queen's rule we, with the exception of one little cloud, have a clear and open sky. You are the little cloud, and that little cloud must clear itself away" (Layard to Robinson, CO 83/6, cited in Macnaught 1971: 24). The optimistic colonial assessment that the hill people had voluntarily entered "into the pale of civilization, law and order" was to be checked by Fijian reaction to an ensuing measles epidemic, unwittingly spread into the interior by the chiefs returning from the meeting and interpreted by the survivors as the anger of the old gods.

A second meeting at Navala in 1876 was held by Governor Gordon.

> I told them that if they abstained from murder and cannibalism, and discontinued the practice of making forays on their neighbors, they would be unmolested in the enjoyment of their lands, the practices of their religion, and the observance of their ordinary habits and customs.
>
> With the concurrence of this meeting, I, immediately after its conclusion, sent my Commissioner, Mr. Carew, and a body of police, to take up a position in an inland district, the villages of which were either nominally Christian, though without teachers, or heathen, but not unfriendly to the Government. (1879a vol. 1:vii)

In the colonial view, these meetings initiated the rule of order in the colony. From then on, warfare in Colo would require colonial attention. And indeed, the interior people did not immediately come within the pale of the Queen's good order.

10. Gordon used the term to refer to the interior tribes to the west of the great range of mountains dividing Viti Levu. Later the three "Colo [hill] Provinces" would come to bound and define the mountain people in the administrative parlance, but "Kai Colo" was generally used contextually to refer to any inland or hill people.

Governor Gordon's despatches to the Colonial Office in London describe his expectations, and the causes to which he attributed the "Disturbance." On the one hand, he portrayed the hill people as legitimately ignorant of the intentions of the colonial government, and even legitimately entitled to question Cession, since they had not been party to it.

> A large proportion of the natives inhabiting this part of Viti Levu had not even nominally embraced Christianity, or been represented at Navuso. They had never submitted to any coast Chief. They but very imperfectly realised the claims or power of the Government. . . .
>
> Unfortunately, too, their neighbors to the south, the people of Nadroga, always jealous of the river tribes, and filled with all the zeal of new Christianity, constantly taunted the heathens of the mountains with their inability to fight for their faith, and told them that, if they did not voluntarily adopt Christianity, they would be shortly made to do so by force.
>
> Nor was the conduct of the white settlers always judicious, and it is to be feared that reason was given to the natives to suppose that the Government was prepared to enforce the most extravagant and unbounded claims of the whites. . . .
>
> Still, when I saw how rapidly alarm and irritation were giving way to confidence and security, in other parts of Fiji, I could not but hope that measures of a similar character to those which had been adopted with success elsewhere might ultimately produce the same result. (1879a vol. 1:viii–ix)

When forced to qualify his optimism, Gordon sought to blame, not Fijians, but outside influences. Fijian resistance to religion or rule was not only due to their evolutionarily simple stage. The taunting zeal of the newly converted, and the evil influence of whites of the lower orders, could explain the interior peoples' resistance without implying that Fijians were intrinsically unlikely to become civilized and take their station in the colonial polity.

The Prototypical "Disaffected or Dangerous Native"

But when Fijians themselves were seen to act willfully in opposition to religion and government, they were conceived to be disorderly and illegitimate. Gordon assigned the blame for the Little War most particularly to two "heathen" chiefs.

> In fact, all the influences of which I have spoken, and others on which I do not greatly care to touch, might have failed to produce any sinister effect, but for the

determined hostility to the Government of the Chiefs Mudu, of Qalimari, and Na Bisiki, of Drio-drio. . . .

On the 12th April, the village of Nawaqa . . . was burned, and during the next few days the frontier towns of the province of Nadi were destroyed, or threatened, by bands under the direction of Bisiki and Mudu; whilst by an evidently preconcerted arrangement, the Christian villages on the lower part of the Sigatoka were at the same time burnt, and a number of women and children killed, by the united forces of the tribes in that vicinity.

The young Roko Tui of Nadroga, Ratu Luki, immediately collected a small force, and, crossing the Sigatoka, made a retaliatory raid on the heathen villages to the east of that river. . . .

It now became evident that a collision was unavoidable. It was impossible to permit the perpetrators of such outrages to remain unpunished, and it was clear that it would be equally impossible to secure them without encountering resistance. (1879a vol. 1:ix–x)

Na Bisiki and Mudu figure prominently in the correspondence of the Little War, not just in Gordon's despatches to the Colonial Office, but also in the voluminous practical correspondence between officials as the campaign was carried on. Ultimately, it was these Fijian leaders, rather than the white settlers, whom Gordon found to be the root cause of the "collision."

The initial account of Na Bisiki is from Carew, who blamed him for the frustration of his negotiations with the hill people, writing to the colonial secretary:

the meeting which was held at Nasue . . . when the Beimana and other tribes sent to inform me that they had decided upon offering no further resistance to the government, has ended unsatisfactorily; chiefly . . . owing to the determined action of a chief called "Na Bisiki," belonging to a small village called Namoli. . . .

This man is a most dangerous and active opponent of the Government and has lately plundered the property of a loyal village in his neighborhood, and acts on all occasions as the leader of the turbulent class of people in the interior, who have drilled themselves during the past two years in imitation of the police, and have placed themselves under his leadership. (Gordon 1879a vol. 1:63)

Carew continued in another letter to the Governor,

Nabisiki, a most determined scoundrel, is down again at Vatumoli, with the Naqaqa and other tribes, who are having a great feast and general slaughter of pigs, which for some time past have been tabu-ed, for any very special event. They have also "vakasi-kataka'd" the Kalou Rere, that is, brought outside for trial their superstitious war rites, which they have been working up withindoors [*sic*] in private for some days past, or rather I should say weeks. I believe myself that they are bent on mischief and are perfectly reckless of consequences. . . .

They are so bad that, no matter what profession they may make hereafter, I would not dare to send the men amongst them, or to visit them myself. They know the power of Great Britain, and confess to that knowledge, but say they prefer to do prison labour to going on without a desperate struggle for their independence and I can place no confidence in anything they say. . . . All the "Ra" consists of a number of petty republics. The chiefs have no power except for evil, and the people declare that they, the people are rulers, and not the chiefs, who are only appointed to carry out the public will. (Gordon 1879a vol. 1:63–66)

Na Bisiki became an obsession to Carew. The Commissioner even arranged to have a special set of handcuffs sent up in anticipation of Na Bisiki's capture, and a price was set for his capture alive (Gordon 1879b vol. 1:253, 303). Governor Gordon and the other colonial participants in the "Little War" shared Carew's concentration on the capture of this leader, and his ally Mudu. But it was not simply because these men "worked eagerly and incessantly against the government." The colonial officials perceived and constructed them as opposite to their image of the proper Fijian chief. Their polities, seen as "petty republics," were the opposite of the chiefly kingdoms the officials admired, and of the colonial chiefly hierarchy in the making.

Contrasting orderly hierarchy and disorderly illegitimacy, Gordon explained his use of Fijian troops, under Fijian and European command, by insisting to the Colonial Office that the Little War was not between the government and Fijians, but between different Fijian groups, describing the campaign as "properly considered, . . . only the repression, by the peaceably disposed and orderly portion of the native community, of illegal outrages, committed by another section of the native population" (Gordon 1879a vol. 1:xiv). Before the "perpetration of illegal outrages" Carew had planned to negotiate with the group he conceived as the legitimate leaders in Colo, writing, "I should like to induce some of the old chiefs, who really rule the interior, to come to me and talk matters over" (Gordon 1879a vol. 1:8). Later, his plans frustrated, he wrote with loathing of the "petty republics" of the Ra area.

Implicitly juxtaposed with the illegitimate leadership of Na Bisiki was a representative of the "orderly portion of the native community," of whom Gordon wrote "Buli Nadrau is a fine and favourable specimen of a great mountain chief" (1879a vol. 2:x). Buli Nadrau and Na Bisiki represent a series of oppositions critical to the British view of proper order in Fiji. Buli Nadrau was constituted, from above, by the government, as a district official (buli), legitimately in authority over a bounded territory and properly subordinate to colonial authority. Na Bisiki, in contrast, belonged to a "small village," yet extended unjustified influence "far greater than that to which [his] mere position as chief would have entitled [him]." Thus, Na Bisiki's influence, over a large, and unspecified range, was unnatural. Gordon called his authority "direct terrorism over his tribe." The colonial self-constitution as arbiter of Fijian tradition created a double argument: Na Bisiki was neither a legitimate leader by Fijian customary right (for Carew had defined customary right as belonging to those "reasonable old chiefs") nor was he sanctioned from above by the colonial authorities as their representative.

The threat of Na Bisiki was not simply revolt against the government but at a more fundamental level a challenge to indirect rule and the arbitration of power and legitimacy by the government. Neither Christian nor a proper chief in British eyes, he embodied a threat to the whole premise of the natural civilizing of the Fijians. The British imagination of Na Bisiki, who, eventually captured, was shot trying to escape before his trial, is a paradigm of British fear of assertions of authority by those they did not control. It is not an exaggeration to see obsession in Carew's letters about Na Bisiki, nor to be struck by the symbolism of the special set of handcuffs, materially instantiating the urge to order and restrain.

Gordon insisted on the death sentence for such leaders. His despatches reveal a continuing optimism, tempered now by a "prudent" concern for exemplary punishments, to secure "future good behavior." He chose to make an example of leaders, rather than any "tribe" as a whole.

> It was open to me to follow the plan of the former Government [Cakobau's], and direct the wholesale deportation of the tribes, without taking life, or to show such severity in a few instances as would allow me to permit the population generally to remain in their own towns and districts. The latter course appeared to me the more truly lenient and considerate toward a subjugated people, as well as more consonant with the requirements of justice. It could not, however, prudently be adopted, unless the future good behavior of the tribe was to be relied on, and this could only be secured by the infliction of exemplary punishment on the most guilty of their number. (Gordon 1979a vol. 1:xvii)

Sir Arthur Gordon could not appeal both to custom and to colonial right in creating the colonial system in the interior and in Ra. As an administrative consequence, Gordon decided that these people were to be ruled at the provincial level by European officials and Fijians from other areas. Further, a broad category of indigenous activity was construed as disordered and unsanctioned. Yet, even if the hill people were not construed as completely blameless, the British attributed the "disturbances in the interior" to outside influences or sinister, terrorist chiefs. Their motives were conceived as political, and they had been "subjugated." But the contradictions and the creation of negative tradition would come to the fore all the more vividly in the British apprehension of further disturbances in the north and the hills: the rise of Navosavakadua and the corollary construction of the "Tuka movement."

Dangerous Disaffection in Fiji: Navosavakadua and "The Tuka"

Like the "heathen," "terrorist" chief Na Bisiki, Navosavakadua challenged British constructions of legitimate leadership, as we shall see as we trace the attempt to contain him. But unlike prior problems, in the British imagination Tuka was a "thing" ("movement," "doctrine," "creed," "superstition of mingled elements," "new religion," "semipolitical movement," or "political-religious doctrine") apart from Navosavakadua and located spatially among the peoples of the interior north and west of Viti Levu. Seeking to control this disorder, in 1887 the colonial administration passed both an ordinance which provided for the "deportation and confinement of disaffected or dangerous natives" and an ordinance against "the practices of luve ni wai, kalou rere and other similar and kindred practices" (*Fiji Gazette* 1887) under which people were later prosecuted for Tuka. These ordinances reified disparate aspects of negative tradition as criminal. In confronting Tuka, colonial policy shifted from blaming and deporting individual leaders in 1878 and 1885 to deporting towns and groups of people in 1891 and 1914, to the reification of this British category of negative tradition, grounds for a potential—but never fully realized—reevaluation of the "nature" of Fijians entirely.

In 1878 when the Rakiraki chiefs brought "Charges against the Roko Tui Ra" and Navosavakadua's *kalou rere* was encountered, Governor Gordon and Wilkinson (and the Colonial Office readers of their despatches) initially blamed discontented local whites and the "malfeasant petty chiefs of Rakiraki" rather than focusing serious attention on the oracle Navosavakadua. The "superstition of mingled elements" as Gordon termed it, or the "*kalourere*-ism," as David Wilkinson called it, was considered to be subordinate to comprehensible political motivations: "This religion was designed as a common bond of union among those whom the leaders wished to make use of for the accomplishment of political ends" (CO 83/16).

Wilkinson conceived the "*kalourere*-ism" as manipulable custom, a vehicle for political disaffection if used by the Rakiraki chiefs, but a vehicle for good if used by the new colonial administration: "The chief cause for any apprehension is on account of the power and means of secret combination it possesses or is the agent of, which if united with, or supporting any disaffected movement against authority would be disastrous to all peace or progress, in fact to the race [? word unclear]" (78/550). He proposed, no doubt to Gordon's interest, that the "*kalourere*-ism" itself be used as a sort of indirect rule (spelling and punctuation are as Wilkinson wrote):

> I would leave its devotees unmolested while there is no breach of morals or good order leave them to pursue their own sweet will subject them to no coercion, restraint or even ridicule. It is a Vakaviti or Fijian affair. Regard it as such, and treat the whole thing Vakaviti. . . . The free operation of the same customs and usages of the country will be the best and most effectual observer controller and restrainer. Every chief in the [government] service of any importance as well as those true chiefs who seek the real will [?] of their people . . . let them feel their responsibility at the same time that they have the support of government, in fact let them feel as far as possible that . . . they are expected to share its burdens and its benefits. In all matters of customs prejudices or superstitions let their advice or recommendations be very well weighed . . . and there is little to fear from Kalourere-ism or anything of the kind. In fact rather than attempt to put the thing down by any form I would make use of the fanaticism as for instance every "tamata dina" is to get ready during the four years, he is to have plenty of pigs, fowls, and good of every kind so as to be able to entertain his ancestors in a becoming manner when they return at the time Vakatavovoki (I believe the millenium is a very good rendering of this word) by all means let him feed pigs, poultry and plant food and if he don't do so make him. Promote their industry and it will form the best correction of superstition and ignorance. Or in other words let the native feel that the government is his friend his protector in the broadest and commonest sense and the most inteligable to his mind that it is Fijian that it recognizes him as a Fijian the customs and habits of his every day life and treats him with a friendly easy freedom not suspicion while it deals summerly and effectively with evil doers and those who do him injury. (78/550)

Wilkinson's rather extraordinary optimism, well received by Gordon, was not shared at the time, or later, by administrators such as Carew and Thurston. Yet this document displays the initial attitude of Gordon's indirect rule: "Chiefs" of Fiji, already part of the governmental structure, are proposed as examples of and arbiters of "custom" for the common people. Custom itself is conceived as benign and positive, because it is manipulable. The notion that "fanaticism" could be used by government as easily as by disaffected Fijian chiefs implied that with the deportation of the Rakiraki chiefs and other leaders including Navosavakadua, and the substitution of the proper leadership of Europeans and their selected Fijians, all would proceed naturally, "and Kalourere-ism and every thing belonging to it will pass away . . . he will be a supporter of the government and a peacefull and respectable member of his mataqali, paying their dues both local and general" (78/550).

But by 1885 when officials found Navosavakadua, returned from the brief deportation, to be leading a "Tuka movement," administrative attention focused sharply on the "prophet" as root and cause of disorder. Like Na Bisiki, Navosavakadua and his northern and interior "votaries" were presumed already lower than coastal Fijians on the racial social evolutionary ladder. But further, Navosavakadua was not even a chief like Na Bisiki ("terrorist" though they may have termed him). Rather he was a "heathen priest hereditarily" wrote Carew. The image of the utilitarian self-interested charlatan, the manipulative priest, prevailing in missionary commentary (see, e.g., Williams 1985 [1858]:226–27) informed colonial interpretations of Navosavakadua's ritual practices (see Brewster 1922 and CO 83/43).[11] Colonial officers focused on his retinue of women (the *Ai Leba,* described by Brewster; see also Carew and Cocks in CO 83/43). And they viewed sacrifices to him as extorted payments. The assistant Native Commissioner framed his report in these terms:

> "Tuka" (immortality) was promised by these men on behalf of Navosavakadua to such as should believe in his doctrines and follow him, and they thus succeeded in inducing a number of people to believe accordingly. From these believers they exacted a "Ka ni bula" or payment for immortality consisting of whale's teeth or such other property as the converts might be able to contribute.
>
> The quantity of treasure which Navosavakadua had in this way amassed may be gathered from the circumstance related to me by the Roko that at a "solevu" (feast) held recently at Valelebo in the Raviravi district where the "Bure Kalou" had been erected (heathen temple) Navosavakadua presented 400 whales' teeth. This story might have been thought incredible, but the Roko told me that it was corroborated by Buli Tavua who was present at the Solevu and assisted to divide the property.
>
> Sums of money were also given, as much as 10s. having been paid by one individ-

---

11. Contrasting with an implicit image of benevolent civilizing colonial rule and the noblesse oblige of true Fijian chiefs. Thurston in particular used similar images of self-interest and illegitimacy to describe Catholic priests who missionized in the highlands.

ual to Navosavakadua, or one of his followers, on the promise of "Tuka" (immortality). Buli Saivou who was lately sentenced to 12 months imprisonment for adultery gave four whales' teeth and some mats as payment for "Tuka." (CO 83/43)

Joske, commenting on Navosa's doctrines, argued, "It may be urged that Navosavakadua is mad and therefore harmless, but it is apparent that there is a good deal of method in his madness. Witness for instance the large amount of presents he has received. His votaries were continually presenting pigs, tabuas, masi and yaqona, and to such an extent as to very much rouse the jealousy of Roko Tui Ra" (CO 83/43).

With typical European concern about ownership and profit, sacrifice was interpreted as clever extraction of goods, which should only have been offered up as taxes, or in proper customary form to proper Fijian chiefs, such as the provincial official, the Roko. Ultimately it was assumed by the British that Navosavakadua sought from self-interest to protect his own status as a now discredited ritual expert, in the face of the new government and true god.

A frequently cited anecdote detailed the reaction of a coastal chief and government official, Buli Tavua, to the powers of Navosavakadua.

> Throughout Nadrau, part of Naboubuco, and from Raki Raki to Tavua the belief in him extends.
>
> Buli Tavua, however, promptly stamped out the endeavours to propagate the belief in his district.
>
> One of the Navosavakadua's "betes" trying to make a proselyte of the Buli, the Buli broke a plate in two and said: "Now Mr. Bete, I give you until evening to return that plate whole, if you can do so, I will believe what you say, if not I will flog you." Evening found the plate unmended, so the Bete was tied up and given 30 lashes. (Joske, CO 83/43)

Having heard the story, Thurston wrote to Carew, "Buli Tavua seems too nice in his estimate of 'Vosavakadua' he shd have broken the prophet's head instead of his own plate" (Carew Papers, Thurston to Carew, 11 December 1885). The anecdote is an exact parallel of the story of the *wai ni tuka bete* told by Fison twenty years earlier, but by the 1880s the alliance of chiefs and government had transformed the image: now the coastal chief was not only Christian but a government official as well. The colonial officer's self-identification with a proper legitimate chief is typical of Thurston. Typical too was his approval of the punishment employed by Buli Tavua. Public thrashings were to become the primary punishment for practitioners of *kalou rere* and *luve ni wai*, and for those "votaries of the *tuka*" who were not deemed dangerous enough to be deported. Punishment through force and example displayed in microcosm the British subjugation of those who asserted illegitimate authority.[12]

As the British saw it, Navosavakadua and his followers were not simply ignorant, but were, instead, subversive. In 1878 it was the challenge to Ratu Isikeli and Ratu Semi, high chiefs of Viwa, with the patina of service in the Cakobau governments as well as colonial appointments to testify to their "customary" place. In 1885 the anecdote about Buli Tavua was as much about the priest's attempt to suborn an official as about the official's probity. Direct contradiction of administrative orders by Tuka "votaries" was as significant as the form the disobedience took. (Told to build a leper's house they instead built a temple; told to move a village they built a *koro ni vuvuni* (settlement for plotting war).) Not only were officials disobeyed and incited to disloyalty and regulations flouted, but also were colonial boundaries and spheres of jurisdiction traversed, as "Ra men" of Ra province, under the jurisdiction of the Fijian provincial Roko Tui Ra Tevita Rasuaki "crossed over the border into Udu" (as all the colonial reports and successive narratives consistently state) and brought discord into Colo North, the jurisdiction of Resident Commissioner Carew. Carew's first report (Enclosure 2 in CO 83/43) identifies Navosavakadua as "a heathen priest hereditarily living at Drau-ni-ivi, Rakiraki, district, of Ra province who has for some time been stirring up sedition in all the surrounding districts." The spatial units (villages, districts, provinces) and the boundaries were sacrosanct in British eyes, imagined to be simultaneously legitimized in Fijian custom and British administrative utility, as was the equally "customary" system of indirect rule itself.

In fact the colonial districting crosscut, marginalized, and dispossessed many small-scale polities, including the Vatukaloko polity. Cakobau government official Swanston was probably the last (perhaps the only) European administrator to have been aware of the polity at all (he sketched out Vatukaloko territory on a map he drew in 1873 (see figures 3, 4, and 5)), unless, of course, some hint is contained in Thurston's assertion that "from Togavere south to Udu there has always existed a set of turbulent benighted scoundrels" (Carew Papers, Thurston to Carew, 11 December 1885).

---

12. In 1885 Carew's flogging of a group of youths in Soloira for practicing *luve ni wai* was questioned by the new Governor. Carew, agreeing that flogging was "repugnant," nonetheless argued that the elders of Soloira had come to him and asked him to discipline the youths, and that he thereby prevented rebellion and upheld the customary leaders (see 85/1668). Although never explicit, I think that colonial flogging also maintained the colonial sense of themselves as adult and the Fijians as childlike.

Navosavakadua far outstripped Na Bisiki in his infamy among the Europeans. Na Bisiki (and Sadiri Nabete too) were "pure" heathens, encountered on the frontiers of the civilizing mission and colonial projects. As well, Na Bisiki was a relatively simple "political" rebel, requiring to be "subjugated." His heathenism, in that curious 1860s European discourse in Fiji, was a simple "political" category. In contrast, Navosavakadua truly threatened the sought-after order of the colonial polity, for he initiated a simultaneous political and religious counter-theory, perceived as a witting creation of "doctrines" and "practices" in imitation of and opposition to colonial government and true god.

Gordon and subordinates had claimed that the Little War was between Fijians. But in the 1880s, administrators perceived Navosavakadua to be explicitly anti-European, opposing both *"Lotu"* (Christianity) and *"Matanitu"* (government).[13] Discussions of his "doctrine" and his "organization" reveal that the colonial officials considered Navosa to be influenced by European ideas and institutions, and to be attempting to mimic them. Religious doctrines, no matter how unusual, were less the justification for colonial alarm, than the activities they did or might give rise to, including, as Joske and Carew were to point out, possible murder and cannibal sacrifice. Practices, not beliefs, were "political," and it was the "armed, drilling men" of Navosavakadua's following who initially impelled inquiry and governmental action. Joske commenting further on the "method to his madness" summarized: "his movement was organised with a great deal of skill, his followers being divided into bands of what were called soldiers commanded by "satinis" and in such villages as believed in him were "betes" who regularly reported to him in the way Wesleyan Native teachers report to their superior officers" (CO 83/43). Colonial observers, and later scholars as well, were to stress the imitation of European military drill, salutes, and the obscure passwords that they could not translate.[14] They postulated Maori influence or influence of white planters:

---

13. By 1885 there is no mention in the minute papers or despatches of Wilkinson's notion of turning *"tuka"* to the service of indirect rule. Indeed, with Thurston as acting Governor (administrator) the rhetoric shifts from Gordon's stress on the upholding of Fijian custom to the rule of the colonial government. (That is not to say, however, that Thurston's notions of what constituted a threat to colonial government were not solidly molded in his projection of British aristocratic hierarchy onto Fijian chiefs.)

14. Many of the practices could have been understood in Fijian terms, however, as Joske himself made clear in CO 83/43. Marching and drilling were war *meke* (gesture chants); the circumambulation by warriors was to *butuka* (tread the land) in order to establish a relationship between Navosavakadua and any community who wished to become his allies (see chapter 5).

It appears to myself and to Mr. Tripp that all these men were bound by an oath not to divulge. This may seem a new departure in Fijian habits, but I would point out that nearly all the people concerned in this have done about three or four terms of indentured service with white men, the Ra province having been from the earliest times the favourite recruiting area.

Whilst among the white men . . . they have heard of Free Masonry and secret societies. This appears to be a humble imitation of them. They seem to use signs and shibboleths as a means of recognition amongst themselves. (Joske to Carew, 18 January 1886, 86/253, Dangerous and Disaffected Natives file)[15]

However humble or crude, Navosavakadua's organization (unlike the hierarchy of the Wesleyan church) was to the British an audacious mimicry. Moreover, its presumed secrecy, unlike the obvious warfare in the hills in the 1870s, was sinister and unpredictable. In a similar vein, the doctrine of "Tuka" and the "compounding of Fijian mythology and belief with the teachings of the Old and New Testaments" seemed to Carew both "very ingenious and dangerous" (CO 83/43). Unlike a simple "heathen," Navosavakadua made use of Christian doctrine, within a Fijian framework, proposing it to be a delusion.

He says [the Twins] sailed away to the land of the white men, who wrote a book about them, which is the Bible, only the missionaries in translating it have deceived Fijians in talking about Jesus Christ and Jehovah, their real names being Nakalasabaria and Namakaumoli [sic].[16] They are shortly to appear and at their arrival the Fijian Millenium is to commence. All who believe in the doctrine that Navosavakadua preaches, are to have life eternal, and their ancestors are to rise from their graves. They are also to be rewarded with "sitoa" (stores) full of the wealth of the white man. Those who do not believe in him are to perish. (Joske Enclosure 3 in CO 83/43)

Like Na Bisiki, Navosavakadua was seen by the British as an agent. Not simply deceived by low-class whites, he himself was an active agent of deceit, corrupting his "votaries." Worse than Na Bisiki, Navosavakadua did not simply assert recognized Fijian "heathen" aims, but, rather, seemed to mimic and pervert colonial and Christian forms. He was a symbol of the vulnerability of the colonial project, whether a sign of the success of low-class whites in cor-

---

15. A separate file of colonial administrative minute papers concerned with Fijians deported under the Dangerous and Disaffected Natives Act of 1886 is held at the National Archives of Fiji.

16. In his original handwritten minute Joske wrote "Nakausabaria and Nacirikaumoli." When the entire despatch and enclosures were later printed up in government records, misreadings of Joske's handwriting were frequent.

rupting Fijians in the face of administrative and missionary protection, or simply a sign that the colonial administration could not completely control the prerogatives of knowledge and authority in the colonial polity. In British eyes the combination of knowledge of European forms with the subversion of them rendered Navosavakadua a truly "disaffected" and "dangerous" native. He was therefore removed "for the public safety and welfare" (Carew CO 83/43). In 1886 the balance of administrative opinion believed that the problems in Ra and Colo could be solved through the deportation of Navosavakadua. It became necessary to pass a new ordinance, in order to confine him to Rotuma, thus affirming and reifying the category of the "Dangerous and Disaffected Native." Not simply dangerous but disaffected, lacking in that affection that the colonial rulers expected to inhere between ruled and rulers (see Kaplan and Kelly 1994), he was removed from the colonial polity, to allow civilization of the Fijians to proceed.

The End of Optimism

Because British perceptions of disorder and ordinances of control focused on the individual prophet, the illegitimate leader, the events of 1885 and 1886, like those of 1878, might have been read as further awkward moments in the transition to civilized participation in the colonial "customary" order. But optimism ended between 1886 and 1891. Years later, Joske wrote that after Navosavakadua was sent to Rotuma in 1887,

> I said in my mind, "Exit the prophet," and I thought I had done with him for at least a considerable period. But I spoke in my ignorance and foolishness of heart. Although the Government had seen to the detention of his body in far away Rotumah, it was not able to restrain his free spirit, and his astral form returned to his native hills and comforted his adherents by ministrations, and his doctrine of the *Tuka* exists to this present day. (Brewster 1922:246)

Joske's retrospective description in his 1922 memoir takes a detached and romantic tone. But confronting the "revival of Tuka" in 1891, the administrative tone was both urgent and severe. Since Tuka had not been eradicated through the deportation of its prophet, the administration now located disaffection more broadly. In an elaboration of the coastal-interior dichotomy, Tuka was no longer regarded as simple heathen ignorance, nor natural political avarice, nor the machination of an unscrupulous leader, nor even crude mimicry but, rather, as an amorphous inherent social characteristic of the "peoples living in the shadow of the Kauvadra range" (Joske 94/2036). The 1891 "reappearance" of Tuka and the deportation of the people of Drauniivi represents this projection of disorder onto groups of Fijians more generally.

Thurston, now governor, amplified the precolonial attitudes of planters and coastal chiefs toward the interior people, seen not merely as political "rebels" but as dangerous and disaffected racial and moral others.[17] Governor Thurston assessed "Tuka" largely as the continuant of objectionable older Fijian ways found among the spatially and socially distant turbulent peoples of Ra and Colo. His despatches consistently characterize the "new religion established by Navosavakadua" as "reversion to heathenism," or "mischievous practice of the old priests of heathen times." His virulent objection to "Tuka" paralleled his objection to another religion whose leaders seemed to challenge his authority, the newly proselytizing Roman Catholic mission in Fiji, of which he wrote, "There is not however, any Magistrate in the Colony or officer of the Native department, who does not testify to the altered bearing of the Natives wherever Dr. Vidal establishes a Missionary. Their first duty is to him, the second may be to the Government or their Chief, but all things must give way to priestly rule" (83/57). Thurston's concern was with the order of the polity, which he had always conceived as hierarchical, privileging his vision of the coastal chiefly aristocracy. Now he sought to implement, perhaps with the zeal of the newly knighted, his aristocratic model of rule from the top, by personally overseeing the arrests and floggings as he made his way through the interior Colo provinces up to Ra. He informed the people of Drauniivi, which he had identified as the "seat of authority" of Tuka, that his patience had run out, and (turning to the practice of mass deportation that Gordon had considered and rejected) he decreed that they be deported to Kadavu, their villages razed, and the very name of Drauniivi forgotten.

The choice of Kadavu as the new residence of the Drauniivi people was motivated in the entrenched colonial vision of the proper native Christian coastal peoples. Unlike the dark, heathen followers of Navosavakadua, the Fijians of Kadavu represented Fijian orthodoxy, as Joske would explain:[18]

> His Excellency deemed it the wisest and most merciful course to remove [the people of Drau-ni-ivi] at least for a while to a more civilized portion of the group

---

17. Thurston's brother had commanded Cakobau's forces in the victory in 1873 over the interior people of Nabutautau (who had defeated an earlier Bauan force sent inland to avenge the Reverend Baker's death). Perhaps in 1891 Thurston felt he had found his chance to achieve a final "subjugation of the hill people" (see Macnaught 1971).

18. These passages have been quoted previously in the Introduction.

where there would be little likelihood of their pernicious doctrines . . . gaining credence . . . to prevent the spread of the "Tuka" superstition among the simple, yet wild, half-Christianized, half-civilized tribes living in the ranges at the back of Drau-ni-ivi. . . .

The Drau-ni-ivi people have therefore been removed, and are now located on good fertile Crown lands in the island of Kadavu.

The Kadavu Islanders, possessing a large intermixture of Tongan blood, are perhaps the most advanced and intelligent . . . of our Fijian population. There is therefore no fear of the "Tuka" doctrines being received by them otherwise than with ridicule and it may reasonably be hoped that finding themselves among a strong but law-abiding and civilised community the Drau-ni-ivi people will profit by their association with them by qualifying themselves for what they will certainly long for — a permission to return to their own mountain district. (Brewster 1891)

The deportation of the people of Drauniivi was meant to remove a root and source of disaffection from the body politic, but neither Governor Thurston nor Commissioner Joske considered that the deportation alone would put an end to disorderly practices in the highlands. Joske portrayed "the Tuka" as a disease, "always smoldering in the Nalawa and Naiova highlands . . . endemic with occasional periods of epidemic activity" (91/1133). Thurston planned roads, and a new station at Nadarivatu to maintain a Government presence in the hills; he also blamed the Wesleyan mission for neglecting to send white missionaries to the remote areas, considering that only leadership and decision making by whites, or aristocratic Fijian chiefs, could keep order in the colony (Despatch 53). Identifying with high coastal chiefs, Thurston conceived the northern and interior people as inferior and substandard. And though Joske's affection for the "simple yet wild" hill people was genuine, he also echoed the long-set colonial framework which saw them as inferior to the coastal peoples on all grounds.

The British administrators who succeeded Thurston, Carew, and Joske inherited these attitudes, but they inherited as well the optimism of the civilizing project, routinized and unquestioned in the structures of rule. In the early twentieth century Tuka was still an administrative problem, but it was becoming a topic of antiquarian and scholarly speculation as well: "Considering that only a brief period had elapsed since the Fijians had practiced heathen customs that made their name a byword in the world, it was not surprising that a recrudescence of their old superstitions should take place in some form. It would have been too much to expect a complete transition from barbarism to peace and contentment as an immediate result of the new order of things" (Sutherland 1910:3). Thus wrote William Sutherland in 1910 (he had been the Native Commissioner for twelve years) in a paper for the Fiji Society on "The *Tuka*' Religion." He told his listeners that even in 1910 "the Tuka" and other kindred superstitions, more commonly known perhaps as "Luveniwai" and "Kalou-rere," were still practiced, warning "they are smouldering always in various parts of the country." Although he concluded his paper on an optimistic note ("the younger generation, let us hope, find it more profitable and less hazardous to devote their time and energy to honest work in which superstition finds no place"), there was to be yet another "outbreak of Tuka" in 1914, and a minor prophet named Sailose troubled the administration by holding a public meeting in Tavua in 1918. These events took place along with rumors of German sympathizers in the hill country, *luve ni wai* prosecutions, and the incipient activities of another "dangerous and disaffected native" called Apolosi Nawai, all grouped together in the British construction of disorder.

The colonial construction of Christian, hierarchical, loyal Fijians has never been completely destroyed, even though categories of negative tradition were established and perpetuated. Ultimately, most instances of negative tradition were and are reconstrued by colonial and postcolonial arbiters as awkward moments, or childlike superstitions.[19] For though I have concentrated here on danger and disaffection, the constructed colonial orthodoxy and its institutions were established, from the top down, by the British and high chiefs with tremendous conviction in its legitimacy in both Fijian "custom" and British policy. Moreover, as time went on the sense of "smoldering" Fijian threats was overshadowed by more heated points of conflict. In vivid contrast to dangerous and disorderly Fijians was a far greater threat to the premise of the British colonial project, the demands for social and political equality of the indentured, and then post-indenture, Indo-Fijians. Crucially united with the Fijians as Christian and hierarchical, the British could always see themselves as the protectors of the Fijians, against the Indo-Fijians, who would argue for equality with whites in colony and empire. Far preferable in the British vision were Fijian chiefs and people who knew their place.

The Tuka as Negative Tradition

In 1910 Native Commissioner Sutherland referred to Joske as his authority on "the Tuka." In 1914, though the Resident Commissioner of Colo West asked

---

19. See my article on "Luve ni wai as the British saw it" for changing administrative perceptions of the degree of power that Fijian deities and Fijian ritual might hold for the administration.

Fijians for definitions of Tuka, new Native Commissioner K. L. Allardyce cited Carew and Thurston's despatches. The reification of Tuka in the routinized administrative form of "minute papers," despatches, and regulations set as authoritative a British vision compiled in the midst of the construction of a colonial orthodoxy and colonial institutions of rule. The circumstances and presuppositions of that construction were uninvestigated by the later administrators — or indeed by later scholars who would begin to plumb the colonial record for "facts" about "the Tuka."

As the British sought to extend their vision of order to disorderly others, many disparate phenomena were linked together in what they called "disaffection," and what I have called negative tradition. Disparate Fijian practices were linked, not because of intrinsic similarity or connection in Fijian culture and history, but because they were problems encountered by British administrators in their organizing project. Only from the British perspective were "petty republics," "charlatans," and "heathenism" necessarily linked. Only in the course of the British hierarchical project of the extension of the state in empire were the Maori Hau Hau, Catholicism, and Freemasonry linked. These connections and comparisons were motivated in the British colonial cultural project, in the vision of the orderly polity led by a defining ruling elite. All were practices of "others" in relation to the British ruling and ordering class.

Further, not all Fijian practices constructed as disorderly by the British were activities of "people of the land." The British rubric of "Dangerous and Disaffected Native" encompassed both Navosavakadua and the Buli Naceva of Kadavu (the government chief of the district to which Navosavakadua's kinfolk were deported in 1891) who was found guilty of excessive oppression of the people of his district.

Nonetheless, there has been created, in the European imagination of Fiji, "a dark substratum of Fijian life," as one scholar has called it, just as the vision of "primitives in transition" has made the Pacific "cargo cult," or "millenarian movement" a reified category. For scholars, Tuka has been a thing, a cult, movement, or practice. They thus followed a reification begun in colonial documents following the 1891 "revival of Tuka" in the absence of Navosavakadua when "Tuka" had become an entity and sometimes even an agent in colonial documents. It was a movement that "arose," "spread," "subsided," and then "recurred" again. Its association with Navosavakadua was always presented, historically as its origin, but it had gained a definition in relation to other Fijian "practices" that were "penal by Native Regulation practices" (as the Commissioner of Colo North minuted in 1914). They were unusual, disorderly practices, outside the expected trajectory of Fijian civilizability. Whether conceived as "new religion" or "reversion to heathenism," as "dangerous disaffection" or "proto-nationalism," the reification of Tuka arises from the colonial history of its invention. The power of the colonial construction has been to make this history seem authoritative. Despite my strongest efforts to the contrary I am sure that my own narrative itself participates in some of its assumptions.

There were consequences for Fijians such as Navosavakadua and the Vatukaloko. Colonial forms and practices of inquiry, regulation, and discipline brought these categories of British discourse into Fijians' imagination and actions in both explicit and covert ways. But did Navosavakadua consider himself to be both a *bete* and a heathen, an autochthon and a purveyor of disaffection?

5

NAVOSAVAKADUA'S RITUAL POLITY

Navosavakadua made history in a complex Fijian colonial field. He left few statements that we know to be his own; there was and is much said and written of him. He was said to have prophesied that "the world would shortly be *tavuki,* which is the Fijian for being turned upside down, and when that occurred all existing affairs would be reversed; the whites would serve the natives, the chiefs would become the common people and the latter would take their places" (Brewster 1922:237). He set about to effect his prophecies by establishing a new polity, through informing people about gods and power, transacting *"wai ni tuka"* (water of immortality), doing miracles, and bringing the dead back to life. Bearing in mind long-term projects of "people of the land" and the colonial reification and criminalization of Tuka, how might we write a narrative of Navosavakadua and Tuka? How can we come to understand him as simultaneously Dukumoi, Navosavakadua, and Moses? How can we understand his transformation of the old polity of the Vatukaloko into the Twelve Tribes? How can the Twin Gods of the Kauvadra be Jehovah and Jesus? Can we read his mobilization, his attempt to free the Vatukaloko as *both kalou rere* and Exodus? Reading nineteenth-century colonial documents and hearing present-day Fijian accounts about Navosavakadua we can feel the articulation of two systems in the 1880s: Navosavakadua's "Tuka" as an attempt to found a new kind of ritual-polity and Navosavakadua's project more generally as the deliberate assertion of identities of gods and powers in the world. In the face of a developing colonial-chiefly Fijian orthodoxy, Navosavakadua acted, making a first move in an ongoing alternative articulation.

The "Tuka" in Historical Contexts

Certainly we could read Tuka in terms of indigenous Fijian culture and history alone. Colonial characterizations of Tuka as epidemic aside, in the 1880s and 1890s, Tuka and interest in Navosavakadua's leadership followed the historically well-defined bounds and relationships of the Vatukaloko *vanua*. We can recognize many of these same peoples, from inland to coast with long-term ties to the Vatukaloko polity, as the "Tuka votaries" of the colonial record (see figure 5). Here Navosavakadua follows Sadiri the invulnerable warrior-priest of the battle of Nakorowaiwai, rallying the Vatukaloko once again. In Fijian terms we could read Navosavakadua's project as an attempt to establish an autonomous ritual-polity in opposition to Bauan-European rule. In Fijian terms continuous with earlier Vatukaloko mobilizations, we could see them still insisting on being *bati* (allies not subjects) in the face of encroaching others. Or we might even understand Navosavakadua to be establishing himself as a chief on the eastern coastal model, his *mataqali* (kin group) Nakubuti taking back the rule. Yet, taking Navosavakadua seriously as a hereditary oracle-priest and the heir of Sadiri, we could also read Navosavakadua's project as an indigenous transformation of the eastern Fijian polity, a transformation with antecedents in the land-centered potential of the Ra and interior peoples. Here we would see it as a major, novel mobilization of people of the land, motivated by and on behalf of Kauvadra gods. Within Fijian terms alone, his mobilization established a new kind of Fijian ritual system, a land-centered polity.

But to read Navosa's polity and project in Fijians terms alone ignores the transforming power of the encounters with the colonial administration and Christianity. Navosavakadua did not call himself Sadiri, but rather Moses. In place of the club of a *kalou rere* ritual expert, he was said to possess Moses's staff, the one with which the biblical figure parted the Red Sea. It would be equally easy to read in his movement a form of resistance that was shaped in the encounter with the constructs and practices of colonial top-down power: in the face of the sustained colonial attempt to subjugate the Vatukaloko, he found in colonial ritual doctrine an icon of leadership of wronged people. But that would ignore the fact that colonial power itself was already a chiefly Fijian-British synthesis.

My interest here is to read Navosavakadua's project as neither indigenous nor colonial, but rather its own dynamic intelligence, a creative articulation of possibilities in Fijian and colonial systems. Here, most crucial of all might be the double valence of "Navosavakadua" (he who speaks but once and is effective). It was the name, Joske says, Fijians gave to the colonial chief justice, in awe of his power over life and death in sentencing (Brewster 1922:239). In the case of the colonial official and of Mosese Dukumoi, the name marked a new notion of the potential power of a new state and its gods. Let us explore the synthesis Navosavakadua articulated, and how it was, briefly, routinized.

Navosavakadua's Cosmology

A first puzzle for colonial officials and later scholars encountering Tuka is its mixture of the political and the religious. Some have seen the political (or political-economic) context as prior to the content and cosmology. I think we should put aside these divisions. After all, nineteenth-century Fijian confederations and chiefdoms were ritual-polities. The British state was then and is now headed by the head of a church (see Fields 1985). And the encounters of Europeans and eastern coastal Fijians throughout the nineteenth century joined Methodism and colonizing political order in an ongoing articulation. So, what is puzzling about Navosavakadua is not that he prophesied to set the Vatukaloko free, but what he prophesied. Why foreign gods, the Twins and Jehovah? Why water of immortality?

The Twins and Degei

As Wilkinson described in 1878, it was the Twins, Nacirikaumoli and Nakausabaria, who chose Navosavakadua as their oracle. These two gods of Kauvadra were the grandsons (in some versions sons or nephews) of Degei. The Twins defied Degei by killing Turukawa, a bird belonging to him. They thus precipitated the war at Kauvadra, which Degei eventually won by summoning a great waterspout to the top of the Kauvadra and causing a great flood to drive out the Twins. Accounts from the 1840s to the present detail how this initial unfilial act caused the founding and peopling of the coastal and island polities as the Twins fled from the Kauvadra by canoe. In 1885 Joske juxtaposed an account of the war at Kauvadra with his description of Navosavakadua as an oracle of the Twins. He did not explicitly state that it was an account given by Tuka adherents, but it seems to me to be a version from the Kauvadra area.

>Degei the "Kalouvu" or Fijian Creator, lived in a cavern at Na Kauvadra. He was a gigantic serpent but at such times as he willed assumed the human form. There was also in Naboubuco a gigantic dove called Turukawa. Degei sent for this dove and told him to live in the Baka tree (banyan) that grew at Uluda, the cavern's mouth. It was Turukawa's sweetly cooing at dawn that daily roused Degei from his slumbers and the bird was very dear unto the God.

>At that time there also lived at Naraiyawa, not far from Nakauvadra, two young godlike Chiefs named Nakalsabarai [Nakausabaria] and Namakaumoli [Nacirikaumoli]. They were in their way mighty hunters, and armed with bow and arrows ranged the country round shooting birds. Soon they had killed all the birds in the country and only Turukawa remained alive. One night they said "Let us go and shoot the bird of Degei."

>The "matasau" or Chief's attendant whose duty it was at dawn to beat the Veitala or big drum of Degei, found Turukawa dead with two arrows in him.

>When Degei heard of it he wept and said, "Oh, how I loved my dove, for his dear sake a moon I'll fast and for two more moons I'll mourn."

>A messenger was forthwith sent to the young Chiefs at Naraiyawa. He said "You two, you two shot Turukawa," but they denied it. The messenger replied, "Ere a moon be past, submission make, or Degei wreaks his wrath." The chiefs answered, "Come war, come flame and fire, we'll not submit."

>The result was that the lands of these young Chiefs and their adherents were wasted and at last their father said to them, "You two are the cause of evil in our land, you have called down upon us the wrath of Degei, build yourselves a canoe and sail away that Degei may be appeased and we have peace." So they built a canoe and hauled it to the sea at Rakiraki, and the gap that they broke in the mountains to haul it through may be seen even unto this day. And they sailed away to the west and the Fijians knew not whither they went.

>But in these days has arisen Navosavakadua to whom it has been revealed the place they went to.

In the 1870s, as Wilkinson described in his report on the protest against the Roko Tui Ra by the Rakiraki chiefs, Navosavakadua invoked the Twins, preparing the way for them in an extended *kalou rere* (invulnerability) ritual. At that time the Twins revealed to Navosavakadua the extent of their travels. Joske continued,

>He says they sailed away to the land of the white men, who wrote a book about them which is the Bible, only the missionaries in translating it have deceived the

Fijians in talking about Jesus Christ and Jehovah, their real names being Nakalasabasai [Nakausabaria] and Namakaumoli [Nacirikaumoli]. They are shortly to appear and at their arrival the Fijian Millennium is to commence. All who believe in the doctrine that Navosavakadua preaches, are to have life eternal, and their ancestors are to rise from their graves. They are also to be rewarded with "sitoa" (stores) full of the wealth of the white man. Those who do not believe in him are to perish. (Joske CO 83/43)[1]

On the one hand, the story of the war at Kauvadra tells a familiar story about Fijian power. It establishes a version of the interior-coast, autochthon-foreign opposition. The two opposing sides are the unmoving Degei in his cave of stone in Ra and the canoe-voyaging Twins who travel by water out to the coast and beyond. The Twins are sometimes called the "foreigners" *(vulagi)*. They were not the *kalou vu* (ancestor gods) of the Vatukaloko people, nor of the Ra and interior people, at least not since 1918, when the Vatukaloko told narratives that traced their lines either from gods senior to Degei, or to more established children of Degei.[2]

The story of Degei can be read and told from different perspectives. From the point of view of Jovesa Bavou in 1918 the interior people were descendants of an autochthonous Degei, or of lines senior to Degei, and the coastal people were powerful upstarts like the Twins. From the point of view of many coastal chiefs their powerful kingdoms are descendants of active superseding lines who successfully usurp the rule. As these powerful upstarts, the Twins are the war gods of coastal polities.

From either point of view, in the nineteenth century Degei was most fundamentally identified with the Rakiraki people, as their ancestor god. As such an interior, ancestral god, located in the Kauvadra mountains on the spatial and social periphery of centralizing, burgeoning chiefly confederations and hierarchies, he was considered to have control over nature and the fertility of the land. People of the coastal kingdoms recognized Degei's ritual authority. Missionary Joseph Waterhouse (1868:362) reported that during a terrible

---

1. For further contemporary descriptions of Navosavakadua and "Tuka" see CSO and CO papers, especially Wilkinson (78/550), and Carew, Cocks, Joske, Thurston (CO 83/43), and many other associated papers. See also Brewster (1922).

2. The myth also describes a dual nature to Fijian power. As Sahlins (1985) might put it, Degei, the unmoving central chief, is the *gravitas* figure and the voyaging Twins are *celeritas* gods. They represent two sides of Fijian chiefship, sacred kingship, and active kingship, which were embodied, in some Fijian kingdoms in two chiefly lines (e.g., as in Bau the Roko Tui (sacred) line and the Vunivalu (active) line).

drought in 1838 the Vunivalu of Bau (Tanoa, the father of Cakobau) had sent offerings to up to Rakiraki to be given to Degei to bring rain.

But if Tuka was a movement of people of the land, why was Navosavakadua an oracle of the Twins who were voyaging gods? Why the gods who had rebelled against Degei? I think the answer lies partly in a reading from a very local perspective that sees both Degei and the Twins as gods from the Kauvadra range and focuses on the specific historical and ritual relations between Rakiraki and the Vatukaloko people. The Twins were Navosavakadua's gods of war. And there is a real parallel between the relationship of Degei and the defiant Twins and the Rakiraki kingdom and the defiant Vatukaloko *bati* (warrior allies). The Vatukaloko repeated this relationship of ambiguous warriors versus chiefs in their resistance to Rakiraki, to Viwa, and to Bau over many years. Since 1918, as noted above, the Vatukaloko have represented themselves in their relationship to Rakiraki (and Bau) as more senior, but superseded lines descended from the elder brothers of Degei. But in Navosavakadua's day, I think that he presented a narrative of Vatukaloko power as warrior power, that of rebellious *bati* such as the Twins against more powerful and established chiefs, such as Degei.

The Twins and Jehovah and Jesus

Further, Navosavakadua centered his project on a novel articulation of the Twins and the new Christian god(s). In 1878 Wilkinson wrote that Navosavakadua heralded the return of the Twins "who are said to have fled Fiji in disgust on the people adopting Christianity and other modern innovations" (78/550). But in the 1880s, colonial accounts agree that Navosavakadua identified the Twins with the Christian deities. Joske wrote,

> When Navosavakadua was arrested he sent an emissary to Roko Tui Ra saying that if he was sent to Suva, all the glorious things which he foretold of would not come off. He says that unless Nakasabasia [Nakausabaria] and Namakaumoli [Nacirikaumoli] reappear the power of Degei (who is the old serpent) will continue in the ascendant, as those two are they, of whom it is foretold, shall bruise the head of the serpent. (CO 83/43)

Carew wrote at the same time:

> He has given out that the return of Degei's two sons, Nacirikau Moli [*sic*] and Nakausabaria, lost at the time of the legendary Fijian deluge, is at hand when the

world is to be upset *(vukica)*, and the Lotu and Matanitu (Christianity and Government) driven out.

> He also pretends that the teachings of the Christian Bible are altogether compatible with Fijian mythology and heathen practices, but that the people have been shamefully deceived by the substitution of the names of Jehovah and Jesus for those of Degei's sons already mentioned. (CO 83/43)

And Cocks wrote:

> On the 29th November 1885 the Provincial Scribe, in the course of an interview with Navosavakadua, elicited from him the following statement: —
> What is reported of me is perfectly true. We have the "Lotu" and the "Matanitu" which were originated by the two who drifted from Nakauvadra. They started the Lotu to put down the work of Degei, but finding that it had not sufficient power they established the present Government as an auxiliary to the "Lotu" in the suppression of the work of Degei. (CO 83/43)

If Tuka was anticolonial and anti-Christian, why did Navosavakadua adopt even more foreign gods, identifying Jehovah and Jesus as Fijian deities? This brings us to a second, more complex reading. Returning to the story of Degei, it can be read as a narrative of the Fijian people-chiefs and interior-coastal division, but it is a very different kind of narrative from the origin myths of voyaging chiefs (discussed in chapter 2). In those myths, stranger kings from the sea marry women of the land and found chiefly lines. Here, in this narrative from Ra and the interior, both Degei and the Twins begin as Kauvadra gods. They represent settled and voyaging actors, Degei stays in the mountains, the Twins voyage *to* the sea, but both are most fundamentally gods of the "land." I think that this is how Navosavakadua constructed the Twins, as pivotal figures who were simultaneously gods of the land and strangers. Their message to Navosavakadua was that the power of foreigners was nonetheless ultimately that of the gods of the land. Thus Navosavakadua preached that the powerful war gods Jesus and Jehovah were to be identified with Nacirikaumoli and Nakausabaria, that they had traveled to the lands of the white men which was the same as the Fijian Burotukula (Paradise), and that they had returned, like Jesus and Jehovah, to vanquish an old enemy, Degei. Thus, also, Navosavakadua's argument that the colonial officers and missionaries were attempting to deceive Fijians on these very points. It was not merely Navosavakadua's claim that Fijian gods were more powerful than foreign gods, but rather that if foreign gods were powerful, then they must be Kauvadra gods.

Chiefly-Centered Fijian Christianity

This Kauvadra-centered and "land"-weighted articulation contrasts with the relations made with Jehovah and Jesus elsewhere in the islands. In the coastal kingdoms the "chiefly" weighting of the great kingdoms enabled the massive conversion to the stranger god. And conversion remade and strengthened chiefly hierarchy (see Kaplan 1990, Toren 1988). In the eastern confederations and kingdoms, conversion proceeded from the top down, especially when Cakobau, ruler of Bau, converted in 1854 (see Waterhouse 1868:223–294). Missionaries proclaimed that false deities were being replaced by the one, true god. In coastal Fiji, Fijians were offered rebirth and life eternal from the foreign Christian god, whose priests were white men and the "native teachers" they trained. Following conversion, the first fruits of the land, due to land gods, were instead offered to Jehovah. Christian chiefs (both self-defined and British constructed) were already linked with European *mana*, when they installed colonial rule at Cession in 1874. They themselves then became part of the emerging Fijian-colonial hierarchy of rule. The majority of Fijians came to portray their conversion in missionary terms as the historical movement from a time of darkness to a time of light (Waterhouse 1868:69), a founding moment also associated with the colonial *"vakarewa na kuila"* (the raising of the flag, the establishment of the colony).[3]

The coastal chiefly people came to accept the British notion of conversion as civilizing and progressive. Further, they viewed the Ra and interior people as refusing the grace of this conversion. Thus Ratu Joni Madraiwiwi, the Bauan Roko Tui Ra, on "Tuka": "Ra is truly a land of black souls. They believe the lies of the devil and even the elders have customs that are like those of little Fijian children" (91/1133). But where coastal Fijians acknowledged the new god to have superseded the old and offered up their land to the Queen, in the hills Navosavakadua denied that the new, more powerful god was new. His assertions baffled and outraged the colonial observers.

> Navosavakadua in going about the country used to tell any one he met to leave their work and follow him, saying that immortality was better than any earthly

---

3. Waterhouse wrote that initially Fijians more generally made the equation Degei = True God, Jehovah = True God, therefore Degei = Jehovah. But the eastern coastal version of "Degei," and chiefship more generally, stresses the foreign, stranger aspect of gods and their earthly instantiations, chiefs. Foreign god and foreign (colonial) rule thus articulated with the "foreign" nature of coastal high chiefs.

possession and that should be the reward of obedience to him. In this he was avowedly imitating the conduct of Christ. Navosavakadua also professes to heal the sick and in payment receives large presents. . . .

They have named the various spots around the Nakauvadra respectively Roma (Rome), Ijipta (Egypt), Kolossa (Colossians), &C. (Joske CO 83/43)

In British and coastal Fijian eyes, Navosavakadua, if not mad, was the charlatan oracle-priest, profanely trying to conflate his own (false) gods with the true Jehovah and Jesus to maintain an increasingly challenged position. Christian missionaries argued that their god was the one, true, and only god (although they often did not deny the power of other gods, ancestor gods now labeled "devils," to act on people in the world). Believing that truth and good order emanated from centralized government under (one) God and the Queen the British and coastal chiefs were bound to construct Navosavakadua's project as claims by an illegitimate charlatan priest, following false gods. But Navosavakadua's "acceptance" of Jehovah's truth was not expected by the missionaries. For them, to accept Jehovah was to reject other gods. Instead, Navosavakadua identified Christian gods as gods of the land, and Christian sacred spots as sites in the Kauvadra mountain range (tenets which continue to shape the sociocosmology of the Vatukaloko to the present). This was a creative reworking of the "land" perspective on the relation of gods, people, and power. Among the Vatukaloko folk, two ideas were confirmed, and even effloresced in the face of the successes of Bauans and white men: first, that there were and are true sources of *mana* (divine power) in the world, and second, that Kauvadra deities and their priests were that authentic source. At the same time, coastal chiefs and their followers were differently persuaded, finding the *mana* of the foreign god to be foreign, and as such, impressive, superior, unprecedented, and useful.

Wai ni Tuka: *The Power of Life*

Well beyond victory in war, what kind of power over life and death did Navosavakadua seek? And why was *wai ni tuka* (water of immortality) the physical form in which Navosavakadua transmitted his power to his people? Of course the idea of a powerful sacred fluid was not new in Fiji. Drinking *yaqona* or kava (the better known Polynesian term), known as the "water of the land," was and still is a central Fijian ritual. By drinking *yaqona* Fijian priests became one with the ancestor gods. In installation, it is the cup of *yaqona* given by the people of the land that poisons the chief to be, but also brings him back to life, now a living representative of the gods of the land. Once restricted to priests and chiefs, *yaqona* now is drunk by chiefs and commoner Fijians at any and every occasion in which power or sociality are at issue. But water as a vehicle of life was also a Christian form, for baptism. To begin to understand these aspects of Navosavakadua's practice we must consider divine power, in the forms of fertility and invulnerability among nineteenth-century Fijians, in the form of salvation as taught by the missionaries, and in the form of control and discipline exerted by the colonial polity.

In 1885 Joske recorded that "all who believe in [Navosavakadua's] doctrine . . . are to have life eternal, and their ancestors are to rise from their graves" (Co 83/43). In 1891 reporting that "Tuka" had been checked in Nalawa, he wrote, "The movement had not gone beyond the presentation of propitiatory yaqona [kava] and feasts to the priests of the 'Tuka,' in return for which the priest had distributed the 'wai ni tuka' or 'water of everlasting life' and had tried to raise the dead." The living received this immortality by drinking the *"wai ni tuka,"* or through visits from Navosavakadua's cadre of "warriors" who would tread through a village, entering each house and thus investing the community with Tuka. Further, the dead were resurrected in rituals in which *bete* (priests) stepped on their graves.[4]

In nineteenth-century Fiji "fertility" (or "life") and "invulnerability" were important aspects of divine power, but "immortality" and "resurrection" did not figure prominently in ritual-political concerns. In the great coastal kingdoms, it was especially chiefs, embodying the gods, who controlled the vitality and fertility of the kingdom, people, and nature (Hocart 1970:60). Their projects were carried out in conjunction with oracle-priests and sacrificers (see Quain 1948:229–32) who communicated with the ancestor gods to convey the will of the gods in the affairs of the kingdom, to diagnose the divine causes of defeat, sickness, or drought, and to supplicate the gods through sacrifice.

---

4. In 1882 a Fijian official at Ba informed the Governor that some people in Tavua had revived *kalou rere* rites, "as they had done lately under Navosavakadua" and had sent a man to stamp upon graves that the dead might rise again. They were led by an oracle-priest who claimed that he could "cure disease, give life to the dead and that the god would soon come and bring the dead friends from the grave again who had died under the matanitu [colonial government]." The people involved also "plotted" against their Buli (Fijian district official), accusing him of adultery (Stanmore papers vol. 41, 1881–1983, "The Tavua Affair"). The Stanmore Papers are held at the British Museum. Microfilm copies are held at the Research School of Pacific Studies, Australian National University, Canberra.

Hocart argues that the entire Fijian ritual system grew out of the urge toward life. In his interpretation the synthetic divine king is the source of all life, of social life (the establishment and flourishing of polity), and of the life, health, and fertility of the people and the land. Chiefs, and sometimes priests too, through their association with the gods, had such excessive fertile power that people were careful not to touch them or to eat their leftover food, lest they swell up or become pregnant. The death of a chief called the sociocosmological system into question, until it could be reconstituted through the installation of a new chief.

It was this notion of divinity as fertility that inspired the challenge of a great Fijian chief (Tanoa of Bau) to a missionary "When you have grown *dalo* (taro) on yon bare rock, then will I become a Christian" (Waterhouse 1868:77). In Navosavakadua's articulation of the Twins with Jehovah and Jesus, these (now autochthonous) Kauvadra gods gave him great power over the fertility of the land. According to colonial officials and also his descendants, he grew banana plants on salt sand, and caused them to grow to maturity in a day. He established pots of food that were eternally full. After his followers had eaten fish or pig, he reconstituted the live animals from their bones. These miracles are nowadays likened to Christ's miracles of the loaves and fishes.

As I have described earlier, in nineteenth-century Fiji power over death, invulnerability, and power in war (rather than "immortality") were also granted by Fijian gods through their priests and oracles. Land people controlled the ability to make chiefs, and to make people invulnerable, by invoking the gods of the land, using kava *(yaqona)* as their medium to do so. Among the inland hill people, priests, as mediums to the gods, invoked the gods, offered them sacrifices, and as mediums or conduits, were identified with their warlike as well as their fertile power. Nineteenth-century officiants of *luve ni wai* or *kalou rere* or *kalou vatu* rites made young men into invulnerable warriors. The gods entered them to make them invulnerable like stones, so that they would not become dead bodies to be sacrificed to the gods of enemies. The earliest description I have of *wai ni tuka,* "elixir of life," the story told by the missionary Fison quoted in chapter 2 of the Rakiraki priest who expected to be invulnerable even if clubbed, makes it clear that he was transacting Fijian invulnerability, rather than salvation and immortality in a Christian sense. Navosavakadua himself was celebrated for his invulnerability. In the 1880s he was known to have survived British attempts to kill him in Lau (Joske CO 83/43). Later, after his second deportation, the tales of the British efforts to drown, shoot, starve, and hang him and tales of his invulnerability to their attempts have flourished among followers and descendants from the 1890s (see, e.g., Brewster 1922:245, Sutherland 1910) into the present.

Thus in nineteenth-century Fiji, it was fertility and warrior invulnerability that were granted by the gods, and immortality and resurrection were of little concern. Among Fijians, the boundary between life and death was reckoned according to the passing of the spirit *(yalo)*. (Sometimes the horrified missionaries observed the burial of sick but still "living" people.) Spirits lingered by their grave sites for about four days, and then set out on a journey to an underworld. Ancestral deities were still in communication with their descendants, and enabled their social activities. *Bete* were the channel to the ancestral gods. Communication with the gods, by *bete*, in concert with the projects of chiefs, was fundamental to the war and sacrifice system, and equally fundamental to the prosperity of the land.

But "immortality" and "salvation" were concerns of the British missionaries in Fiji. It was no accident that Fison mistook "invulnerability" for "immortality." Beginning in the 1830s, the missionaries introduced to Fijians the idea of eternal life and offered Fijian converts eternal life through Christ's grace, and the resurrection of the dead. They also introduced the figure of Christ who made possible these miraculous blessings. Eventually the missionary concern for the salvation of the soul became a concern for Christian Fijians. For example, the missionary Waterhouse reported that Lydia Vatoa, newly converted wife of the chief of Viwa, "besought her kinsman Cakobau to join the *lotu* which he sought to destroy. She told him how happy the religion of Jesus made her and how it fortified her against all fear of death" (1868:128).

What links the missionary project and the colonial project, I think, is the concern for control over truth and hierarchy. Both insisted on one true god and one true sovereign. For the missionaries truth was moral salvation, for the colonials it was proper civility and obedience to administrative codes. Both insisted on a centralized, top-down organization, with power over life and death flowing from the top. Both found the hinterland disorderly, the possibility of complementarity of ritual roles inconceivable. In the course of his deportation in the Lau islands, among a Fijian community that had been Christian for decades, did Navosavakadua study the Bible and also gain a sense of how one Fijian-Christian polity was organized? Is this where he came to be concerned with truth in a sense rather different than the Fijian idea of *mana* (effectiveness), and to argue that the missionaries were "deceiving" Fijians? And might it have been in the experience of deportation itself that he came to see the link between power over bodies and power over morality that animated the British notion of body politic?

How then are we to interpret Navosavakadua's ritual-political practice? On the one hand, based on his miracles of fertility we might consider that he created a new chiefly polity. Stressing his rites of invulnerability, we might consider that he simply mobilized the land for war. Instead, I think that he created a novel polity, not a chiefly polity but a land-centric polity. In this land-centric polity just as Christian gods were identified with land gods, Christian themes of resurrection and immortality were made continuous with both chiefly fertility and land warlike invulnerability. It was a centralized hierarchy, with a one-way flow of power, on the model of the Christian or colonial top-down forms, but this polity located its central source of power in the hinterlands, the interior country of the Kauvadra, which had become the biblical landscape as well.[5]

In the form of *"wai ni tuka,"* I think that Navosavakadua combined land control over invulnerability with chiefly constituting fertility and with colonial-Christian control over salvation and morality. On the one hand, the missionaries infiltrated bodies with water in baptism, used other liquids in communion, and offered liquid medicines as well. And, on the other hand, in Fijian usage, kava and other forms of water of the land had their own effectiveness. In the myth of Degei, the water flowing from the Kauvadra is simultaneously fertile and dangerous. Degei himself controlled the fertility of the land through his control over rainfall, acknowledged by people throughout the islands. His control of water had also enabled his triumph in the war of the Kauvadra. To defeat the rebellious Twins he caused a giant waterspout to flood the land, to wash them down from the Kauvadra. This warlike use of water shaped the geography of the southeastern side of Viti Levu. Understanding Degei's control over water, both warlike and fertile, illuminates the link between the miraculous water of life *(wai ni tuka)* and Navosavakadua's mobilization against "foreign chiefs." In the *"kalourere* business" in the late 1870s, Wilkinson tells us young men struck rocks with spears and water sprang forth. In the 1880s Navosavakadua and other *betes,* called "fountains of life" *(va ni bula),*[6] dispensed *"wai ni tuka"* water (explicitly spring water; see Wilkinson 78/550 and Macnaught 1982). It was power in manifest form, as fertile life, warrior invulnerability, and now also immortality, from the Kauvadra gods, controlled to an extraordinary degree by Navosavakadua and his followers.

His miracles reflect a power or fertility not dependent on the "sea" or

---

5. Nowadays too some of Navosavakadua's descendants can point out biblical sites on the Kauvadra landscape.

6. Some accounts say "source of life" *(vu ni bula);* both are in CO 83/43).

"stranger chief" aspect of the chiefly synthesis. In fact, they suggested the power of people over chiefs and foreigners. In his system the land controlled the sea (as Moses he had possession of the staff that parted the Red Sea); and even the fertilizing power of the "sea" was derived from the land itself, water spouting from the unmoving rocks of the Kauvadra. His one-way, hierarchical polity did not depend on a synthetic relationship of land and sea, because, having constructed Christian gods as Fijian, Navosavakadua could draw his power completely from the land side, from autochthonous gods.

Finally, while his prophecies spoke of the future, it has always seemed to me that Navosavakadua was less concerned with fertility and birth than with communication with ancestors and resurrection.[7] Adapting the model of Christ's power of resurrection and enlarging upon invulnerability to proclaim it "life without end," the raising of the dead was integral to his mobilization. I think that this vision of the future as return to the past may have emerged because Navosavakadua, like the Vatukaloko more generally, was born and raised in the originating center of all life in the world. He located biblical sites in the Kauvadra range and equated biblical gods with Kauvadra gods, thus locating them in a spatial and cosmological original past. In seeking to resurrect the ancestors and make his people immortal he sought to reinstate an earlier order, which he now constructed as a polity in which the autochthonous people of the land would triumph over newer chiefs. His desire to return to an earlier order was compelling and innovative, and the past it sought existed only in an imagination that, however persuasive in Fijian terms, reflected on colonial experience.

Navosavakadua's Ritual Polity

Over a decade, Navosavakadua's new polity came into being, and began to be routinized. Fijian sacrifice and colonial criminalization shaped its institution.

The flow of newly constituted "land" power passed from the Kauvadra gods through Navosavakadua by means of *wai ni tuka* and ritual to the peoples now called the Twelve Tribes. From various reaches of the old Vatukaloko polity and along networks of alliance, messengers came to Navosavakadua at Vale Lebo or Drauniivi offering *tabua* (whales' teeth) asking for *wai ni tuka* ritual authorization and entrance thereby into this new ritual polity. In response to

---

7. For example, as I will discuss later in this chapter, he does not seem to have intended to found his own dynastic lineage: apparently the women who attended him were promised eternal virginity.

the requests for *"tuka,"* Navosavakadua sent out groups of men, dressed in *masi* (bark cloth) and painted. The purpose of such visits "was to *'butuka'* (tread) them, that is, to enter into a compact," wrote Mr. Carew. Joske elaborated:

> When a community desired the promised blessings they sent a messenger to beg the tuka or gift of immortality. If the request was granted a body of so-called soldiers was sent, who by treading the ground of the place and performing certain ceremonies conferred the boon.
>
> Thus it was at Udu; by treading the ground there and filing through every house in the village, they gave immortality to the inhabitants and the promise of the resurrection of their ancestors.
>
> The latter is greatly desired by all the old Natives, as it is by it they hope to regain what they consider their ancient power and prestige. (CO 83/43)

Much was made in the colonial record of the presentation of goods to Navosa himself. Roko Tui Ra told Mr. Cocks, angrily, that "at a solevu (feast) held recently at Valelebo in the Raviravi district where the Bure Kalou [temple] had been erected, Navosavakadua presented 400 whales teeth. . . . Sums of money were also given, as much as 10 s. having been paid by one individual to Navosavakadua or one of his followers. . . . Buli Saivou . . . gave four whales teeth and some mats as payment for 'Tuka'" (CO 83/43). "Payment" in the European sense is unlikely, reflecting European categories rather than Fijian. Rather, it was sacrifice: pigs, whales' teeth, bark cloth, kava, money—and women of the land—were offered to Navosavakadua (and in 1891 to other priests). In return, he provided *wai ni tuka*, miracles, and immortality.[8] Thus sacrifice to Navosavakadua created the ritual and political relations of the new polity hierarchy. Following Navosavakadua's example at Vale Lebo each new group within the system built or rebuilt a *bure kalou* (temple) to reinstate the gods.[9] Local priests (Navosavakadua's "lieutenants") were renewed in inspiration and tended these temples to receive the messages of the gods, sitting behind curtains or beneath string baskets through which the gods descended.

But in so doing they acted in opposition to the rest of Fiji, where Wesleyan churches were supplanting the temples. And, from 1878 on, they may have

---

8. Although in the 1878 accounts it is suggested that *tabua* (whales' teeth) were sent out by the Rakiraki chiefs, and perhaps from Drauniivi as well to enlist the aid of allies, in the 1886 accounts we see *tabua* going *to* Drauniivi.

9. Not unlike the earlier Fijian practice of refurbishing a much neglected temple and resurrecting a neglected god during mobilization for war (see Williams 1858 [1982]:223).

acted in (to some degree) self-conscious opposition to the colonial polity. Informers were everywhere. They were not simply individuals like the man who freely told Wilkinson of Navosavakadua's powers in 1878, but Christian teachers, village headmen, district heads, "Native" policemen who, to a greater or lesser degree, conceived these practices dangerous and disaffected. In nineteenth-century Fiji, plans for warfare were covert, but perhaps the colonial scrutiny, searching for Tuka, had a different effect on Navosa and his people. Did it, like deportation, create a sense of objectification, of novelty in practice, among the people of the Twelve Tribes themselves?[10] Might they have felt themselves to have the power to baffle or terrify coastal Fijians, missionaries, and colonial officers? Was incitement of Christian and colonial anxieties and imagination an intention, or merely an unintended consequence of Navosavakadua's practice?

Until 1886 Navosavakadua himself was the focal leader of this new ritual polity. Like the Navosavakadua of the colonial system for establishing truth (the Chief Justice) he sat at the apex of a system of administration and morality. Like chiefs of synthetic ritual polities, he was the central focus of sacrifice and redistribution. The "people" presented him with their virgin daughters to live with him and to be his attendants, like the retinue of a coastal chief. These women chewed and prepared the water of the land, the *yaqona* that kept Navosavakadua in a perpetual state of communication with the deities. But unlike the eastern polities, Navosavakadua's relations with these women of the land would not necessarily result in a line of chiefs. Instead the women were promised that they would remain virgins perpetually (CO 83/43). Unlike a synthetic coastal chief, Navosavakadua did not seek to expand the polity through conquest, nor to create new chiefly lines through his own descendants. Unlike the colonial polity or the old Fijian coastal polities, it was Navosavakadua's intention that "people of the land" should rule over chiefs. The fertility of his project was inverted and genealogically retrospective, focusing on the preservation of the present and the return of the ancestors.

Sacrifice in the Land-Centric Polity

The principles of sacrifice that underlay Navosavakadua's ritual system similarly invert those of the stranger chief-centered polity. It is said that Navosava-

---

10. I do not mean to imply that before the colonial encounter Fijians had never been self-conscious concerning their own practices. After all, I have discussed the indigenous opposition of

kadua's *tanoa* (kava bowl) had two *sau* (the cord with shells attached which is extended toward the ruling chief during a chiefly kava ritual).[11] The typical *tanoa* has only one such cord, which extends toward the chief. But according to the story, in Navosavakadua's kava ritual one *sau* was extended toward Navosavakadua and the other was extended to the people who served him. Thus *veiqaravi* (respect, sacrifice, or worship between chiefs and people) was atypically equal between the two sides. This unusual *tanoa* suggests that Navosavakadua viewed his relationship with his people as radically different from that between a "chief" and "people." It would have been even more radically different from the colonial and Methodist hierarchies, where authority, truth, and effectiveness were held to flow only from the top down. Rather, it suggests a land-centered system of relations, in which power passed between gods and people through the oracle-priest.

Even more strikingly, the alleged symbolism of the white pig aside (see Carew's suggestion that it stood for the sacrifice of Europeans in CO 83/43), there was apparently no human sacrifice among the Vatukaloko in the decade before Navosavakadua was deported. Colonial officers, keen to point out the dangers of Tuka, remarked on the "consecration" of the various temples, but they warned only of the future likelihood of cannibalism: none claimed that bodies were buried for the posts of god houses, or that any other form of human sacrifice was involved. Navosavakadua's polity was without *kai wai* (chief's fishermen), the essential third term, representing the chief's sea side, who would provide bodies for the oven. Indeed, Navosavakadua's most important miracle was a complete inversion of cannibal sacrifice. Under his direction, a man was baked in an earth oven along with taro and a pig. But the man emerged uncooked, and was not consumed. Sutherland wrote in 1910: "A man whose name was Atunaisa was baked alive with some food in an oven. All who witnessed it were horror stricken, but not so with Navosavakadua! When the usual time had been allowed for the food to cook, the oven was uncovered and everyone crowded around to see if Atunaisa were dead, but there lay Atunaisa, laughing. All the food with which he had been baked was properly cooked." In 1984 Osea Ravai, a Vatukaloko man of Wakalou *mataqali* (ritual kin group), wrote and published a version of the story:

---

hill and coastal people and a host of culturally constructed attendant differences; and surely as well some Fijians constructed certain kinds of "Fijian" identity in relation to Tongans, and so forth. Here I simply want to suggest that this was an occasion in which such reflexivity might have taken place.

11. This story was told to me in 1985 by a man of Nakubuti *mataqali*.

What follows here is the second miracle *(cakamana)* Navosavakadua (or Mosese Dukumoi) performed. One day he called together the people of his *yavusa* [ritual-kin group or polity, but he is writing in a biblical mode and would probably chose "tribe"], and told them that they should give one of their *yavusa* to be baked and that they would know the strength of the god he was worshipping and not Degei, Dakuwaqa or Waicalanavanua but Jehovah only.

They then agreed, they would give a man for Navosavakadua to bake, and they gave a man whose name was Atunaisa for baking. . . .

The people then started the earth oven. When the stones in the earth oven were heated well, they took Atunaisa, the man, and they laid him there in the middle of the oven and buried him. The oven was covered at the time the sun was standing right above (noon) and when it was afternoon Navosavakadua ordered that the oven be opened. . . .

When the oven was about to be opened Navosavakadua told them that when the oven was opened they should not open the leaf covering, but should come back to him and call him that he might decide what to do.

Navosavakadua was then called and he went straight to the oven before they opened the leaves and held one more of his prayers.

When the prayer was finished then Navosavakadua called Atunaisa three times. After calling three times the voice of Atunaisa was then heard. Navosavakadua then told him to stand and then to come to him.

Navosa then blessed him and the people of the yavusa when they saw this thing that was done by Navosa they touched his hand and didn't doubt.

You, the gentlemen and ladies who read *Nai Lalakai* [the Fijian-language newspaper in which the story was published] this man Atunaisa, we two met and I knew him because he is a member of my *mataqali* (kin group). He died in the year 1944 in the time I went to the war in the Solomon Islands. (*Nai Lalakai,* my translation)

Navosavakadua's power over bodies seems to have rejected Fijian cannibal sacrifice, but it did not transform body disciplines in the way that colonial Christians did. It did not replace power over life (fertility, invulnerability, immortality) and power over death (cannibal sacrifice, conquest, and redistribution of feast and warfare goods) with the body disciplines (from handcuffs, hair-cutting, and clothing to road-building, imprisonment, and deportation) that the colonial system employed. Instead, I think, Navosavakadua retained the power of potential cannibal sacrifice, but subsumed it, by offering salvation to the potential victim, just as he retained the warrior power of the Twin Gods, but remade them as Jehovah and Jesus.

Inverting succession, *veiqaravi* (chiefly ritual), and sacrifice, in Navosavakadua's polity life flowed from the land gods to the land people, mediated by a priest rather than a chief. His polity did not center on a synthetic chiefly figure combining land and sea, but rather on a land interpreter of the gods, already identified with the land gods. In installation a chief drinks *yaqona,* the water of the land, and is ritually "killed" by the installing people and is reborn as a god. Navosavakadua was instead constantly *"mateni"* ("dead" from kava). Through his hereditary nature, and his ritual use of kava he was already of the substance of the gods of the land.[12] The new polity was far less an alternative chiefly polity than it was a transformed version of the power of *bete* and the land side. Like the gods of the Kauvadra, Navosavakadua proposed not simply to reconstitute, but to overturn the world.[13]

Navosavakadua mobilized a polity of reversal, in which the people of the land were to rule the chiefs, driving out all foreigners. This new land-centrality did not simply continue Vatukaloko land-centrism, but also took its form from the new colonial polity as local syntheses and balanced relations between "land people" and "chiefs" were negated by the British chiefly centrism. Facing the new hierarchically absolutist colonial polity Navosavakadua created an opposite to their annihilating sea power. If the colonial polity was to be top down and foreign, his was to be centered on the hinterland and passed-over sources of power, and equally uncompromising.

The Consequences of Intervention

The Twelve Tribes polity differed from the old Vatukaloko polity, as well as from the evolving chief-centered, top-down colonial forms of the big coastal kingdoms. Formed initially, as early as 1878, as a mobilization for battle instigated by the Rakiraki chiefs, Navosavakadua's polity, developing out of the relatively land-oriented Vatukaloko polity, was more radically land-centric. Whether in a noncolonial context it could have emerged as a novel polity or maintained its structure beyond the lifetime of Navosavakadua's leadership I do not know. Nor can we know whether Navosavakadua's ritual system could have mobilized sustained warfare against the colonial government. Perhaps,

---

12. As Valeri (1985) says of the Hawaiian *kaula:* "[he] really has no need to sacrifice; having a direct relation with the god he needs no mediating term."

13. A man told Mr. Joske: "Navosavakadua, otherwise Degei, is to overturn the world *(vukica na vanua)*."

instead, it would have become protest in ritual form, like the delimited ritualized assertion of authority of the superseded mother's brother's (land) line at the installation of the chief. Perhaps, on the other hand, had warfare begun, human sacrifice would have followed. Perhaps a line of leaders would have followed Navosavakadua, or perhaps another new form of leadership and power would have developed. And in the absence of active British questing after Navosavakadua we would certainly have gained a better sense of how directly Navosavakadua would have sought out and overtly challenged the colonizers.

But Navosavakadua's developing new ritual system was formed in engagement with British projects and was constantly interrupted by British top-down punitive action: the deportation of Navosavakadua to Lau in 1878, his final deportation to Rotuma in 1886, the deportation of twelve *bete* and the entire village of Drauniivi in 1891. The British outlawed Tuka and sought its source in order to excise it. By 1891 they had determined that the source was not simply one charlatan leader, Navosavakadua, but rather, his kin group, the people of Drauniivi and associated settlements, and a group of "charlatan" priests and "ringleaders." What happened to Navosavakadua's ritual polity?

Certainly from his deportation in 1886 to the deportation of the Vatukaloko people in 1891 the ritual polity continued to center on Navosavakadua. His return replaced the advent of the Twins in ritual expectation, says Joske. The organization of prophecy, distribution of *wai ni tuka,* and admission to the ritual polity were still directed from Drauniivi and Vale Lebo. Invocations at *yaqona* presentations were directed to the Kauvadra range, and to Navosavakadua's places at Drauniivi and Vale Lebo. Navosavakadua had designated no one successor, but Joske describes a group of priests who carried on the ritual practices,[14] who moved back and forth from Drauniivi on the coast to the ritual center inland at Vale Lebo, and who traveled to stay in the newly built *bure kalou* (god houses) that were being built inland at Nadrau, Nasoqo, and Bobuco. Joske was told that the priests were organized in two divisions, the *"Lawa ni mate"* (which he translates as destroying angels) and the *"Lawa ni bula"* (angels of life). Some were to tend to the interior people, while others were to be active on the Ra side. When Fijian policemen arrested a man called Dresa in Rewasau (in Bobuco) they found a written list of twenty-two place names, with a title at the bottom of the page reading *"Na i wiliwili ni koro e 21"*

---

14. See 91/2344 (Report of Proceedings for the Suppression of Tuka in Colo East by Joske) for a comprehensive listing of *"bete"* and "ringleaders." See also 91/1852, and CO 83/46.

("A list of the twenty-one villages"). The list, beginning with the name Vatukaloko, included villages from the coast all the way to the interior district of Bobuco.

Even following Navosavakadua's deportation, Fijians still sought to join the new ritual polity. The Nasoqo people, who were the interior border *(bati)* of the Vatukaloko polity, who had been living at Drauniivi from the early 1870s until Carew resettled them inland, became a path to other groups, including the Bobuco people farther inland. As the Nasoqo people reestablished themselves, Raicula their priest oversaw the building of a temple for Tuka ritual. Through Raicula, requests for Tuka were transmitted back to Drauniivi.

In the interior district of Bobuco, a priest named Senileba had been holding conversations with Navosavakadua, and had received letters from him, carried by birds (91/2344). In 1890 the government-appointed Buli (district official) at Bobuco and his brother sent whales' teeth to Raicula, the principal priest at Nasoqo, who took them to Drauniivi. Back from Drauniivi came the word that "Buli Bobuco's services would be acceptable to the Gods" and that he should build a temple at his town Navuniwaiwaivula. The temple was presided over by a local priest, Peni Nacolauli. The Buli's brother solicited kin and old allies to help in the building. The *bure* was built and "consecrated" when the Vakatawa (Fijian minister) was away.

Convinced of a spreading phenomenon, the colonial government took action by striking at its core. Joske had begun his reports in 1891 with assurances from local Wesleyans that what appeared to be Tuka was actually proper Fijian ceremonial due to leaders of *mataqali*. But by the end of his investigations, he and Carew and Thurston saw a well-orchestrated "revival of Tuka." They determined that Tuka still had a central source, based in Navosavakadua's old village, among his kin, and among the priests who had worked with him. They decided to deport the people of Drauniivi, Vale Lebo, and Vatunisala villages and twelve other "ringleaders" to the southern island of Kadavu.

Two Trajectories of Tuka

Before following the ensuing history of the Vatukaloko folk, in exile and return, I would like to consider what became of Navosavakadua's ritual polity, here noting two trajectories to Tuka. In coming chapters we will look at the history of the Vatukaloko folk deported to Kadavu to chart a history of a continuing but unstable land-centric polity, in which people of the land side in many senses prevented their chief, the Tui Vatu, from returning to the fore, and in which, throughout colonial vicissitudes, Navosavakadua's land-weighted construction of the relationship of the Christian god and the gods of land continues to be most salient. In this trajectory, Tuka is denied, and Navosavakadua is constructed as a Fijian-Christian martyr. But before we continue this history I would like to note briefly another trajectory of "Tuka" in the Ra and hill areas, the colonial districts of Ra and Colo North, East, and West, which seems to have involved local chiefly-led polity struggles rather than land-centric inversions of the ritual political system.

Despite the colonial hope that the deportations of Navosavakadua, and then the priests and the people of Drauniivi by 1891, would root out Tuka, the local dynamics of Navosavakadua's ritual-political system had become more varied in the years after he was deported. First of all, although Joske was told that Tuka was run from Drauniivi by the two divisions of priests with their delimited domains of influence, in the 1890s various local chiefs, several of whom held colonially designated offices, themselves had begun to make claims to leadership through Tuka. Such chiefs included the previously mentioned Buli Bobuco (government-appointed official of Bobuco district) and his brother, and Navulalevu of Lamisa, who was assistant Buli of the Tokaimalo district. According to Joske, in 1890 Navulalevu came to Nasoqo

> attended by five women called "Leba," the usual cortege of a "Tuka" leader. . . . Navulalevu upon his arrival took up his abode at the Tuka bure with the priest Raicula. Raicula assembled the Nasoqo people and said "This is a very great chief of the Tuka who had come over he is senior even to Navosavakadua and Qaluma. . . . You must bring food for him, those who do not will assuredly die." Then yaqona was nightly made by the Leba women. . . . When the yaqona was strained and ready and the customary libation to the gods poured out, the priest Raicula offered up the following dedicatory prayer:
>
> . . .
>
> This [wrote Joske] I venture to translate as ——
>
> An offering of all we chiefs who are
> assembled here. Let the offering proceed
> downward/onward. Until it reach
> Vale ni Lebo and its house at Draunivi
> It is now the offering of the
> root of it, who is now with us, he of
> Lamisa. A prayer for those who
> hold Government Appointments
> that they may be punished at

the day of Judgement whether they
be magistrates or bulis may they
be turned into pillars of salt. I
finish this that there may be no rain [?]
Mana dina — e — dina

(Joske in 91/2344)

In contrast to Navosavakadua's priestly-led system, I think that in Nasoqo and Bobuco in 1891, and in Qaliyalatina in 1914, Tuka became the vehicle for the competing chiefly claims of local leaders, in response to local specifics of indirect rule. Just as in 1878 the Rakiraki chiefs had consulted Navosavakadua, here Tuka seems to have become a means in competition by local chiefs.

In both Nasoqo and Bobuco, local chiefs had quarrels with British-appointed chiefs. Navulalevu "was not a Tuka practitioner," he protested at his trial, but rather he had been prosecuted because "Roko Tui Ra had a grudge against him about some fish" (91/2344). Similarly in Bobuco in 1891, the Buli and his brother were in conflict with Native Stipendiary Magistrate Ro Qereqeretabua. Qereqeretabua's people were historical enemies of the Bobuco people. Even Resident Commissioner Carew remarked on the arbitrariness and harshness of his sentences. The government-appointed Buli of Bobuco and his brother sought to defy him. They proclaimed in his open court that "only the Buli and [his brother] commanded in Bobuco, and that the Government had nothing to do with it" (91/1852). Neither Navulalevu nor Buli Bobuco were priests. They made offerings through locally inspired priests both to the source of power at Drauniivi, and to the Kauvadra gods.

In Qaliyalatina in 1914, Buli Qaliyalatina himself (Joseva Bebe Tube, who had been a clerk to Joske) was identified by officials as a member of the Bai Tabua, a group of men who had continued to pray to Navosavakadua and the Twins, through their priest Osea. Osea had sent ten whales' teeth to Drauniivi in 1892, shortly before the Vatukaloko people were deported. In this case Osea the priest seems to have also intended to assume the rule of the people. Deported by the government, the people converted en masse to Catholicism.

The contrast between Navosavakadua's polity and these other examples is one between a transformation of the synthetic Fijian polity form and a simple variation on it. Navosavakadua's ritual system was an assertion of land priority at so fundamental a level as to invert the chiefly polity totally, by suggesting that the people would rule the chiefs and that the world would be overturned. In contrast, the events in Rakiraki in 1878, and in Nasoqo and Bobuco in

1891, were more simply assertions of local autonomy or enmities, on behalf of competing chiefs.

It is possible that if I had done fieldwork and heard narratives of the past in Nasoqo, Bobuco, or Qaliyalatina I would have discovered that what appear to have been chiefly projects were, as in the Vatukaloko case, a far more complicated matter. But based on the colonial descriptions, it seems to me that in the Rakiraki, Nasoqo, and Bobuco mobilizations, chiefs — as local ruling chiefs — sought relationships with Navosavakadua and the Kauvadra deities, through "Tuka" priests. The priests who were Navosavakadua's heirs could not, or did not, maintain Navosavakadua's dual role as leader and medium. They did not sustain or extend the land-centric ritual system, in Ra and Colo as a whole. Among the Vatukaloko people themselves, as we shall see, the power of the installing group, and the *mana* (power) of Navosavakadua would continue to rival that of the Tui Vatu, particularly through a reinterpretation of Navosavakadua as Christian. I think that there is a real difference between the sort of complete transformation effected, if only briefly by Navosavakadua, and the local, chiefly-led ritual-political struggles which did not fundamentally challenge the prevailing orthodoxy of the chiefly-led polity. In these differences, I think we also see the beginnings of a real plurality of articulations of colonial and Fijian systems, by means of different narratives of Navosa, ranging from the government's demonization, to a local chiefly version in the less controlled districts of the north and interior, to the Vatukaloko versions.

Reconsidering Navosavakadua and "Tuka": Articulating Plural Systems

In these last three chapters I have been reconsidering Navosavakadua and "Tuka." We can read Tuka as a movement of the "land" within the flow of indigenous and contact historical trajectories in Fiji, in the face of a colonial project which never really knew who "land people" were but formed their own constructions and codifications of Navosavakadua and his practice. While it would be possible to write a narrative that stresses only indigenous continuity or a narrative that gives most weight to colonial power, in this chapter it is Navosavakadua's own creativity that has interested me most. And I think that his creativity reflects one of the most interesting kinds of agency possible in colonial societies. Navosavakadua looked at multiple systems of power and created a new articulation. By stressing creativity, I do not mean to suggest that I read Tuka as a random formulation, or that I think that this colonial society was a fluid chaos. Instead, I think that Navosavakadua's project was the product of structures (the Fijian and colonial systems in a real historical conjuncture). But it is not reducible to, or completely dependent on, any of these structures. I am convinced that creativity is possible in "indigenous" contexts, but I also think that colonial conjunctures create spaces where new possibilities are thrown open. These are rarely happy possibilities, as colonized people face colonial power. But in spaces and arenas such as hinterland Fiji, new kinds of history were and are made by the colonized. And creative making of history did not end with Navosavakadua for the Vatukaloko, any more than Navosavakadua's own significance was fixed by his own acts or intentions. We turn now to the aftermath and consequences of Navosavakadua's career, for the Vatukaloko in particular, and also for others in Fiji.

6

ROUTINIZING ARTICULATING SYSTEMS: JEHOVAH AND THE PEOPLE OF THE LAND, 1891–1940

This chapter and the next two are about the consequences for the Vatukaloko and others of Navosavakadua's project and the colonial suppression of his polity, and, more broadly, about ritual political power in twentieth-century colonial and post-colonial Fiji.

In this chapter in particular, we examine struggles to articulate and wield ritual political power early in this century in Fiji's emerging colonial society, these struggles viewed from the atypical yet revealing vantage point of the Vatukaloko experience. This is a story of competing articulations of gods, chiefs, and people of the land, and how such articulations were routinized. By routinized, I mean that some visions of Fiji's order were established and institutionalized, and became more or less enduring systems in which people led their lives. But these established systems were plural. No single complete colonial orthodoxy has ever emerged, though some are more dominant than others. The means of routinization are also part of our story; they included colonial institutions such as the Native Administration and the Native Lands Commissions and public colonial commissions claiming to authorize the truth. But other forms of routinization existed as well, including privately held manuscripts and ritual relations inscribed on local landscapes, both insisting on potent alternative visions of Fiji's order laid down by Jehovah and the gods of the land.

Within this period there were many resounding historical moments, critical in the history of Fiji, which go unaddressed. But from the Vatukaloko perspective much is made clear—about British constructions of negative tradition and about Fijian constructions of "people of the land"—that might otherwise be obscured.

As a brief look at the emerging colonial society of Fiji,[1] this is the story of a colonial government (or at least its "Native Administration" and its land tenure system) that depended on a version of the Christian Fijian chief as colonial authority, constituted from the top down. As *"turaga"* was so redefined, this new class of chiefs came to administer provinces and subdivisions. Simultaneously, new meanings were also being made for "land," notably people of the land as owners in something like a capitalist sense. But "land" was a far more disputed category.

As a history of the Vatukaloko, this chapter sometimes reveals how sparse a record there is about many aspects of their lives in this period. (Much more was written by the colonizers in the era in which they tried to exorcise full-fledged Tuka, and today's Vatukaloko folk too prefer to tell the stories of Navosavakadua's lifetime.) Nonetheless, I have found and brought together sufficient material to write of the Vatukaloko deportation to Kadavu, their return to Ra and then to Drauniivi itself, and their involvement in two major social projects: a business venture (the Fiji Company of Apolosi Nawai), and the colonial codifications of the Native Lands Commission. These topics bring us into complicated cultural and even theological matters: emerging, contesting understandings of the relationship of Jehovah, Fijian gods, and the people of the land.

The Years of Exile

In 1984 at Drauniivi I interviewed an elderly lady of *mataqali* (kin group) Nasi who was one of the last of the Vatukaloko people who had been in exile in Kadavu.

> (Where were you born?) I was born at Kadavu.... We stayed there. I was a child. I saw their church, I saw the big house of Taivesi. When we used to play on the

---

[1]. This is indeed a brief look at this historical period in Fiji, a period in which there were many resounding moments, critical events that shaped the colony and the nation. They include the political and economic implications of the end of indenture for Fiji's South Asian migrants who worked the colonial sugar plantations, colonial concerns over the declining Fijian birthrate, and the effect of world conditions including World War 1 on the colonies. For an excellent general history of Fiji's twentieth century see Lal (1992).

beach there was his big house, near the sea at Kadavu. And I saw the church when I was young. (Whose church?) That of the people of Drauniivi. There was a big grave there. I asked my mother why are the flags raised? Our house had flags. She said "Our chief Naivalulevu [the Tui Vatu] is being buried there."

I wasn't yet three when we left Kadavu. Just a small child. . . . We rode in a big boat from there, how many boats, there were three, one *mataqali* one boat. We of Nasi, they of Wakalou, they of Nakubuti. We rode to Nanukuloa. (Translated by Vika Tagivuni and myself)

Lifted surgically from the Ra landscape the Vatukaloko people[2] were sent to exile in Korolevu, Naceva district, on Kadavu island, off the south coast of Viti Levu. They would spend ten years there (see 02/2057). Then from 1903 on they spent six years back in Ra province in the Roko Tui Ra's town Nanukuloa under the watchful eye of Ratu Joni Madraiwiwi. Finally in 1909 they were allowed to return to rebuild the site called Drauniivi, on the northwest coast of Viti Levu.

In Kadavu and Nanukuloa the Vatukaloko faced a mixture of extreme prejudice and optimistic neglect. Thurston had minuted that the name Drauniivi was no longer to be used and that all the "Tuka villages" should be leveled (see, e.g., 92/2258). Articles in *Na Mata,* the government-produced Fijian-language newspaper, were intended to make an object lesson of the Vatukaloko for all other Fijians (October 1891). At first the Kadavu officials were alert to spot any incipient practices of Tuka. But the Vatukaloko came to conform, outwardly at least, to church and governmental expectation. They built a large thatch church, the one remembered by the elderly lady as one of the two major buildings of the settlement, which was described approvingly in the 1893 Methodist Mission Report of the Kadavu Circuit:[3] "They have built a commodious church for themselves and a teacher's house. Their attendance

---

2. The deportees were Vatukaloko people in the inclusive sense, that is to say, members of Nasi, Wakalou, and Nakubuti kin groups and others from the "Twelve Tribes" who had been living at various Vatukaloko villages, including Vale Lebo. In 1902 the ten year maximum period of deportation allowed by Ordinance had expired. At that time the colonial officials sent some of the deportees back (some Wacakena people returned to the Naraviravi villages in Tokaimalo district and Nabaqa village in Nailuva district, the Nacolo people (deported from Vale Lebo) went to Vatukacevaceva village in Naroko district). The Vatukaloko people proper, deported from Drauniivi, were given the choice of returning to ancestral lands inland, returning to live at Nanukuloa, the Roko's town in Ra, or staying in Kadavu. They remained an extra year in Kadavu and then initially resettled to settlement at Nanukuloa which they named "Kadavulailai" (little Kadavu) (for further details see 02/2057 and Kaplan 1988).

3. Volume 1879–1884, Mitchell Library, Sydney.

at the various services seems all that can be desired and many have recently been admitted into our classes on trial. There is reason to believe that while their banishment is very humiliating to them, it will drive them to seek comfort in One who 'sticketh closer than a brother.'"

Like the missionaries, colonial officials expected the Vatukaloko to become Christian and civilized in their healthy new environment. But where the missionaries hoped the Vatukaloko would find God, colonial officials explicitly anticipated the moral influence of high chiefs, first the Roko Tui Kadavu (see, e.g., 96/4498) and later the Roko Tui Ra. As for the Vatukaloko people, in 1891 they had chosen Taivesi Mamaqa of Nakubuti to be their village headman (Turaga ni Koro). It was he who occupied the big house on the coast that the elderly lady remembered. In this position he represented them in correspondence with the British authorities, and in interactions with the Fijian provincial head (the Roko Tui Kadavu), with the local district head (Buli Naceva) in Kadavu, and with the provincial head in Ra (the Roko Tui Ra). In another sense he represented them in the colonial imagination, for as village headman (Turaga ni Koro) of the Vatukaloko people he became the focus of the British projection of possibilities for proper Fijian leadership and a barometer of the progress toward civilization of all of the Vatukaloko. What it may have meant in the Vatukaloko imagination to create a new position of intermediary between Vatukaloko and colonial authority is equally important to explore. Two incidents in the mid-1890s reveal the British projection. They reveal as well how some of the Vatukaloko categories were changing during their experience, in deportation, of the colonial vision for Fijians.[4]

In 1894 Taivesi was accused of practicing *luve ni wai* by the local Christian Fijian teacher. The Roko Tui Kadavu immediately investigated and reported to the Secretary for Native Affairs, who summarized "These rumours proved to be utterly false and seem to have had their origin in a half witted man of the

---

4. These two incidents, recorded in the Colonial Secretary's Office and Kadavu and Ra Provincial Records, National Archives of Fiji, seem to me to be the most important points at which the Vatukaloko came to administrative attention during their exile in Kadavu (at least as far as I can glean from the colonial papers). Further correspondence concerns an accidental fire, reports of the terrible effects of influenza (see Missionary report for 1892; Provincial Council Meeting 22 July 1896 Kadavu Provincial Records, National Archives), thievery, and the activity of "one Sesevu a bad character." There was a long correspondence over resettlement (two main series: Files Relating to Deportation of Natives case no. 24, containing CSO 91/2858 and following, and in the regular CSO series 02/2057 and following) in the later years. (See also 92/2258, 96/2797, 96/2822; and Native Department Fijian Letter Book 1893–1894, outgoing and Kadavu Provincial records available for this period at National Archives, Suva.)

name of Kolinio. This however would probably not have amounted to anything had it not been for the conduct of Joave the teacher whose antipathy to Taivesi the chief of the town resulted in his circulating false reports and assisting to concoct a heathen song which was attributed to Taivesi." Another official noted "Being brother or cousin of the man who called himself Navosavakadua (Dugumoi) Taivesi is liable to be suspected of heathen practices." Governor Thurston himself sympathized, writing, "Something is due to Taivesi. The office might write saying he appears to have exonerated himself from the charges made and that so long as he acts straight and honestly as the Matanitu requires he need not fear that anything will happen to him. If any of the people have conspired against his authority they must be punished" (94/925).

Thurston's comment (vintage Thurston) ascribed authority to Taivesi, seeing in him a proper leader, innocent of charges, subject to conspiracy by grumbling people. But in an abrupt reversal in 1896 Taivesi bore the brunt of administrative actions when it was discovered that the Vatukaloko had "tied a dead man to a tree for two days." The local Buli reported the matter to the Roko, who called Taivesi before a provincial council. In the course of the investigation Taivesi was accused by some of the Vatukaloko of ordering "customary *(vakavanua)* practices" to be carried out. He defended himself by claiming that the only customary practice he had ordered was to require people to work on his garden. At the same meeting, the Vatukaloko were accused by some Kadavu people of stealing from their gardens. The European Stipendiary Magistrate reported that

> the Roko severely censured him [Taivesi]. He was told that he was not to "lawaka" [levy] anything from the Vatukaloko people in future and that if the Roko again heard of their treating a corpse as they had treated the one referred to he would immediately report it to His Excellency the Governor and request that they should no longer remain on Kadavu. That they robbed the taukeis [*sic;* Kadavu people's] gardens and behaved generally in a disgraceful manner.
>
> Taivesi seemed very penitent (or frightened) — wept — and said it would not happen again. (94/925)

The Native Commissioner immediately minuted that the situation must be nipped in the bud. Implicitly following Thurston's paradigmatic personal and physical assertion of top-down authority when he deported the Vatukaloko people, the high-ranking Roko Tui Kadavu was told to visit the Vatukaloko people at Nakorolevu and to lecture them. It was hoped that his rank and forcible manner of speaking would "inspire them with fear."

The Vatukaloko people told Roko Tui Kadavu that the dead man Isikeli had been treated specially at the insistence of his wife. Asked by the Roko "What is the significance of treating a corpse in this manner?" they told him: "If a chief dies it is the custom to build a raised 'vata laqalaqa' — a moveable vata — a bier. It is only done for chiefs deceased.[5] One end of the bier rests on the side pole of the house and the other end protrudes into the middle of the house and the corpse is laid thereon."

Taivesi told the Roko that this was a custom he had often seen in Ra when he was a boy. Reading this, Allardyce therefore summarized that it was an attempt to "revivify an old heathen custom." I do not know what the Vatukaloko intended to achieve by this ritual treatment of a dead man. Navosavakadua had raised the dead to life through the power of his words. Others had attempted to do so by treading on ancestor's graves (Stanmore Papers vol. 41). But the descriptions of the treatment of the dead Isikeli in the colonial reports are brief, and reveal more about British fears of heathenism than Vatukaloko ritual practice.

From 1894 to 1896 Taivesi and the Vatukaloko had rapidly shifted in the British estimation from their civilizing course. They were "backsliding." Crucial elements for a British judgment of disorder appear in this case: Taivesi's untrustworthiness in concealing the incident, his alleged abuse of power for gain, an inexplicable reversion to heathen custom, theft from the gardens of the stable and Christian Kadavu people. Thus it was decided to charge Taivesi with "*luve ni wai* and kindred practices," the colonially reified category for disorder or what I have called negative tradition.[6]

Among the many ironies of this incident is the fact that Kaliova Banivalu the Buli Naceva (the local district chief on Kadavu who began the inquiry) would several years later be tried and deported for abusing his position, specifically for excessively levying work and goods from the people *(lala)*. A letter from the Buli to Roko Tui Kadavu charges that Taivesi levied work from the people, but it also suggests that Taivesi had written to the Roko to complain about the Buli. It is indeed possible that, as in the incident with the Fijian

---

5. The dead man, Isikeli, was apparently a member of kin group Nasi, the chiefly *mataqali*, and was survived by his wife who was known as Adi Alisi (see 04/1473). "Adi" may have been her name, rather than a title. I do not know how closely Isikeli was related to Naivalulevu the Tui Vatu of the time.

6. This charge was made even though Taivesi himself was not implicated in the treatment of the corpse, or in the thefts from the Kadavu people, and his levying of work would not have come under the *luve ni wai* regulation.

teacher, Taivesi was falsely accused, and that in this case he was accused of doing what the Buli himself was doing.⁷

The incident also reveals internal Vatukaloko dissensions. While in Kadavu, Naivalulevu the Tui Vatu (Vatukaloko chief) grew old and weak. He died in the last year there. Meanwhile it was Taivesi, of the installing group Nakubuti, who became the interpreter and the conduit between the powerful colonial government and the Vatukaloko, who regarded themselves as prisoners at Kadavu (*vakavesu mai Kadavu*). Perhaps influenced by Kadavu practices of using honorifics for chiefly leaders, Taivesi was sometimes addressed as "Ratu Taivesi." This honorific may suggest that the old tensions between the superseded chiefly line of Nakubuti and the Tui Vatu line of Nasi had again emerged, and may have become significant as the Nasi people pressed for the installation of Naivalulevu's successor, once back in Ra. In particular Taivesi was the first Nakubuti man to use the position of Turaga ni Koro (village headman), a creation of indirect rule having no indigenous Fijian ritual-political standing, to enable an active, organizing role in village life for a member of the installing *mataqali* group, who are also the superseded chiefly line.

Taivesi's position as Turaga ni Koro is interesting also because it suggests that—despite internal tensions—the Vatukaloko did not try to distance themselves from the authority of Navosavakadua, or to shun his kin. While I do not know what ritual-political role Naivalulevu the Tui Vatu was accorded, and to what degree Navosavakadua was a focus of ritual activity in the exiled community, we know at least that Navosavakadua's kinsman was given a central role in relation to the government. The British assumed this to mean he had heroically reformed himself. As we shall see later in this chapter, learning more about Taivesi's participation in the Fiji Company of Apolosi Nawai in the 1910s and 1920s, and considering later constructions of Navosavakadua in the next chapters, it instead suggests that the Vatukaloko were continuing to fashion new articulations between British categories and their own.

In particular, these incidents—the colonial questions and the Buli's inquiry in particular—reveal new Vatukaloko formulations of categories of *"vakavanua"* (in the way of the land) custom and authority. The British wanted to know what the Vatukaloko had done with the corpse and whether and why it was a customary practice. They had already assimilated the incident to their

---

7. See Files Relating to Deportation of Natives case no. 14 "Kaliova Banivalu dismissed for excessive *lala* [levying from the people]."

category of *"luve ni wai,"* a form of ritual reified as criminal disorder, and had set in motion their response of arrest and intimidation. But the records of the incident begin to reveal that while the Vatukaloko were increasingly aware of what the colonial administration considered heathen or criminal, they had not accepted the colonial definition of themselves as heathen, and that they were in the process of creating new categories of authority and custom. Note Taivesi's use of *vakavanua* (in the way of the land, or customary) in Buli Naceva's account of his interrogations of the Vatukaloko:

> I asked them, the Kai Vatukaloko, if they had been performing again the heathenish practices for which they were removed from their land at Ra to Nakorolevu and one of them named Osea replied as follows: —
>
> "The things which were done at Ra Taivesi is now doing—that is the heathen performance." I then asked "What heathen practice." Osea then said "The ordering of gardens to be planted and other work by which money can be obtained." Osea also said "Two men were the root of all the Luveniwai at Ra, Navosa who has been sent to Rotumah and Taivesi who is here at Nakorolevu." This sir was what Osea had to say.
>
> Filimoni also spoke, and said "The "Lala" which Taivesi exacts is not Government and not "Lotu" [Christian]." I asked Filimoni questions but he said he had nothing to tell me.
>
> I questioned Taivesi concerning what these two had said and he replied "No the only thing which is true is that I levied my garden from them and it is not a heathen practice but merely a ka vakavanua [customary thing, in the way of the land]; I told the heads of the mataqali [kin groups] and others and they approved of my garden being made. (96/4498)

New categories of practice were being established. Here, quite apart from the schemes of the Buli and the prejudices of the colonial authorities, the Vatukaloko themselves were beginning to use appeals to things *vakavanua,* as justification in the face of questions from the government. Filimoni claimed that Taivesi's exaction of work from others *(lala)* was sanctioned neither by government nor religion. Osea thus called it "heathen." But Taivesi called it *"vakavanua."* In the colonial polity an authoritative category of Fijian custom *(vakavanua)* had been established by the British themselves. The British presumed *vakavanua* to be defined by rank, Christianity, and relationship to the government. Using it, the Vatukaloko could escape condemnation. But for the Vatukaloko and in Ra, the category did not necessarily mean what it meant to colonial authorities. It could mean other things, accommodating Christianity, but still challenging the eastern-coastal Fijian claims to rank, and excluding the colonial government.

Colonial Contradictions and the Return to Ra

Was Taiveisi honorable or was he a *luve ni wai* practitioner? Were the Drauniivi people disorderly, or were they no longer dangerous and could therefore be returned to Ra? The about-faces of the colonial administrators mirrored the contradiction of their project. Still, at the turn of the century, as administrators held to a teleological view of the Fijian future, even the "Drauniivi people" were civilizable. They chose to interpret optimistically such signs as the Vatukaloko people's participation in church activities and the transformation of Navosavakadua's cross-cousin Taivesi into a responsible Turaga ni Koro. In 1904 the Vatukaloko were permitted to return to Ra—even though Ra was still the site of numerous new and different rituals and prophets—to live under the supervision of the Roko Tui Ra at Nanukuloa.[8] Once there they petitioned to be allowed to return to Drauniivi.[9]

Governor Thurston had wanted the very name of "Drauniivi" obliterated. Moreover, at first, officials claimed that return to Drauniivi was pragmatically impossible, minuting that there was not enough land available for the thirty-two households of deportees to settle and plant and that in any case the Vatukaloko had no rights to the land on the coast (02/2057). By 1909, however, the Vatukaloko had successfully argued for the right to some of the land earlier alienated to the Thomas brothers.[10] Mr. Joske and William Sutherland the Native Commissioner explicitly chose to supersede Thurston's directive of sixteen years before, and sanctioned a return to "Drauniivi," so named. Joske minuted: "it is of no use to proscribe the name of 'Drauniivi.' The Government might order the discontinuance of its use, but the people would secretly disobey and the importance of it become enhanced. . . . It should now be

---

8. I have often wondered whether one consequence of the Vatukaloko sojourn in Kadavu may have been the later inspiration of a man whom Cato (1947) pseudonymously called Kelevi, who preached a new religion in Kadavu in the mid-1940s. All I know of this "new religion" is from Cato's article, but it seems to me that Kelevi's articulation of Jehovah, Jesus, the Twins, and Kalinamolikula might be interestingly compared with the articulations following Navosa developed by different Ra groups that I contrasted at the end of chapter 5.

9. These petitions and discussion concerning their return constitute the only references to the presence of the Vatukaloko people at Nanukuloa I found in the records held at the National Archives for those years.

10. They thus had a small but temporarily adequate amount of planting land to which the thirty-two households residing at Nanukuloa could move. One official noted that these Vatukaloko land claims were supported by local planter Thomas Frederick Burness who wanted to foil the Thomas brothers' claims to that land (see 07/6293).

treated as a place with no past history, just as an ordinary every day Native village. But in advocating this I would also advise that Nadrauniivi should be quietly kept under severe scrutiny" (6293/07).[11] But the severe scrutiny ebbed and flowed, with the wider course of events in Ra and more importantly, with widening contradictions in colonial expectations of the civilizing progress of Fijians.

Everywhere in Fiji, Fijians were subject to incessant and peculiar supervision in certain aspects of their lives (see Macnaught 1982:64–74, Brewster 1922:154, Thomas 1990). The early twentieth century saw an efflorescing bureaucracy and practice of village inspections, yearly, monthly, and weekly timetables of work owed to government (crops for taxes, road maintenance, maintenance of provincial officials, and village, district, and province work) and a parallel set of obligations to the Methodist church. The colonial assessment of Fijians as uncivilized children to be led into civilization stultified into contradictions. Beginning in the twentieth-century new administrators challenged the self-described paternalist colonial policies established by Governors Gordon and Thurston. When would the Fijians be civilized? In the face of such regimentation, how were Fijians to become free, self-governing, productive individuals? No provision had been made for them to be free, even those in the admirably civilized provinces such as Kadavu. So argued critics such as Sir Everard im Thurn, governor from 1904 to 1910. However, continuing administrative worry over the declining Fijian birth rate, and the developing utility of using concern for Fijians to reinforce control over the large "free" postindenture Indo-Fijian population, combined to preserve the Native Administration and "rule by custom."[12]

In Ra and the hills, however, routine supervision was mixed with special attention. Second only to colonial fear of the postindenture Indo-Fijians was the threat posed to colonial order by the various Ra and hill people whose indigenous projects and varying constructions of the way they were to live as Fijians continued to flourish. *Luve ni wai* and Tuka prosecutions were carried out sporadically into the 1930s. The Bobuco people were deported in 1914, in 1918 a Tavua man, Sailosi Ratu, convened large crowds promising the return

---

11. See also Buli Saivou's comments, namely that "he did not care to say more than that should they be allowed to go he would be sorry for a better people could not be found," and Roko Tui Ra's comment that "he thought they had a severe lesson and no danger need now be apprehended from them" in the 1907 Records of Ra Provincial Council Meetings (Ra Provincial Council Meetings and Resolutions of Meetings 1908–1918:20–22, National Archives, Fiji).

12. See also France (1969) on Sir Arthur Gordon's role in nullifying im Thurn's policies.

of Navosavakadua. Most important of all in the lives of the Vatukaloko and the fears of the colonial government was the Viti Kabani (Fiji Company) organized beginning in 1913 by a man called Apolosi Nawai.

The Vatukaloko and the Fiji Company: Articulations of "Owning" and *"Itaukei"*

Unlike Tuka the Viti Kabani began as a self-consciously "Fijian" project, on behalf of a general class, the *"itaukei"* ("Fijians, people of the land, owners of the land"). From the beginning Apolosi's project was couched in opposition to economic exploitation of Fijians by whites and to colonial strictures on Fijian life. And from the beginning his project was couched explicitly in European terms of organization (as a company) and purpose (seeking economic parity for Fijians). He sought to organize Fijians to sell bananas to exporters, replacing European middlemen with his Fijian-owned, cooperatively run Viti Kabani. His base was the western side of Viti Levu, but he found support throughout Ra and Colo, and in other parts of the islands as well. Claiming authority from Jehovah and Kauvadra gods, associating with certain "disaffected" high chiefs who supported him, he formed not just a company, but, it seemed, an alternative government *(matanitu)* from national to village levels.[13]

Among the Vatukaloko, Taivesi Mamaqa became the local manager for the company. Another Nakubuti man recorded a transaction made on 15 December 1914 when two Vatukaloko men each paid two pounds for shares in the Fiji Company.

> Four pounds have been given, in the presence of Peremi and Ralali [name unclear] as witnesses on the day that the flag of the Company of Fijians [Kabani Taukei] has been raised in the village of Vatukaloko, Raviravi, Ra.
>
> Jovesa Bavou
> The scribe and revenue collector.

Monckton, the local District Commissioner,[14] believed that Drauniivi was

---

13. Concerning Apolosi see CO and CSO minute papers (many of which are confidential) from 1913 to 1946; also Macnaught (1979, 1982), and Scarr (1980). By requirement of the Archivist, National Archives of Fiji, I do not cite minute paper references for confidential files.

14. In an administrative change, District Commissioners (young British administrators) replaced the European Stipendiary Magistrates and supervised aspects of local life. Their authority frequently usurped and conflicted with that of the Fijian Provincial heads (Roko Tui) (see Mac-

the center of Viti Kabani activity in Ra (14/8968 14/10837) and Taivesi Mamaqa its instigator. He minuted:

> 1. I feel it is my duty to inform you of various rumours that have been filtering through this province for some time—they all tend to show that some anti-Government agency is secretly at work. People here do not feel safe.
>
> 2. The Centre of dissension among the natives here is Drauniivi town with Togovere close by. The leader is Taivesi with whom I have already had some trouble.
>
> 3. There have of course been many rumours ever since the Viti Company has been started which I have given in my monthly reports to help show the disquiet of the natives. This movement should be put a stop to I think, before it gains any further hold, it is at present gaining in power.
>
> 4. At the beginning of this month I arrested Taivesi for counselling a breach of the Native Regulations but on [words unclear] I was obliged on the evidence before me to dismiss it. I am nevertheless convinced that Taivesi is at the bottom of all trouble at Drauniivi although I have warned him particularly to have nothing to do with the Fiji Company he sends men round to try and collect money . . . but I can get no satisfactory evidence against him. After the case against him the other day I spoke to him at length in my office re Fiji Company and he promised to leave it alone until it should be proved a good company then he would like to join it, but he would consult me first. I now hear that they are having secret meetings at Drauniivi to which no one can get admittance—the subject of the meetings is not known.
>
> 5. Taivesi was the ringleader and cause of the trouble at Drauniivi in, I think, 1891, which led to the deportation for ten years of Drauniivi town to Kadavu for "Luveniwai." It is significant that Kadavu men have [word unclear] their protection to Apolosi at the Yasawas lately.
>
> 6. The removal of Taivesi from Drauniivi at once is I think an urgent matter and also a few of his fellow townsmen, to a place where they can do no harm. Taivesi is a cunning man and difficult to catch. It is stated that Luveniwai goes on there but it is being kept dark and I can find out nothing. I nevertheless [word unclear] that the risks at stake would justify strong action in this matter.
>
> 7. When Mr. and Mrs. Spencer [Seventh Day Adventist missionaries perhaps?] came round here they camped at Drauniivi and raised a Fiji Company's flagstaff there, it was put up with Fijian heathen custom of burying tabua, yaqona, &c. (C37/1915)

He added that a German man at Tavua was spreading news of British

---

naught 1982:76). The brash "take charge" attitude of a number of them was also in contradiction to earlier colonial reliance on indirect rule through Fijian officials.

defeats in the war and that likely such Germans were behind Apolosi. He reported as well that the planter Tom Burness had applied for a stockpile of ammunition, that "the Tavua and Ba people (Europeans) are in a high state of nervous excitement" and ended with the rumor that a young girl had been killed, cooked, and partially eaten in Colo West (C37/1915).

In response the Native Commissioner visited Ra, and a European Constabulary Officer was detailed to Ra to keep an eye on the situation. Certain administrators thought that overwork had "placed a strain on Mr. Monckton and have perhaps tended to make him take a gloomy view of the situation," and no steps were taken to deport Taivesi. But other administrators shared his alarm. Ultimately, though Monckton's letter reveals how the dangerous and disaffected Vatukaloko history had condensed in the colonial imagination of the 1920s, it was not Taivesi and the Vatukaloko, but rather Apolosi himself who was the focus of their attempts to restore order, and whose project I now briefly address.

Much has been written about Apolosi and the Viti Kabani by historians of Fiji (especially Macnaught 1979, 1982, and Scarr 1984; see also a serial biography in *Siga Rarama* in 1985). Apolosi has been proposed as the inheritor of Navosa, and the Kabani as a successor "movement" to "the Tuka." But this history has yet to be studied fully in its indigenous and colonial contexts.[15] The colonial reaction to Apolosi (and in microcosm to Taivesi) was an extension of the horror at disorder that was evoked by Tuka. Fijian chiefs at the Great Council of Chiefs resented chiefly ceremonial in his honor, just as the government fumed over his use of official sounding titles for company agents (Macnaught 1982:89). Writing during World War I, Ratu Sukuna, son of Roko Tui Ra Ratu Jone Madraiwiwi, a second-generation colonial official and chief, evoked Fijian chiefly loyalty in contrast to Apolosi when he minuted:

> Thinking Fijians look to the Government for help, vaguely wondering, with their autocratic views of government, why Apolosi and his followers have not been suppressed. His utterances and letters have been shown to be clearly against constituted

---

15. Here I do not offer any analysis of the history of the Viti Kabani in relation to the polity forms and cultural principles of the peoples of the western side of Viti Levu. Instead my concern is both to suggest how the Viti Kabani related to "Tuka"—not as succeeding "cult," but within the wider flow of cultural change—and to consider its importance in the life of the Vatukaloko people. It should be noted that while some Fijians nowadays collapse tales of the miracles of Mosese Dukumoi and Apolosi Nawai, and believe that they were both "Navosavakadua" who lived in the early colonial days, most Vatukaloko people carefully differentiate the two, well aware of Navosavakadua's genealogy and specific ties to their polity.

authority and yet nothing is done. . . . Apolosi is trafficking with racial feelings for position and gain. . . . It is a crime of the worst kind. It is an example of life unthinkably vile. (Sukuna 1983:57).

The transgression of the British expectation marked by Tuka was denial of chiefly authority and Christianity, essential presuppositions of the civilizing trajectory of Fijians. But Apolosi's Viti Kabani, I think, struck even more fundamentally at colonial assumptions about their civilizing relationship with the Fijians. The early governors had decided that in order to civilize the Fijians they must be saved from economic exploitation and kept from becoming enmeshed in the market. They believed that Fijians were rooted in the land, thus they reserved Fijian lands for kin groups and made them inalienable. They also constituted provinces, districts, and land ownership to keep Fijians rural and in their "customary" places. These policies prevailed against the nineteenth-century planters and early twentieth-century administrators who sought to "free" Fijians for economic development and exploitation. But though Gordon's perspective triumphed among colonial administrators, it was not resolved in the lives of Fijians. In founding the Viti Kabani, Apolosi denied that Fijians should be protected from business. In British eyes he claimed the right to engage in unsupervised, irresponsible, exploitative, and above all chaotic economic behavior. His seizure of freedom was regarded as an ungrateful, irrational response to a history of protection. Even to those administrators who disagreed with Gordon's policies, Apolosi's leadership was a threat to constituted order that could only be resolved by identifying him with the very sort of disorder that demonstrated the need for a protective paternalism.

To diagnose the colonial fear of Apolosi as fear of his challenge to basic assumptions of the colonial project in Fiji is not, however, to say that the Viti Kabani was a counter colonial capitalism mirroring colonial practice. Quite the opposite, Fijian cultural constructions of goods and power also animated Apolosi's Viti Kabani, most particularly through his reliance on deities and his attempt to accrue *mana* (effectiveness, power), to constitute himself as chiefly in order to make the Kabani effective. Looking at the Viti Kabani, I think that we see an attempt to arrange new access to money and profit within an explicitly "Fijian" social hierarchy.[16]

A nineteenth-century Fijian system of "generalized reciprocity" (Sahlins 1972, cf. Thomas 1991) was reinforced by colonial notions of Fijian commu-

---

16. Here Burridge's 1969 suggestion that we attend to the juxtaposition of money and other goods in these sorts of Pacific rituals is relevant in a way that it was not in his consideration of Tuka.

nalism and perhaps as well by indigenous readings of the missionary tenet of kindly love *(loloma)*, the term with which Fijians nowadays characterize "life in the way of the land" explicitly in opposition to European or Indo-Fijian "life in the way of money." But in the Fijian system, goods had circulated not just for use, but also hierarchically: chiefs had the right to levy and the duty to redistribute. What Apolosi created was the idea of a levy that benefited the people more directly. This new form was enabled through the power of the Christian god. As Apolosi said, "I alone am the chief of Fiji: it is the will of God. These other chiefs only work for themselves; they don't spare a thought for you or your welfare" (cited in Macnaught 1982:89).

What Apolosi seems to have addressed was the relationship constituted between the British and chiefly Fijians, which made it legitimate for chiefs to profit off the people. In early contact and colonial times, Europeans made economic relations with the chiefs, from the top down. Simultaneously, the *itaukei* were called owners, in a society in which ownership, in the British sense, was increasingly possible, but in which by reified "custom" they were unable to own much besides their (inalienable) land. Over and over Apolosi held mass meetings in which he simultaneously presented himself as "Apolosi Nawai na kai Ra" (the man from the west, or the ritually prior leader) and as "the chief of Fiji." In the meetings held by the Viti Kabani, the people treated Apolosi as a chief, offering him the goods and ceremonies of respect that so irked Ratu Sukuna, and contributing money to the company. In his person Apolosi thus combined the standings of people *(itaukei)* and chief. He represented the frustration of Fijians (who to this day complain "we the owners have nothing") and the right of chiefs to receive goods (as sacrifice) and to transact them (made legitimate by colonial sanction).

The Viti Kabani was an elaborated form which has a descendant in the present-day fundraising festivals *(soli)* by which Fijians most comfortably amass money for communal purposes. In the typical *soli*, following the form of precontact chiefly *solevu* (presentations of goods), a chief is the focal point of the ritual. By virtue of the chiefly presence, the people can be collected together. They conduct the rituals of respect, and offer up the appropriate goods, as sacrifice; and then they also give previously specified amounts of money, which will be returned to and used by the collectivity (province, village, school). In the absence of a chief, in a small fundraising ritual (e.g., a *mataqali soli* (fundraising for a ritual-kin group) to raise money for petrol for a generator) some other sort of chiefs-people distinction will be drawn. For example, men will be honored, women will give, or vice versa. Through this process the money is transformed into a sacrifice and is made subject to "Fijian custom." It is thereby made clean and usable for Fijian purposes. I suggest that the structure of Apolosi's Kabani was similar. In order for Fijians to properly acquire money for their bananas and other crops they had to offer the crops and the money to a divine figure. However, Apolosi's claim to chiefship and divinity had to be created, in his great ritual meetings of the company, in every instance where he raised a flag. Because of the opposing colonial-chiefly hierarchy his claims were constantly in question as indeed was the entire novel project of creating "owners of money" from *itaukei*.

Apolosi's ritual authority came from the people of the land and from the gods. It had no basis in the colonial hierarchy of chiefly Christian custom. Instead, his *mana* was attributed both to the Twins and to Jehovah. He himself claimed Jehovah publicly, and he likened himself to persecuted Jesus and spent his later years in various sites of deportation in what Macnaught has called "a forced retreat into messianism." But what is most critical is that Apolosi's movement proposed that Jehovah and the people of the land could authorize a leader. His Jehovah was not a foreigner's god, but, as among the Vatukaloko, a god of the land.

Apolosi's constructions of *"itaukei"* (owners of the land) and *"vanua"* (land) were formulated quite explicitly in opposition to British constructions. In his movement the concept of the *itaukei* as owners of land and of their labor explicitly challenged British profits. But as I have tried to show above, his articulation of the relationship of people of the land and money, goods, and profit continued to assume that communal and hierarchical relationships based in divinity must be invoked to create or take control over money, goods, and profit. This version of profit-making practice was not particularly effective. Perhaps the peculiar economics of official colonies may have inspired him. "Private" enterprises like the Colonial Sugar Refining Co. and the efficacy of the colonial government itself may have presented a top-down image of capitalism in which powerful rulers created prosperity by assigning roles and collecting products. In any case, if Marx and others see mystification in all capitalist relations, Apolosi's company was as or more mysterious in its workings than most. The Viti Kabani's finances were apparently a shambles, the money, in colonial terms, squandered. The *itaukei* probably got little or no financial return on their bananas. No doubt European businessmen took advantage of Apolosi where they could, and certainly colonial disapproval circumscribed the Viti Kabani's potential. But a crucial reason for the Company's limits as a profit-generating enterprise is that frequently values established by the market (money) can be less important to Fijians than values of hierarchy and communal solidarity being expressed. This alignment of two sorts of values continues in *soli* (fundraising festivals) of the present day.

Yet if Apolosi's misapprehension of the way to generate profits was shared by the *"itaukei"* of Fiji, the Fijian chiefs who long made business accommodation with Europeans had and have equally culturally inflected notions of economic relations in a colonially constituted polity to this day. If Ratu Sukuna claimed an ascetic and aristocratic chiefly Christian vision of colonially constituted order, it must also be remembered that many Fijians nowadays believe (with sorrow and incomprehension) that he died poor. In any case, his inheritors in political power in 1970s and 1980s Fiji subscribed instead to a concept of the accumulation and then redistribution of wealth by chiefs which relies on a combination of levying from the people of the land, extorting from the Indo-Fijian economic sector, and producing wealth, miraculously, from outside sources, foreign money in many forms including subsidies and aid.[17]

In Drauniivi today there is a house in the Nakubuti section built on a high foundation, signifying ritual preeminence. An informant explained to me that this was the place where "the flag of the Viti Kabani was raised" in Drauniivi. Along with Taivesi Mamaqa, many of the Vatukaloko joined Apolosi in the work of the Viti Kabani, but as we shall see in the following sections, Apolosi's goals of economic parity and ownership were probably only part of the Vatukaloko vision of themselves as people of the land. Their concern, following Navosavakadua rather than Apolosi, has also been with their ritual political standing. What they have drawn from Apolosi has been his explicit call to the *"itaukei,"* his call to all Fijians in opposition to Europeans and Indo-Fijians, and his insistence on his (and Fijians') inspiration both by Kauvadra gods and Jehovah. Of course, in joining Apolosi the Vatukaloko also became subject again to colonial labels of heathenism, rebelliousness, and criminality.

Articulations of Jehovah and the Gods of the Land

I will end this chapter on articulations and routinizations with two narratives about the Vatukaloko and being *"itaukei"* ("owners" of the land). One is from

---

17. I thank an anonymous reader of the manuscript for pointing out that up to 1960 capitalist development took a very limited form in Fiji, and chiefs were able to accumulate much more power than wealth. The main external sources of money came directly from the Colonial Office in England, and were not directly accessible to Fijian chiefly colonial officials. The situation changed radically after independence.

the official government commission of inquiry into Native Lands "ownership" in 1918. Those who wrote these "records" thought they were codifying custom and property. But over the years some Fijians have come to call the documents they produced "Bibles," proof that they were also producing new forms of authority — seen by Fijians as divine authority — in the colonial order. The other narrative is a manuscript written by a Vatukaloko man around 1918. In its discussion of land, kinship, and divine genealogy, it is a contrasting version of the true forms of power that ordered the lives of the Vatukaloko, Fiji, and the world. Just as Apolosi invoked Jehovah and the gods of the land, the Vatukaloko and other Fijians found the power of deities to be intrinsic to any project, colonial or hinterland.

So, before I turn to these two narratives, I would like to describe four contesting ways in which Fijians came to imagine divine power and the fate of the gods of the land in the early part of this century. First, in the coastal chiefly articulation, it was said that the true god had replaced heathen superstition, abolishing attention to old gods. Second, among those who continued to worship the ancestor deities, sometimes the old gods formed a secret mirror image of the top-down centralized colonial order. Third, in other cases the old gods became marginalized spirits, consulted in secrecy. Fourth, as Navosa (and Apolosi Nawai) preached, some found that Jehovah himself was already a god of the land.

In the chiefly coastal articulation, colonial expectation was apparently fulfilled. Chiefs installing foreign gods and the foreign government created well-known moments of conversion, dividing time into before and after Christianity, just as time had also been divided into before and after Cession. Certainly Fijian chiefs, especially high chiefs, remained divine. But their divine source of authority is more complex. On the one hand, in the installation ceremonies of Christian Fiji, a Christian preacher (Talatala) lectures the newly installed chief. On the other hand, of course, founding ancestor deities *(kalou vu)* are still remembered, as are the constituting relationships with women of the land which found the lines of "child chiefs," reborn as gods of the land. But chiefly ancestors may now be reckoned more as heros of myths, founders of lines, and political talismans than as divine figures. In colonial reifications, the active participation of the people of the land in choosing the chief has been de-emphasized in favor of the top-down designation of the true inheritor, by agencies such as the Native Lands Commission, on the basis of ultimate knowledge of genealogy. Through this colonial process chiefs thus became less dependent on priests, and more dependent on the authority of bureaucrats of the colonial state. Christianity became the necessary divine sanction for chiefs, but it is not necessary to the definition of any particular chief, not distinguishing in any way. Thus chiefs, who have come to have definition as a class, are now different from their grandparents, who were more specifically the synthetic representatives of particular polities, the embodiment of specific gods of the land.

By the early twentieth century Christian churches were found on the central greens of all Fijian villages. They were generally Methodist churches, for the very possibility of choice among missions came late in Fiji's nineteenth century. Governor Thurston wrote of Catholicism in hostile terms similar to his descriptions of Tuka; later colonial officials feared that Seventh Day Adventists were in league with Apolosi, and that Jehovah's Witnesses were bolsheviks (see, e.g., 91/2877, CO 83/54, Kelly 1991). Missionary alternatives scorned or criminalized by the colonial orthodoxy offered Fijians multiple forms of expression. The Bobuco people converted en masse to Catholicism after deportation for Tuka, and on return from Kadavu, many Vatukaloko people chose Seventh Day Adventism. (Finding Adventism unsatisfactory, around 1918 Sailosi Ratu of Tavua preached what he called "Religion Eight," which invoked Navosavakadua and other deities of the Kauvadra.) New forms of relationship to the old gods of the land were equally important.

In areas where long-term local struggles and assertions of autonomy were unresolved, the old gods were leaders in opposition to colonial government, and sometimes in opposition to Methodism too. But often, in this struggle, the gods of the land had adopted colonial forms. In Nadrau, Colo North in 1908, Kauvadra gods were invoked by a medium attended by a group of so-called "officials of Tuka," "sergeants," and "scribes." The "officials of Tuka" included a man called the Vuki who was to supervise the inversion of the world at Navosavakadua's decree. The sergeants and scribes mirrored provincial officers. The medium, Ruveni, invoked the gods and reported that

> his spirit had flown to Vugala [a site near the Kauvadra, called Rome by the Vatukaloko].... At Vugala Ruveni found Navosavakadua in council with the ancient gods of Nakauvadra. He presented a tabua to Navosavakadua and was then asked what was his report, or rather, as it was put "What news from the mountain tops" —. "The desire of the mountain tops is that all mankind perish, Foreigners and Natives, that all die —." "Not so replied Waicala [one of the gods of Nakauvadra]. I extend my love to mankind and they live." Then resumed those of Nakauvadra, "What about the request of we seaside gods that the mountain tops come within our jurisdiction, in that we helped Nadrau in former times to conquer Naloto?" "Nay,"

rejoined Ruveni, "I give not up my sway over the mountain tops until I perish." (F/50/47)[18]

The issues in the consultation were local issues involving Nadrau's autonomy in the face of relations made with coastal peoples for support in a former war.[19] The colonial authorities too were attempting to codify Nadrau's allegiances, having reassigned it from Colo West province to Colo East. But as important as the specific assertion of autonomy by the Nadrau people was the form in which the gods of the Kauvadra were conceived to exist. They formed a sort of council, to be consulted by the people about their affairs. These councils had Fijian antecedents called *so kalou* ("meeting of the gods"). In Nadrau they took on the aspect of an alternative government, a Fijian god council as a secret mirror image of the provincial and national councils instituted by the colonial government.[20]

We could trace a version of this centralization, the council of gods, back to Navosavakadua's era and the "yalo spirits" reported by Wilkinson to be congregating at the Kauvadra range in 1878. And it is tempting to view them as an alternative central authority to the new colonial body the Great Council of Chiefs. However, the model of the alternative government of ancestor gods existed alongside an increasing individualization of deities,[21] for personal luck or gain, for curing and divination. Such were the gods invoked in the *luve ni wai* rites (sometimes simple invocations of deities over a bowl of *yaqona*, by a seer) of the twentieth century, who increasingly granted individualized skill, attributes, and good fortune to the participants rather than creating invulnerable warriors in a war system. These deities would identify the cause of illnesses as particular social infractions, retrieve lost objects, or even give luck to a gambler or to a student taking an exam (see Hocart n.d.a.:336-A-H). Whether alternative council or personal spirits, these deities were, in the twen-

---

18. Minute Papers from 1930 on held at the National Archives have a different system of designation from the early year/number in series. This system is subject based, and the prefix F/50 denotes Fijian affairs.

19. These issues are like those involved in the "Tuka" of the Bobuco people in 1914 discussed in the previous chapter.

20. A similar Kauvadra council, even more explicitly in opposition to the colonial government, took place in Ovea in Tailevu at the turn of the century where anthropologist A. M. Hocart attended a *yaqona* ceremony that he called a "seance." The medium, who had invoked the Twins and the "Noble lords and noble ladies of the Kauvadra," reported that the Kauvadra gods were meeting in a council to discuss twelve items on an agenda (Hocart n.d.a.: 336A-H, see also Kaplan 1990).

21. Again, see Hocart's account for examples of the assignment of individual deities to participants.

tieth century, consulted carefully and secretively, for Fijian Methodist teachers and local officials were often informers, and prosecution was likely.

Since Christianity insisted on only one god, one place for the old gods was in the emerging category of "the way of the land." *Vakavanua* itself was a disputed category. On the one hand it was reified and codified in the colonial chiefly model. On the other hand, as used by Taivesi in the inquiry in Kadavu (and in other Tuka inquiries too: see the 1914 Bobuco Tuka record) it was possible to claim that certain acts were simply customary, not sinister. Some Fijians reached an accommodation of one sort, defining as in the way of the land *(vakavanua)* those gods and customs that were "very close to" Christianity, separated from other aspects of a heathen past. Thus in a Fijian-language Methodist magazine, an article differentiated ancestors and proper rituals from criminal and heathen gods and their rites such as *luve ni wai, kalou rere,* and Tuka (Rokowaqa 1935).

Elsewhere in Fiji the contradiction was resolved by redefining the British concept of disorder, bringing to words such as *"vakatevoro"* or "witchcraft" ambiguous — or even positive — meanings. Early on in my fieldwork in Drauniivi a Fijian younger brother, simultaneously proud and apprehensive, said to me in English, "We do witchcraft here in Drauniivi, we respect our ancestor [Navosavakadua]." In Ra and the hills especially, many Fijians came to identify and glorify opposition to the British, and assertions of various sorts of autonomy with illicit British categories such as heathenism and witchcraft and — during the two world wars — support for Germany. Throughout the first part of this century officials would be shocked by one or another local prophet who would proclaim the solidarity of Germany and the people of Colo, or even the oneness of Navosavakadua and Hitler. Although colonial observers ascribed it to Fijian irrationality (see, e.g., the assessment of Sailosi Ratu as a lunatic) we might see this articulation instead as an acceptance but revaluing of colonial categories.

In the early part of this century, however, the Vatukaloko people found a different resolution (not itself without contradictions) to the relation of old gods and new, the way of the land, and the labels of heathen and criminal that have categorized them. They have, like most other Fijians, accepted Jehovah. But they have done so in their own way — not by postulating an initial break, a transition from darkness to light, but rather, by proposing (following Navosavakadua) that the Christian god is ultimately a Fijian god, located in his first creative moment in the Kauvadra range. In so doing they reconstruct the old gods of Fiji, as created by Jehovah and sanctioned by him. Their Christianity as a way of the land attempts in a sense to be hypercorrect, always in dialogue with the possibility of being categorized as heathen or criminal — but nonetheless equally incapable of simply assimilating to the colonial chiefly model. To continue to explore this current Vatukaloko sociocosmology, we will end the chapter with the 1918 Lands Commission Enquiry, and a vision of the place of the Vatukaloko and gods old and new, recorded at that time by a descendant of Navosavakadua.

Land and the Land:
Colonial Codifications and Vatukaloko Claims

Commissions were probably the preeminent ritual-political means used by the British to establish authority and order in colonial Fiji. Their issues of inquiry were many; here we are interested specifically in the Native Lands commissions and the resolution of actual land ownership. But we should not lose track of the way in which these inquiries produced a form of colonial order, no matter what their topics were. As commissions heard "testimony," and in the lands cases "allowed" Fijians to claim lands, they set terms and relations of authority among all participants, routinizing colonial power in ways well beyond what any force might have accomplished. Custodians of these records have called them "Fijian Bibles." But, as we shall see, even among those who participated in the commissions' forms, other visions and forms of authority and order were still possible.

The Lands Enquiries held in Ra in 1917 and 1918 were conducted by G. V. Maxwell and two Bauan chiefs.[22] Their procedure was to record a *"tukutuku raraba"* (sometimes glossed as "tribal statement," or "tribal history") which included a description of an original ancestor, his travels and marriage, the founding of distinct *mataqali* groups (which the Commissioners had arbi-

---

22. Inquiries were held in Ra in the 1880s to establish claims made by Europeans to land purchased previous to 1874, when Fijian lands were declared inalienable. In Ra in 1917–1918 the Native Lands Commission sought to codify the Fijian ownership of the remaining Native Lands, according to owning *mataqali* groups. In 1924, a further commission sought to reserve Fijian-owned lands. This commission was led by Ratu Sukuna (son of Ratu Joni Madraiwiwi the Roko Tui Ra in Navosa's time, and paradigmatic second generation representative of the Christian, colonial, high chiefly articulation). Here the goal was to have Fijians surrender control of their lands to the government which would lease them, or encourage their development, on their behalf, rather than allowing them to make individual arrangements, particularly with the growing population of "free Indians" now that the Indian indenture system had ended. In the 1950s, a further commission inquired into "customary" ownership or usufruct of fishing privileges, waterways, etc.

trarily determined to be the land-owning unit; see France 1969) by his sons, the current membership of the *mataqali* group, and a statement of boundaries. The commission also asked how the group was connected to larger local kingdoms or confederacies (*vanua* or *matanitu*) and what chiefly sovereignty they had acknowledged in the past and present. Next, if claims were disputed, evidence and argument were recorded. These were recorded in separate "Evidence Books." The commissioners then wrote out their own decisions as to the correct constitution of the *mataqali* group and its land boundaries.

At the Lands Commission meeting the initial Vatukaloko "tribal history" was given by Jovesa Bavou (Nakubuti), Fereniki Dela (Wakalou), and Viasi Naitura (Nasi). Their statements set forth one of the most elaborate histories of any of the hinterland polities of Ra and Colo. Like all of the statements by representatives of Ra and Colo polities it began with an ancestor who came from the Kauvadra mountain range, not an ancestral voyager from the sea.

Jovesa Bavou's testimony—

> My village is Drauniivi my district (tikina) is Raviravi. I know my ancestor god (vu), his name was Rasare and he was at Vatukaloko [the *yavutu* in the Kauvadra range], his wife was Naikanivatu. They had three children, 1. Lewanavanua [Rule the land], 2. Bulibulivanua [Maker or Installer of the Land], 3. Saumaimuri [The Chief to follow]. These last two were twins. I am the descendant of Lewanavanua.[23] I will tell of his travels and the spread of his descendants up to the time of those of us living today.
>
> Lewanavanua married Soro and had four children 1. Leka, 2. Qisoya, 3. Degei, 4. Naivilowasa (female). Degei's children are those whose descendants are the Rakiraki people. And the descendants of Qisoya are today the carpenters at Dorovaka at Rewa. But I'll just speak of the descendants of Leka, for he is my ancestor. (My translation; I have broken up the statement into paragraphs for easier reading; NLC 1918)

The representatives of Nasi and Wakalou continued the testimony, tracing their descent from the other two brothers: Maker of the Land and The Chief to follow. Later Jovesa Bavou was asked whether the Vatukaloko owed fealty *(vakarorogo)* to the Rakiraki or Navatu people. He answered no, despite different testimony from Rakiraki representatives.

There is much that is unusual about the Vatukaloko testimony, and its

---

23. In this testimony, the Nakubuti people claimed descent from Lewanavanua, the older brother, and the Nasi people from Bulibulivanua, the younger. In the 1980s these names are reversed. This shift is discussed below.

reception. Here I will discuss the Commissioners' decisions, Vatukaloko conformity to the Commissions' forms of inquiry, and finally, the Vatukaloko alternative version.

Control of the Land through Codification of Custom

The Land Commissioners chose not to authorize the Vatukaloko versions of their history, authority, and lands. Just as colonial districting had ignored the old Vatukaloko polity, the Lands Commission decisions failed to record Vatukaloko as a *vanua* or to take seriously statements of autonomy vis-à-vis neighboring chiefly polities. In 1926 Ratu Sukuna referred to "closely connected proprietary units collectively known as the 'Kai Vatukaloko'" and acknowledged their claim to Nakorowaiwai. And the older history of Vatukaloko paramountcy in the area, from the inland border of Nasoqo to Togavere on the coast, had been documented in the European Land Claims inquiries of the 1880s and expressed implicitly in the "tribal histories." But they were irrelevant to the questions of ownership of land asked by the inquiry, and were therefore never a part of this record of "tradition."

Nor did the Vatukaloko receive ownership, in the new colonial terms, of land they called their "own." Some was claimed by other Fijian groups. Some, that had been "sold" to local planters in the 1860s and 1870s, was resold by them, in particular to powerful interests such as the Colonial Sugar Refining Co. that established a pastoral company called "Yaqara" on the land. The denial of lands to the Vatukaloko created real problems for their subsistence, it also denied them "ownership" of important origin sites in the foothills of the Kauvdra range, including Vatukaloko the origin village, and Korowaiwai.[24] The premise of the Lands Commission was that Fijians were rooted in the land, and that their communal, "pre-capitalist" form of ownership should be

---

24. As was common in Ra, they did not manage to claim sufficient land for a growing *yavusa*. In 1924, when Ratu Sukuna was conducting lands hearings to create Native Reserves, Koresi Nataranuku, newly installed Tui Vatu, tried to claim the land at Nakorowaiwai. Sukuna's comments make it clear that he believed the claim justified, but since the land had been sold to the Colonial Sugar Refinery for the Yaqara cattle run, "the claim is, with regret, not recommended for approval and the Government is faced with the difficult duty of finding suitable land for this Yavusa under Chap 86 section 19" (NR 44). At independence in 1970 the Colonial Sugar Refining Co.'s holdings were nationalized; consequently Yaqara Pastoral Company is now owned and operated by the Fiji Government.

maintained. The Vatukaloko were twice deracinated by colonial authorities, in deportation and in the denial of their land claims.

The Vatukaloko are of course not the only people in Fiji whose polity, autonomy, and lands were altered or diminished by colonial codifications. And certainly some polities were augmented and effloresced, as the new forms of commissions and districting were successfully used by claiming groups, or mobilized by Fijian officials of the Native Administration. In the 1980s the original records of Native Lands Commission testimony (especially the Evidence Books) were not publically available. Published listings of *yavusa* and *mataqali* groups with constituent subdivisions and the boundaries of the lands they own were available, as were maps keyed to these books. And the actual records recorded by G. V. Maxwell (including "tribal histories" and Evidence Books) are part of the entire set of Native Lands Commission records, held in the Native Lands Commission building in Suva. A bust of Ratu Sukuna is set in the front wall. But access to the actual records was through permission, and often, only via selections, of the Native Lands Commissioner. Fijians who were dissatisfied with or had questions about land apportionment frequently came into the building. They were seated, records were fetched and read to them, and they were told that there could be no reopening of lands matters. "These records are like the Bible," several staff members said.[25]

In the mid-1980s, the Native Lands Commissioner himself took on the duty of settling succession disputes and land disputes, and told me that he had to take the volumes and read them to the people, who, he said, often are ignorant of their true history. Yet from Sukuna's time on, certain lands questions have been reopened. Indeed, in 1986 the Vatukaloko were given permission to use Yaqara land for planting, after having appealed personally to the Governor General and to the Prime Minister, in an election year. Dissatisfaction with individual judgments of the Commission, past or present, is hard to raise, since it seems to call into question the rights of Fijians as "owners of the land," a status authorized through the truth of the recording of custom in the Commission's Bibles.[26]

---

25. Ironically, the lands commission inquiries might be read as having desacralized many ancestor-gods, turning them into ancestors and legitimators of property rights. But simultaneously, property rights themselves, at least Fijian land ownership, became sacralized in Fijian eyes, through the workings of the commissions.

26. Any questions about land ownership in the 1980s took place in the context of tactics of divide and rule by Fijian politicians and chiefs who presented themselves as custodians of Fijian rights in the face of purported Indo-Fijian wishes to change the landholding laws. But it is my sense

Vatukaloko Accommodations to the Chiefly Model

The Vatukaloko testimony at the Lands inquiries constructed a history of kinship and ownership in terms that the Commission's assessors could assess. No other Lands Commission testimony in the Ra or Colo volumes contains ancestors with such elaborately and literally descriptive names (e.g., "Rule the Land" for the chiefly kin group), and indeed none of the other ancestors of the Vatukaloko have such literal names. The "tribal history" of the Wakalou and Nasi people which followed Jovesa Bavou's testimony fitted neatly into the genealogy of relations established for the three aptly named children of Rasare and Naikanivatu. The story of the three brothers may have been explicitly constructed for the Lands Commission, to explain the relationship of the three *mataqali* groups. In the 1918 self-presentation, the long history of competition between Nakubuti and Nasi was characterized in the designation of Nakubuti people as "Lewanavanua" (Rule the Land), even though they had already historically taken on the standing of the installers of the Tui Vatu of Nasi. By the 1980s, oral versions of this narrative I heard in Drauniivi called Bulibulivanua (Maker or Installer of the Land) the elder brother and the ancestor of the Nakubuti people. Lewanavanua (Rule the Land), I was told, is the younger brother and the ancestor of the Nasi people. Bulibulivanua gave Lewanavanua the chiefship, and thereby constituted his descendants as the installing people. These relationships were actually of little interest to the Commissioners except as they had bearing on questions of priority of occupancy of land and on succession. I suspect that the swap of Lewanavanua for Bulibulivanua reflects the inevitable fixity of the Tui Vatu of Nasi, installed or uninstalled, since in the colonial and post-colonial orders, every *yavusa* must have an unambiguous chief. The current version of name and birth order denies past ambiguities.

The Vatukaloko presented an anomalous case to the Commission because of their Tuka and deportation history. But in the course of the Lands inquiries they were, ostensibly at least, normalized. Jovesa Bavou identified himself by village and by *tikina* (district) — thus as a proper "Fijian villager." Seeking to conform to a model of one village one *yavusa*, the Vatukaloko spokesmen constructed a working model of descent from one ancestor for the three *mata-*

---

that only rarely were the individual inquiries so routinely managed by the Commissioner concerned with Indian ownership of anything. The issues are very frequently internal Fijian disputes, or as with the Vatukaloko, issues from the colonial past.

qali groups now under the leadership of the Tui Vatu.[27] The inquiry structured responses, a focal point of the process by which colonial indirect rule more generally bounded, codified, or criminalized different aspects of Fijian life. In the lands testimonies, the Vatukaloko spokesmen did not refer to the ritual-political authority and leadership of Navosavakadua except implicitly, when as above, Jovesa Bavou claimed that his ancestors were the older brothers of Degei, ancestor of the Rakiraki folk. This genealogical claim was not debated, perhaps not noticed, though in response to the assessor's specific question about fealty it was argued by Rakiraki spokesmen that in practice the Vatukaloko had performed specific acts of fealty to the Rakiraki chiefs. As with the assessment of the Tui Vatu, the ambiguities were resolved in favor of the centralized, simplified chiefly model. The Vatukaloko were counted in to the Rakiraki kingdom and have since participated in it.

The Vatukaloko continued to attempt to gain colonial authorization of their status as a polity. In 1935 they applied to be recognized as constituting a *tikina* (district) with its own buli (Fijian district officer) (31/768). Far from the 1860s, when they would have asserted autonomy through warfare, and equally far from the visions of Navosavakadua's all encompassing "land"-ruled polity, it would seem that colonial impositions had reconstructed and reduced their vision of the shape of autonomy. (In post-colonial 1991 they were finally "recognized" as a *tikina* district of Rakiraki which has been named Naiyalayala.)

But, while the public inquiries were progressing, and Maxwell and the two Bauan chiefs created a record in which the impression of chiefly-colonial categories on the Vatukaloko is very clear, in a separate local project Jovesa Bavou used the form and impetus of the inquiry to begin to establish and codify a body of Vatukaloko knowledge which reveals the alternative Vatukaloko articulation of ritual-political relations.

Jovesa Bavou's Book:
The Vatukaloko-Centered Ritual-Political Order

If colonizers sought to order Fiji, the records of colonial inquiries both made and displayed this order, seeking to fix and record set boundaries, to contain

---

27. Though in the published Lands Records they are listed as separate *yavusa,* throughout the inquiry they were called *mataqali,* and they call themselves and are known as *"mataqali"* in all circumstances, ritual, administrative, etc., in daily life nowadays.

Fijian land and Fijians in set hierarchies of province, district, and village, and kin group. In contrast the record kept by Jovesa Bavou[28] beginning in 1918 might at first seem to be disordered. In a large bound volume (about seventy-five pages of text, including about twenty loose sheets kept in the back) he compiled a record of Lands Commission business and of other business of importance that transpired in Drauniivi.[29] He recorded genealogies or "tribal histories" prepared for and given at the Ra Lands inquiries, and the boundaries of Vatukaloko lands. He recorded important ritual moments among the Vatukaloko including visits from ancestors and meetings of Apolosi's Fiji Company. His "tribal histories" move from close replicas of the Vatukaloko, Raviravi, and Rakiraki testimonies recorded by Maxwell at the public Lands Commission hearings, to representations of relations with far-away peoples of Bau, Cakaudrove, Verata, that could have had no bearing on Lands claims, but instead represent the pursuit of a different kind of project, namely the specification of the ritual precedence and centrality of the Vatukaloko people among the different peoples of the world. In this vision, the Vatukaloko have temporal, genealogical, and ritual precedence over far-flung peoples and polities, whether Bauans in Fiji, or colonial powers, no matter how powerful they may be.

Jovesa Bavou's records are ordered by this vision. His inclusion of dreams and ritual moments reflect their connection to the relationships between ancestor gods, peoples, and polities in the world. Where the colonial inquiries altered the divinity of ancestor gods in the service of the specification of ownerships, the Vatukaloko pressed Jehovah into service to create a framework for their universal claims.

An entry dated 24 January 1917, written in Jovesa Bavou's precise handwrit-

28. Born in 1882, according to his book, in the Lotio subdivision (*matanibure* or *tokatoka*) of Nakubuti, he was a classificatory son of Taivesi Mamaqa and thus called him "father." Further entries in the book are by his (true) brother Tomasi Rainima born c. 1903, at Nanukuloa. Jovesa Bavou vanished mysteriously in the early 1920s. He went out one night to fish, and the next day his small boat was found, but he was gone. This mysterious end is connected nowadays with his closeness to Navosavakadua. After his death Tomasi Rainima wrote in his book that Jovesa was the biological son of Navosa, but other informants do not agree. Bavou sometimes returns in dreams to give messages to people in Nakubuti. In 1984 he appeared to a Nakubuti lady and told her that certain people were holding back money from a fundraising project *(soli)* to raise money for a generator for the *mataqali* of Nakubuti. In the same dream he told her that he approved of her husband (his son) telling me about the history of the *mataqali*. He was to tell me all the history, and one of their sons was to attend to the *tanoa* (kava bowl) at our meetings.

29. I most gratefully acknowledge the kindness of Mr. Jone Tuiwai, Turaga ni Koro, Drauniivi, who allowed me to read and copy this book.

ing, is headed: "History of the beginning of the *yavusa* [ritual kin group] Vatukaloko and the *yavusa* who share its descent from the beginning of the world in the olden Days"

> The Lord Jehovah (Na Kalou ko Jiova) made two people. A man and a woman. He named the man Rasari and named the woman Naikanivatu. He gave them land of which they were owners *(me rau taukena)*. And it was called VATUKALOKO. Then they had three children. First LEWANAVANUA was born, then later the twins BULIBULIVANUA and SAUMAIMURI were born. When they were grown their father decreed that they should have different lands. He gave LEWANAVANUA the land called BUKELELEVU, he was the eldest. He gave BULIBULIVANUA the land called NARAWARAWA. He gave SAUMAIMURI the land called NASARO. They then went their separate ways and married and their descendants multiplied over time and became people [rather than ancestor gods]. Of the three *mataqali* of our *yavusa* of VATUKALOKO and of all the different *yavusa* of all the parts of FIJI and the WORLD. (My translation, his capitals)

This particular genealogical sequence then traces the origin of the three *mataqali* of Vatukaloko, and their subdivisions. After those histories, he turned to other peoples of Fiji, through accounts of the many wives of Degei and the lands founded by their children. His genealogical scheme is unusual in two interrelated ways. It begins with creation by Jehovah (who does not appear in his "tribal history" as recorded by the Lands Commission). Further it presents a Kauvadra-centric vision of the world, claiming that from the ancestors of the Vatukaloko spring all the different groups of people of Fiji and the world.

Looking at the relations of ancestor gods, peoples, and polities that Bavou portrayed genealogically, the most striking point is the assertion of Vatukaloko autochthony, seniority, and authority in relation to other more powerful chiefly polities, including Bau. This point is made implicitly in the reference to Degei as a younger brother of Leka in the Lands Commission record. And it is found again in Jovesa Bavou's manuscript,[30] here in fuller and more complex genealogies (see figures 9–12).

His accounts of different polities differ markedly in specificity and elabora-

---

30. The entries by Bavou clearly and sequentially trace the genealogical lines and relationships diagrammed in the accompanying figures. The form of the tales is that of the above sections, giving the ancestor, his wife or wives (a woman of what land), their descendants, and where they went. Since some pages of the book are loose and perhaps out of sequence, I have deciphered some connections — checked against present-day accounts and Native Lands Commission accounts. The diagram is based on Bavou's texts, since those by Tomasi Rainima consist mainly of copies and alterations dealing with the Bulibulivanua-Lewanavanua naming question described above.

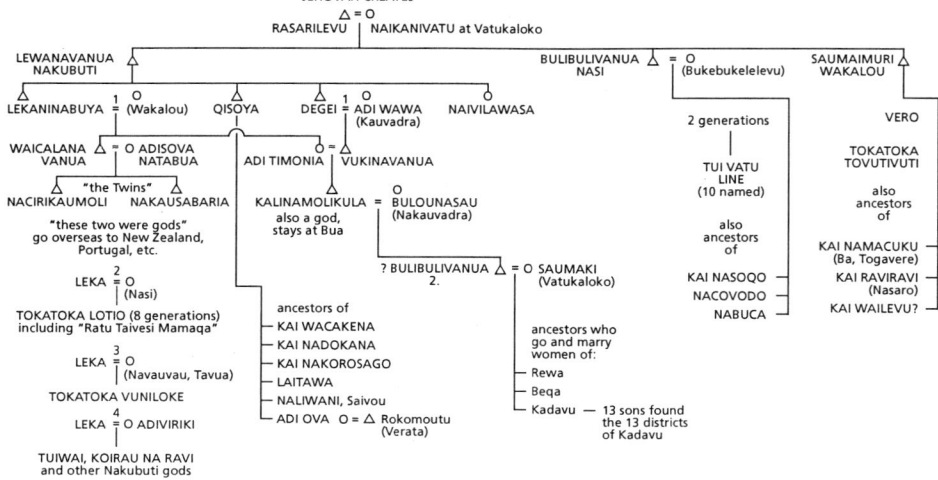

Figure 9. Origins and Relations of the Vatukaloko.
Source: Jovesa Bavou, "History of the Beginning," c. 1918.

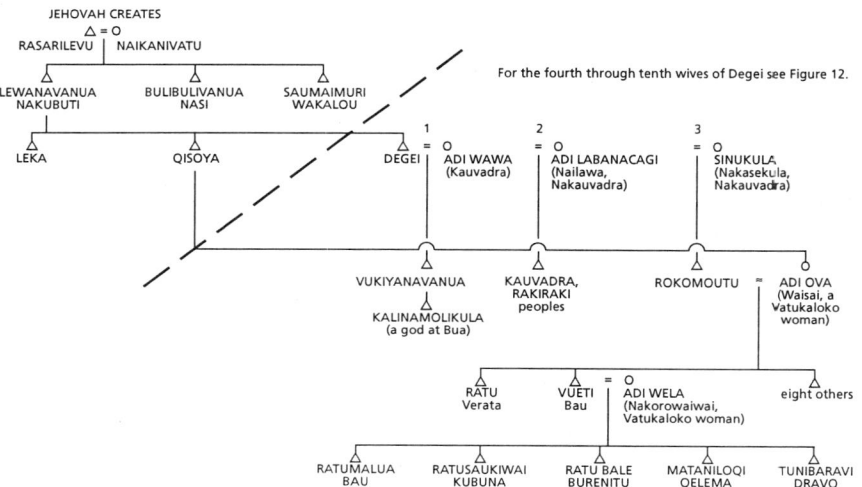

Figure 10. Relation of the Eastern Coastal Kingdoms to the Vatukaloko.
Source: Jovesa Bavou, "History of the Beginning," c. 1918.

Figure 11. Wives and Descendants of Degei.
Source: Jovesa Bavou, "History of the Beginning," c. 1918.

1. Adi Labanacagi (Nai Lawa, Nakauvadra)
   Various Kauvadra, Rakiraki vu (ancestor gods)

ancestor god	descendants' ritual-kin group	
Nasema	Rakiraki (Tuinamo)	*book lists descendants*
Kanaiwai	Rakiraki (Cakova)	
Leka	Rakiraki (Wailevu?)	
Rasuaki	Natoka, Navolau	
Tui Boga	Navitilevu	"
Nawaqabolabola	Nacilau (near Togavere)	"
Kuruloa	Vatuqoro	
Bogileka	Vatu?	
Bokadroti	Naqilaqila (at Vunitogaloa)	"
Coci	Narawa	

2. Sinukula (Nakasekula, Nakauvadra)
   Verata, Ba and Vanua Levu vu (ancestor gods)

Rokomoutu	Verata	*see figure 12*
Raikadruka	Ba and Bulu	
Uaniwaimaca	Vusuvusu	
Rokowai	Naicobocobo	
Igaigavanua	Bua	
Uneunevanua	Macuata	

3. Nasau (Vugala, Nakauvadra)

Ketewai	Loqa (Nasi stronghold)	"
Waqabalabala	Nadi	
Nawakanimali	Nadroga	
Tunovoli	Nadroga	
Toka	Natuatuacoko	"

4. No fourth wife named.

5. Adi Sinu (Nakasekula, Nakauvadra) [same as Sinukula the 2nd wife?]
   Kalinamolikula   "Okoya na sau ki Ba" [he is the god at Ba]

6. Adi Lomaiwai (Bukelewa)
   ?

7. Adi Kasala (Bokadrala)
   ?

8. Adi Kula (Tabalenakula, Nakauvadra)
   Cautata, Tailevu vu

9. Adi Vono (Nakauvadra)
   Votua, Ba vu

Also listed variously as wives of Degei: Adi Mamaca Cakaudrove vu; Adi Lolo Wailevu vu; Naikolo (Nacolo) Naloto vu; Adi Kamanalaqi (Nakauvadra) Tui Nakauvadra

Figure 12. Descendants of Rokomoutu and His Son Vueti.
Source: Jovesa Bavou, "History of the Beginning," c. 1918.

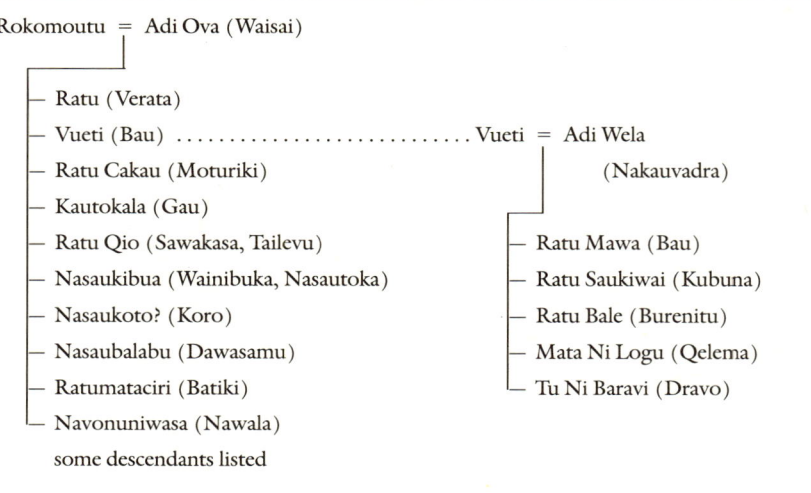

tion. The most detailed accounts are those of the ancestor gods and people close to the Vatukaloko. Through accounts of the travels, lands, and marriages of Lewanavanua, Bulibulivanua, and Saumaimuri the *mataqali* groups of Nakubuti, Nasi, and Wakalou are traced from their initial constitution at Vatukaloko to the contemporary members (in 1918) of the three *mataqali* groups, in their subdivisions. Their land boundaries are given. The Nasi people (including ten Tui Vatu chiefs) are listed as the elder line directly from Bulibulivanua, and the Wakalou people are the elder line of Saumaimuri. Junior offshoots of each of these lines (the Nasoqo people and the Namacuku people) are included, and some of their boundaries are also given.

It is the line of Lewanavanua (Nakubuti) that is most elaborate. As reference to figures 9 and 10 shows, this is the line that sets up major relations between the Vatukaloko and other peoples. Birth order and order of marriage both create relative autochthony and rank. Lewanavanua's first two sons are ancestors of Ra and Colo people in the Vatukaloko polity. His third son Degei is ancestral to most of the other people in Fiji. This thus makes the ancestors of small Colo (interior) polities such as the Wacakena people (descendants of a second son) elder to the people of the major kingdoms such as Verata, Rewa, and Bau. Among the descendants of Degei (see figures 9–12) several lines, including one of a god, and those of the Rakiraki, Verata, and Kadavu people too are senior to Bau. Moreover, the lines of Bau are formed through three marriages with Vatukaloko women including one which is incestuous.

To return to the line of Lewanavanua: The Nakubuti people are descendants of Lekaninabuya, his oldest son, but by his second wife. Through his first wife (a woman of Wakalou) were born eternal gods of the Kauvadra range: Waicalanavanua, Adi Sovanatabua, and Adi Timonia. From the improper intercourse of Waicala and Adi Sovanatabua (brother and sister who bathed together in a pool) the Twins, Nacirikaumoli and Nakausabaria, were born. (Thence perhaps also the other peoples of the world, for a paragraph elsewhere in the book records that the Twins went to New Zealand and Portugal, and oral narratives in 1984–1985 have them marrying women in England and America, thus constituting these peoples. However, these other accounts by Vatukaloko people (oral narratives recorded in 1984–1985) that explicitly name the Twins as the founders of European lines also situate the twins as junior lines to the Vatukaloko.) It is then the second line of children by a woman of Nasi *mataqali* who are the eight generations of *tokatoka* (subdivision) Lotio including "Ratu Taivesi Mamaqa." The third line, by a woman from Navauvau of the Tavua people, are the people of *tokatoka* (subdivision) Vuniloke.

The representations of ancestors and places beyond Ra and Colo are extremely schematic, for example, "he went to Nadroga." Of these, the account of the ancestors who constituted the relation of the Vatukaloko to the Kadavu people, and of Kadavu ancestors themselves, is the most detailed, likely because of the Vatukaloko deportation to Kadavu (see figure 9). Thirteen ancestors are named, reflecting the thirteen divisions at Kadavu. While there may be a more widespread *tauvu* (shared ancestor, joking relationship) relationship acknowledged between Ra and Kadavu peoples, here the specific relationship of the Vatukaloko and Kadavu people, historically born in the colonial deportation, is genealogically conceived as arising through an incestuous relationship. The second daughter of Leka and the son of his younger brother Degei were the parents of Kalinamolikula, a god like the Twins, the product of an improper relationship, the union of children of two brothers (Leka and Degei). This is the line of the founders of Rewa, Beqa, and Kadavu.

Bavou follows the lines of the first born. He writes "state the eldest," occasionally, as though responding to questions of the Lands Commission. What he creates is a wide genealogy growing out of the central origin point. Such a genealogy, incorporating Fiji or the world (*"ko Viti se Vuravura"* as he puts it), owes its national and international scope in part to the colonial era. While "Fiji" surely existed prior to European contact (in relation, for example, to

Tonga) the concept of "Fiji" as a unified polity came into being in the years of European contact (see, e.g., Cakobau's claim to be King of Fiji "Tui Viti," or the ever more elaborate origin myths printed in *Na Mata*.) And certainly as well Bavou's genealogies present a centralized vision of Fiji and the world: the Colo and Ra hinterland polities elaborated and made powerful by Jehovah, the great coastal chiefly kingdoms merely the far-flung descendants, via incestuous unions, of Kauvadra lines.

Yet in another sense, though centralized, this genealogy of Fiji and the world is no simple inversion of the "tribal histories" of the Bauans or Veratans or other coastal groups. That is because, from the Vatukaloko perspective, they remain at the center, at the Kauvadra, close to Jehovah. They are not foreign, they are not far-flung, they still could tread the ground of their origin place *(yavutu)*, and all the spots Jehovah had created nearby in the lands stretching from Drauniivi on the coast to the lands they formerly occupied closer to and in the Kauvadra range: Rome, the Dead Sea, and the place where Lot's wife turned to salt. In 1918 when Jovesa Bavou set down these texts, the Vatukaloko had been resettled in Drauniivi for nine years. Sakiusa Qarau, the Tui Vatu, had decreed that they spatially order their village according to *mataqali* groups, following the (newly constructed) ancient pattern established by the three ancestors, at that original village of Vatukaloko that Jehovah made (see figures 6 and 13). Each *mataqali* was to have its own space within the village, and at the center was the Methodist church. At that time the ownership of land was of concern to the Vatukaloko, but perhaps more important still was their vision of their place in the world. They were still people of the land, foremost among the people of the land, defined and chosen by the highest god of the land, Jehovah.

What then is the significance of Jehovah in the text written by Jovesa Bavou? It was his own book. He had no need to refer to the Christian god to placate or persuade others. But of course, his version of the creation was unusual. God created Rasarilevu and Naikanivatu and gave them the land called Vatukaloko. Is this simply an Adam and Eve story grafted, in conformity to colonial or Methodist expectations, onto the indigenous genealogies? Or instead, is it, as I proposed earlier, that following Navosavakadua the Vatukaloko further claimed Jehovah as their own, redefining him and themselves in the process?[31] One clue comes from Bavou's book itself.

Upon their return to Ra, most of the people of Nakubuti converted to

---

31. The same story of the special place of the Vatukaloko in the creation was told to me by a regular preacher in the Methodist church in Drauniivi in 1985.

Seventh Day Adventism. The Nasi people remained Methodist, and the Wakalou people were divided.[32] Even when they were Seventh Day Adventists, the Nakubuti people were levied to help build the big Methodist church in the village (I have been told), which was regarded as a duty to the government and to custom. As elsewhere in Fiji, Methodists and Seventh Day Adventists disputed which day or days to respect as the Sabbath. The Methodist and government-ordained Sunday was institutionalized in language as *Siga Tabu* (Holy Day). The Adventists sought to rename it *"Sade"* (Sunday), since their "Holy Day" is celebrated on Saturday. It was Navosavakadua who resolved one such dispute in favor of a Sunday sabbath.

On 2 August 1924, Jovesa Bavou recorded a communication to the Vatukaloko people from Navosavakadua, which came as a dream to a village resident.

> The Dream of O. R.   August 2, 1924
>   Vatukaloko, Raviravi, Ra
>
> Listen people of my yavusa, we held a meeting at NABUYA.[33] Navosa has written to us and it was read by Lewanavanua [a Vatukaloko ancestor god]. It has been agreed in Suva that you keep the day of Sunday (Sade) [as the Sabbath]. Read it and think about it. You will see its signs and when these words were finished lightning and thunder came. The report is finished.

Thus, as Bavou recorded it, Navosa now spoke to the Vatukaloko to resolve Christian dilemmas in favor of Methodist ritual observance. Though some Vatukaloko rejected the colonial chiefly orthodoxy by turning to Seventh Day Adventism (as the Bobuco people articulated *vanua* and Jehovah through Catholicism), many among the Vatukaloko, from the days at Kadavu on, were staunch Methodists. But of course this Methodist observance was not the same as that the missionaries brought, and eastern chiefly Fijians accepted. For this Vatukaloko version insisted, as had Navosa, that Jehovah was a Fijian deity, a god of the land, in a truly alternative vision of the world and their place in it.

---

32. Conversions have generally involved entire *"tokatoka"* rather than individuals (except in cases of marriage). Adventist membership remains strong among many Nakubuti members, and a large Adventist church was completed in 1990, built on land adjacent to where the Nakubuti people build their houses. The Assemblies of God are a more recent popular denomination.

33. Nabuya was the name of Jovesa Bavou's house; it was named after the land near the Kauvadra range that was given to Leka, the Nakubuti ancestor. The land is a flat with a number of large stones across a stream from Navosa's pilgrimage site at Vale Lebo.

To complete this point, let me contrast Bavou's narrative of Jehovah creating the first of the world's people at Vatukaloko with an alternative narrative from the chiefly Christian perspective. In this second narrative there is a point of transition, in which Europeans brought God to Fiji, and Fijians moved from a time of darkness to a time of light. This narrative integrally involves the conversion of the major Fijian chiefs. In 1987, a popular lay preacher presented this history of the relation of Christian god, people and chiefs:

> When first God's religion came to our land the chiefs of that time were strong and successful in war. God decreed that those true chiefs of the land should convert to Christianity. They welcomed the religion then, and it was fortunate that they did, we nowadays have received its blessings. We are enlightened thereby, our land was developed thereby and we have learned much nowadays. If we approve of and welcome this, let us welcome the fact that these chiefs were the source of our blessedness. Their descendants who are leading today, they are blessed because their ancestors who have passed on before them welcomed Christianity. (Colonel Sitiveni Rabuka (leader of the 1987 military coups in Fiji), *Nai Lalakai* 16 July 1987, my translation)

This chiefly Christian vision clearly reveals its roots in the mission and colonial civilizing project. For much of the colonial and postcolonial era it became the basis of official state power. Centralized control through institutions of religion, law, and land ownership all invoked truth and custom, defined from the top down. And more important than the doctrines imposed and the particulars of the decisions reached were the institutional forms that created official power and constrained challenge. Activities claimed as *vakavanua* (customary) activity but deemed inexpedient by colonial authorities could still be labeled "*Luve ni wai* and kindred activities," punishable by law. Arguments about land ownership are still arbitrated by the Commissioner.

In 1919 the Vatukaloko privately rejected the chiefly-Christian articulation, but acknowledged the ritual forms of the Lands Commission. If they had refused to testify at the enquiries, if they had not built a Methodist church in the center of the rebuilt Drauniivi, they would have been scrutinized and punished as "disaffected." It seems fair to say that once the Vatukaloko became participants in the exercise of testimony, the substance of their testimony was of little concern to the Commission. But it is equally clear that no one kept a close eye on what was being preached *inside* the Methodist church.

We might make the argument that the Vatukaloko, in building a church or submitting to the ritual forms of the Lands Commission inquiries, had thereby submitted completely to the power of the colonial state. But we could also see their participation in these constraining arenas as moments in which they routinized alternative articulations, that is, learned and created new ways to organize their own versions of power and truth: in rebuilding Drauniivi to map genealogical relations, in texts written and oral. In a sense, the conformity and participation required by Methodism and the Lands Commission literally created new spaces and forms for Vatukaloko creativity. Constrained participation in the Lands Commission incited Bavou to write his private codification of the relationship of the land, and the gods of the land, as ultimately made powerful by Jehovah, himself a god of the land. Jovesa Bavou and his sons and daughters held fast to this understanding of their place in the world, which, as we shall discuss in the next chapters, is in many ways a continuation of Navosavakadua's project.

On Articulations and Their Routinization

Focusing on narratives of gods, chiefs, and people of the land, this chapter has explored the rise of multiple, contesting, differentially held versions of power and truth in twentieth-century colonial Fiji. Some were and are "orthodoxies" confidently proclaimed and enforced by administration and church bureaucracies, others have been more private and quiescent, but powerfully held. From the nineteenth century on into the twentieth, then, the people increasingly entwined in Fiji's colonial society articulated versions of Fiji's order, drawing on multiple colonial and Fijian possibilities. In this chapter we have considered articulations that were routinized, established institutionalized systems in which communities of people led their lives (although none, of course, were uncontested, whether "orthodox" or otherwise).

But some articulations, however coherent or persuasive, are not routinized. In the following chapters we will trace the ongoing routinization of plural chiefly and land versions into the post-colonial present. But we will also consider, next, an interesting failure, an attempt by an Indo-Fijian Fiji citizen to articulate Fijian, colonial, and Indo-Fijian cosmologies and to routinize them through national ritual. As we shall see, his unsuccessful attempt focused on Navosavakadua as a key source of power and inspiration for Fiji.

7

NARRATIVES OF NAVOSAVAKADUA IN THE 1980S AND 1990S

On 15 March 1984, the *Fiji Times* carried an article with the headline "2000 WAIT ON RETURN," subheadline "Police investigating." The article began:

> Two thousand villagers gathered at Drauniivi in Rakiraki last weekend and heard proclamations about a "return" of legendary Fijian chief *Navosa* of the 1930s.
>
> They heard claims that *Navosa* was coming back to life to form a new government and lead Fiji.
>
> But the police Special Branch has been investigating the meeting, looking into whether national security was affected.

I read the article while sitting in the National Archives of Fiji, in the capital city of Suva, where I was reading colonial accounts of Tuka, and of Navosavakadua, Apolosi Nawai, and various other Fijians whose activities had grouped them under the rubric of "cult" or "criminal" in the colonial imagination and record system. I speculated, along with others in the city who read the article, as to whether a long smoldering local belief had flamed once more into activity.

The article itself was full of puzzling information. It continued: "Sources told The Fiji Times one of the organizers of the meeting was a Fiji Girmit Association official, Mr. Harigyan Samalia." Mr. Samalia, I found when I asked around, was an Indo-Fijian gentleman, head of an association for the preservation and celebration of Indo-Fijian indenture history.[1]

---

1. As I noted more briefly in chapter 1, South Asian Indians came to Fiji from 1879 to 1916 as indentured laborers to work on British plantations. At the end of indenture many stayed in Fiji and

Skeptical of "cult theories" at the time I still wanted to study "the Tuka movement." And the power of the names Navosavakadua and Drauniivi as they had come down in colonial narratives into the scholarly concept of cargo cult affected me as well. I wanted to know whether Navosa was coming back. By the summer I had arranged a pathway of introductions to Drauniivi[2] and in August 1984 I went there to begin field research.

I came to find that there was much less and much more to the *Fiji Times* account than its few paragraphs conveyed. Navosavakadua had come back to Drauniivi, but only because an Indo-Fijian visionary, an outsider, raised his name and a flag, and as far as the Vatukaloko were concerned, he had not come back to overturn the world.

There are still plural understandings of Navosavakadua in Fiji. Some of these versions are direct descendants of older Vatukaloko and colonial narratives, some have different roots and purposes. In this chapter and the next I want to tell the stories of four of these versions of Navosa and their intersections in the 1980s. In this chapter we will read of the place of Navosa in an unusual national vision of an Indo-Fijian mystic, the fearful reaction of official Fiji to the possibility of Navosa's return, and public debate among Fijians about gods, power, and history carried out in newspaper correspondence columns. In the next chapter we will consider the quiescent and largely private current Vatukaloko versions. These chapters are about routinizations, and unsuccessful attempts to routinize.

---

became the backbone of Fiji's sugar industry as well as a growing urban middle and working class. British policy kept "Indians" and "Fijians" separate in the colony, and there has been very little intermarriage. Indians, who bore the brunt of colonial exploitation, were anxious for independence. Certain Fijians, such as chiefs in positions of authority in the Native Administration, were less so. Since independence in 1970 the two groups (roughly equal in size) have had a troubled relationship politically. Most recently in 1987 military coups toppled the first government in which Fiji Indians had political representation even close to their proportion of Fiji's total population. On Fiji Indian history see Gillion (1962, 1977), Lal (1992), Kelly (1988a, 1988c). On the coups see Lal (1988), Kelly (1988b), Kaplan (1988b), Howard (1991).

2. Though I had research permission from the government I was determined not to go to Drauniivi with the sponsorship of provincial officials of the Fijian Administration (the post-colonial continuant of the indirect rule "Native Administration"). I did not know whether people in Drauniivi would trust someone coming in with official sponsorship. Instead, I had introductions to schoolteachers at the Drauniivi Public School, who introduced me to the village. In the village I was asked why I was there, and I responded that I had read colonial accounts of their history and wanted to hear their own stories. Although initially I may have been suspected as an agent of the Special Branch, it soon became clear that I had no privileged acquaintance with local authorities — and that my language skills in the local dialect were far too poor to make me a good spy.

Advent of a Mystic:
Mr. Samalia's Vision of Navosavakadua

Why an Indo-Fijian to raise Navosa's flag? I had sometimes wondered whether the Vatukaloko anti-colonial history might not lead to a sense of common cause and history with Indo-Fijians who during and after indenture also struggled against the British. Ironically, however, Vatukaloko articulations of Christianity and the idealization of non-capitalist systems of exchange have not created such a historical narrative. Instead, in Drauniivi, I often heard of the differences between the European and Indo-Fijian world of money *(vuravura vakailavo)* and the Fijian Christian customs of the land, also called (in Drauniivi) the world of kindly love *(vuravura vakaloloma)*. Moreover, there has been no widespread interest in Navosa on the part of Indo-Fijians past or present. However, in the 1980s, one idiosyncratic Indo-Fijian visionary invoked Navosavakadua in his efforts to create a harmonious Fijian nation.

The late Mr. Harigyan Samalia, president and dominant force in the Fiji Girmit Association, is said to have spent much of his life in the Lau island group among Fijians. He lived in a Fijian squatter settlement in Suva in the 1980s. In that decade Mr. Samalia began to introduce his vision of Navosavakadua to others in public ritual, posters, and newspaper advertisements.[3] In his narrative, Navosavakadua is an avatar of god in a cosmological history centered on Fiji's "racial crisis."[4]

Early in 1984, Mr. Samalia wrote to the Tui Vatu and the Turaga ni Koro saying that he wished to visit Drauniivi:

> We are hoping to convey to you the men of Vatukaloko some important news. We also ask you to prepare a flagpole in order to raise the flag of the Government of the New Age of the Chief Sir Navosavakadua, King of Fiji, King of the World (Matanitu ni Gaunavou nei na Gone Turaga ko Ratu Navosavakadua, Tui Viti, Tui ni Vura-

---

3. See, e.g., advertisements in the *Fiji Times* 3 December 1983, 16 May 1986; and holdings in the National Archives of Fiji under the collection name "The Fiji India Girmit Council"; also miscellaneous flyers and publications from Mr. Samalia in my possession. For accounts of the *Syria* Monument ceremony see the *Fiji Times* and *Fiji Sun* 12 May 1987. I attended this ceremony. For accounts of Mr. Samalia's visit to Drauniivi, see the *Fiji Times* 15 March 1984, *Nai Lalakai* 22 March 1984. My account is further based on interviews in Drauniivi during fieldwork, and on an interview with Mr. Samalia conducted by John D. Kelly and myself. For a fuller discussion of Mr. Samalia and his project see Kaplan (in press [a]) "Blood on the Grass and Dogs Will Speak: Ritual Politics and the Nation in Independent Fiji."

4. It will be recollected that "race" is the term used in Fiji, following colonial usage, for groups who might elsewhere be called ethnic groups.

vura). Let the flag be raised at four o'clock. (Copy of letter kindly supplied by Mr. Jone Tuiwai, former Turaga ni Koro, Drauniivi, my translation)

Mr. Samalia believed that Fiji is "the little Jerusalem of the Pacific," a product of a cosmologically ordained union of "India the Motherland" and "Fiji the Fatherland." In 1984–1985 he prophesied that Fiji would undergo a violent change that would then lead to a new government or kingdom led by a returning Messiah, the "King of Kings." Navosavakadua is that Messiah. Here, repeated from chapter 1, is a summary of his prophecies, from notes made during an interview I conducted with him at his home near Suva in 1984.

> The King of Kings began as Krishna of the Mahabharata who when he had finished his work in India disappeared and changed his form. He sent a snake to Fiji then went to Fiji himself and became incarnated as Navosavakadua, there he performed miracles, and was deported. . . . Navosa said to the people of Drauniivi "Don't worry if I am gone for long. My flag will be raised." He pushed two stones into the ground, saying "When the stones rise it will be time." Those stones are now two feet above the ground. Then he went to Germany and became Hitler, he shaped the world, it was growing fast at that time. At another time he was incarnated as Jesus Christ. He returns each time in different forms. His next incarnation will be as a Fijian, to found the new Kingdom on Maqo Island in the Lau Group. The living God will arise from earth, flowers will sing, dogs will speak like humans. Fifteen thousand flyers have been distributed prophesying this.

Many of Mr. Samalia's stories of Navosavakadua were stories which have been well known throughout Fiji since the turn of the century. He stressed two themes. First, he retold many of the commonly reported tales of miracles which Navosavakadua performed (bringing the man alive from the oven, surviving British attempts to imprison or kill him). Second, more idiosyncratically, he told stories in which Navosavakadua promised to return, and preached that this return was imminent. His sources for the first sort of stories were certainly Fijians, some from Ra, but he was never associated with the Vatukaloko people until he came to visit them.

In the early 1980s Mr. Samalia created a stir by taking out newspaper advertisements claiming that Hitler, Krishna, and Navosavakadua are all avatars of god and will found a new kingdom in Fiji. (His attention to Hitler drew upon the historical moment from the 1940s when many colonized people in the British empire were at least briefly interested in Hitler and Hirohito as potential allies in anti-imperial struggle.) The ads contain pictures of Mr. Samalia, wearing a white uniform with medals and a blue sash. He describes himself as "Junior counsellor delegated by the Supreme counsellor on earth" (the Supreme Counsellor is the Krishna-Hitler-Navosa figure). In May 1984 at Nausori bridge (in the town adjacent to Suva) he organized a ritual which had the dual purposes of unveiling a monument to commemorate Fijian-Indian cooperation in the "Syria disaster" of a hundred years before and "bringing the goddess of wealth from the harbor of New York to the harbor of Fiji." The *Syria* was a "coolie" ship that struck a reef in 1884. A number of Fijians came out to help to rescue the drowning indentured Indians (some also came out to pillage the ship). At the unveiling of the monument Mr. Samalia presented medals to purported descendants of the benevolent Fijians. Ratu Sir George Cakobau, Vunivalu of Bau and former Governor General of Fiji, was the guest of honor at the occasion, during which Mr. Samalia identified the carved female figurehead from the ship as both the Hindu goddess Lakshmi and the Kauvadra goddess Adi Sovanatabua (mother of the Twins). A recurring theme throughout Mr. Samalia's discourse is the oneness of Fijian, Christian, and Hindu deities.

Mr. Samalia's goal in his rituals and publications was to establish a vision of a harmonious Fijian nation, in which Fijians and Indians were brought together by the will of divinity. Most Fijians (and Indo-Fijians) view the coming together of the two groups in Fiji as a contingent history, a matter of chance in a colonial context (the result of Sir Arthur Gordon's experience with indentured workers during his previous time as governor for indentured labor plantation colonies Mauritius and Trinidad). Many Fijians think that the arrival of the Indo-Fijians was simply unfortunate, ignoring the plantation exploitation Indo-Fijians suffered in the Fijians' stead. Many Indo-Fijians consider emigration a more attractive future goal than residence in the islands where they are discriminated against. But for Mr. Samalia, the history of Indian immigration to Fiji was necessary, not contingent. He believed that it was a blessing for all, and ordained by god. In the mid-1980s his prophetic articulation took some of its urgency from his sense that Fiji would soon be rent by a racial war. Only a visionary such as he spoke so clearly in Fiji of developing contradictions in the political situation. In essence he predicted the coups. When we interviewed him in 1984 he said that

> 1987 would be the most dangerous election. The military was advancing. Fijians were fighting with themselves. Chiefs failed to control the people, they were criticizing Indians. Chiefs used to command the Kai Colo (hill people) but now the educated Kai Colo (hill people) spoke back to the chiefs. Fijians newly in power thought they knew what to do, but Indians and Europeans too had sacrificed and should be respected. That was why he founded the Girmit organization, so that Fijians would realize the truth about Indian sacrifices for Fiji. Fijians are in a greedy position now

as thieves but should be on reserved land. The world was made by god for the people living on it. Now city Fijians were chased off when they wanted to go back to farms.

Mr. Samalia described contradictions in "racial" relations in Fiji which he hoped to resolve. He identified with both Fijians and Indo-Fijians and wanted Fiji to be a synthesis of both. He wanted Fijians to recognize and acknowledge Indian contributions to the creation of Fiji, but he did not seem to believe that they could or would do this, and thus instead foresaw "a cloud of blood in Suva." Shrinking from this vision, ultimately reassured by belief in divinity in the world, and the inevitability of Fiji's oneness, he predicted the rise of the King of Kings (formerly incarnated as Krishna, Jesus, Navosavakadua, and Hitler) to unite the islands following the disaster.[5]

In the political field through the early 1980s Mr. Samalia was a supporter of the ruling, Fijian-chiefly-dominated Alliance Party, where his interest in things Fijian (although idiosyncratic) was welcomed. (The Alliance Party did not have a large pool of potential Indo-Fijian members and spokesmen.) In the rhetoric of multiracial harmony relied upon by the Alliance Party in the early 1980s, Mr. Samalia was sometimes advanced as a representative of Indo-Fijian history and interests. It was probably because of his long connection with the Alliance Party that Ratu Sir George Cakobau, the former Governor General and Vunivalu of Bau (himself elderly and idiosyncratic), was willing to unveil the *Syria* monument and to participate in the eccentric ceremony. But Samalia's world view and prophecies did not convince most Fijians or Indo-Fijians. He was known because of his use of media and public ceremonies, not because he had a large or convinced following. His acceptance as a legitimate public figure was a product both of the public media, and of Fiji's peculiar post-colonial political and symbolic arena, where the Alliance Party required some sort of Indo-Fijian representation to maintain its facade as an "alliance" party. Mr. Samalia—wrapped in a symbolism that is very far from the mainstream of Indo-Fijian history or interests—seems to have served for a while, ironically enough, as the necessary Indo-Fijian presence.[6]

---

5. To be clear about these predictions: While Colonel Rabuka's pro-Fijian military coups did entail violence against people and property, there have been no massacres, no "cloud of blood." Further, in the few years following the coups, national leadership was assumed by Colonel Rabuka and those he installed; the King of Kings did not appear.

6. Part of his authority came from his own sense of conviction. An informant of John Kelly's said of Samalia that "he is not afraid of anything and will say anything" (personal communication, 1988). Fragments of his narrative could convince different groups in Fiji. Hindus would accept his presentation of the historical recurrence of divinity in different forms, but are unlikely to accept Navosavakadua as an avatar. Fijians nowadays would not accept avatar theory in general, finding

Accounts of Mr. Samalia's visit by Vatukaloko people say little about his unifying cosmological history; they focused instead on his message of impending disaster and his claims about their ancestor. When he first wrote to Drauniivi about his plans, the village headman (Turaga ni Koro) was concerned and asked a friend to telephone to Suva to Mr. Samalia to object that Sunday was the Sabbath. "But Mr. Samalia responded 'I know it is the day of the Lord, the day Jesus rose again.' Those were his words, 'Tell them that day, it can't be held before or afterwards. That day is the Lord's day, the day on which to raise the flag.'" He also instructed them to pray in the church before he arrived. The Turaga ni Koro sent messages to the peoples of the old Vatukaloko polity — whom he calls the Twelve Tribes *(Tini ka Rua na Yavusa)* — to come to Drauniivi on Sunday, 13 March 1984.[7]

When Mr. Samalia arrived, he bathed in the river adjacent to the village, and then put on a suit of white clothes, with a blue sash, like those worn by the Governor General in days past. The headman directed the ritual preparations, from food and housing for visitors to the actual chiefly welcoming ritual *(veiqaravi)* itself. Several thousand people are said to have attended.

> When he came here, there was a ceremony of *vakasobu* of entering here [they presented whales' teeth *(tabua)* to him]. The choir made a great noise, the choir of this village. They sang a hymn. When finished we prayed. When the prayer was finished then the rituals to honour a chief *(veiqaravi vakaturaga)* were performed [for Mr. Samalia]. Each of the stages of the ritual were done. He then asked to present his *sevusevu* (offering of kava) then he spoke. "This is not only my *sevusevu*. This is my speech to show that I am going to raise the flag. When I return I will speak. This is what he said. He said that then he went. He came here [to this place in the village], the elders of the village were here, then he raised the flag, it was raised. Many said it was the Girmit flag, the flag of an association or whatever, we don't know. But we just know, the lamp on it is bringing light to us . . . because of the lamp the light of God is with us. (Account by a Nakubuti man, my translation)

In his speech Mr. Samalia, who was fluent in standard Fijian, had also told the

---

Jesus to be paramount. The identification of positive divinity with Hitler derives from the melding of anticolonial sympathies with pro-German sentiments during both the first and second world wars. The anti-colonial sentiment is very real to some Fijians and some Fiji Indians who opposed the British, but it does not serve to make the total cosmology acceptable. The two groups are in general unpersuaded by the claim that they were meant by god to create a single nation. However coherent, Mr. Samalia's vision remains idiosyncratic.

7. This account is compiled from accounts by participants in the ceremony who live in Drauniivi.

people of his vision of India the motherland and Fiji the fatherland. He said that a red cloud in Suva portended bloodshed, that Ratu Mara's government would be changed, that Fijians would lose their land. He spoke to them about Navosavakadua, whom he said would be King of the World.

He gave the people of Drauniivi the flag with a lighted lamp against a blue background (the flag of the Fiji Girmit Association, the representation of the lamp reminiscent of the little clay lights used at Diwali, a Hindu yearly ritual). He told them to fly it always. If it were to become torn or weathered, they were to send to him for another. The Vatukaloko accepted the flag. They raised it, singing a hymn, on the flag pole that they had prepared, at the opposite end of the village green *(rara)* from the Methodist church and the village meeting house.

Mr. Samalia's visit to Drauniivi sparked a series of events that reveal curious articulations and accommodations with the memory of Navosavakadua among the Vatukaloko, in Fiji, and in the world. In Drauniivi, a young man of Nakubuti *mataqali* was visited by Navosavakadua and began to cure the sick and prophesy. The national government took note of the events, and Fiji's "Special Branch" investigated. A reporter wrote about the meeting, and the article was published both in the *Fiji Times* and in the Fijian language newspaper *Nai Lalakai* published by the same company. A man of Wakalou *mataqali* then began to send stories about the miracles performed by Navosavakadua to *Nai Lalakai* where they generated a certain controversy. I read about the imminent "Return of Navosa" in the *Fiji Times* and went to stay at Drauniivi and inquired into the history of Navosavakadua, Tuka, and the Vatukaloko polity. But anyone who expected, hoped for, or feared a major movement, like that of Navosavakadua or Apolosi, would be disappointed. Mr. Samalia rallied few if any Fiji citizens to his vision. Anyone looking for a continuant of the colonially reified Tuka would also be disappointed. Instead, Mr. Samalia's visit briefly foregrounded the routinized place that Navosavakadua and the history of the Twelve Tribes hold for the Vatukaloko today (and also therefore how they are different from other Fijians). Let us look first at what official inquiries did not find.

Official Inquiries

In the mid-1980s the Fiji government, headed by Fijian paramount chiefs, carried on the colonial concern for top-down order. "National security matters" was the phrase used to name the threat posed by the meeting at Drauniivi. In the *Fiji Times* the article headlined "2000 WAIT ON RETURN — Police Investigating" painted a picture of an incipient revolutionary movement, to be headed by the charlatan priest.

> "It was a meeting and flag-raising ceremony by someone who is trying to convince people that Navosa is coming back to life" [one person who was at the meeting told the *Fiji Times*].
>
> "They were saying there will be a new government formed after his return and they had a lot of talk about the present government," the person said.
>
> "They said there will be changes in the chiefly status and the Native Land Commission and what not. . . ."
>
> A senior police officer who confirmed report of the meeting said he could not go into details because "it deals with Special Branch matters."
>
> It is being looked into but from a different angle," he said. "It's not a normal police inquiry but a specialized thing."
>
> Asked whether it concerned national security matters, he said, "yes."

Over the next year, the Vatukaloko were the focus of a series of inquiries. The local police inspector (a Lauan) had attended the meeting at Drauniivi, and reported to his superiors. The Roko Tui Ra instructed the head teacher of the local primary school (a Bauan) to write an account of the events, "by order of the Prime Minister." But the head teacher had not even attended the meeting, saying "as a Civil Servant, I should not go." Several members of parliament who are also chiefs came to Drauniivi to question the people about the events. Finally, in September 1984, the local police inspector held a meeting in the village hall:[8]

> The heads of the *mataqali* (ritual kin groups) were there, many men, youths and women. The Inspector presented a kilo of *yaqona* (kava) requesting the people to help him. He said the Prime Minister was investigating. He told them not to be afraid, he said that he wanted to help them, to protect them. He asked for accounts of the meeting. He said anyone who didn't want to speak in the meeting could come to him privately. It took ten minutes for them to begin to talk. . . .
>
> J.T. said they didn't know anything, two letters came [to the Turaga ni Koro and the Tui Vatu] informing them that Samalia would be coming.
>
> Old O.R. said "Whatever Samalia said we just heard it. Believed some of it, but mostly we just heard it and then it was gone." This pleased the inspector.

---

8. These are my notes of a description of the meeting told to me by someone who attended it. I have checked the account with others who were there.

When the Inspector summed up, he said he was very pleased that they only listened, did not believe.

He asked them about the flag. They said Samalia gave it to them.

T. asked the Inspector the difference between Ratu Cakobau's government [by which he meant the Colonial Government] and the present one. He was worried about the nation borrowing money. The Inspector said that when Fiji was a Crown Colony it was like a child, relying on Britain. Now it must think, trade, develop for itself.

They asked the Inspector how Samalia got the Governor General's clothes [Samalia wore a uniform like that the Governor General used to wear when opening Parliament]. The Inspector said, "Anyone can buy white cloth and gloves and go to a tailor."

The police were concerned because Samalia said "Ratu Mara will be nothing. There will be bloodshed. No more Fijian land, all Crown land."

They said they did not cross-examine Samalia, just heard it, and went.

The inspector said he wanted to protect the Drauniivi people.

The investigations at Drauniivi simply showed that Mr. Samalia had instigated the events. On the surface, Mr. Samalia's predictions were read as revolutionary, predicting a change in government accompanied by violence. As with many parties in power the Alliance government took a prediction of their own defeat to be a challenge to national security. Deeper still, official concern over Mr. Samalia's message may have been stirred by his alternative national message. While he had ties to the Indian Alliance within the chiefly Alliance Party, the Alliance Party had begun to pursue a strategy of increasingly racist rhetoric, seeking to keep Fijian members from defecting to strongly Fijian nationalist parties. In the mid-eighties, aside from the newly formed Labour Party, Mr. Samalia's was the only message of Fijian and Indo-Fijian interdependence on the national scene. And perhaps most important, even if listeners did not follow or accept Mr. Samalia's national narrative, his use of constituting national symbols — flag raisings, the uniform of the governor general, and public monuments — conveyed the general message of an alternative polity, an alternative national vision. British colonial authorities were always alarmed by "mimicry" and alternatives, no matter what the content, since order in their polity was constituted from the top down. Post-colonial national leaders in Fiji sought to assert the same kind of control. But Mr. Samalia was able to carry on with his prophesies and to mount public events (perhaps because of his other ties with the Alliance Party). Indeed, the unveiling of the *Syria* monument was held several months after the meeting in Drauniivi, and was nonetheless attended by the former Governor General.

As to the Vatukaloko, they have ignored or rejected the syncretist reading of Navosavakadua. The paradigm of "India the motherland" and "Fiji the fatherland" is not adopted in their vision of the world. India and Indo-Fijians come into Fiji's cosmological-history not during the age of the *kalou vu* (ancestor gods), but instead in recent years, as the servants of the British, as heathen Hindus or Muslims, and as clever people living a life of money. In the year following Mr. Samalia's visit the Vatukaloko people, and Fijians of the Rakiraki district more generally, affirmed their relative loyalty to the Fijian chiefly system by hosting first Ratu Sir Penaia Ganilau, the Governor General (in 1985), and later Ratu Mara, the Prime Minister (in 1986), as they came through on tours of governmental business which allowed them to visit the land in chiefly style. The Vatukaloko people used the opportunity of these visits to petition *(kerekere)* them for the use of government-owned Yaqara land, which they were granted. Further, following Ratu Mara's visit, in that pre-election year, he sent the villagers a check for one hundred fifty Fijian dollars, a personal thank you for their hospitality. If the Alliance Party had anything to worry about, it was not the prophecies of Navosavakadua's return, but rather, support for the Fiji Labour Party.

But, if the Vatukaloko are not separatists, if they were not swayed by Mr. Samalia's vision of a coming disaster and new kingdom, why did they participate? Why did they welcome Mr. Samalia to Drauniivi, and what did his visit mean to them? In part, they welcomed him because they are still hinterland people who are used to obeying directives and who are sometimes unclear on the specificities of chiefly and national power relations. Moreover, Mr. Samalia, who was "not afraid to say anything," creates an authoritative presence. On the one hand, they were afraid of being arrested or deported if they responded to Mr. Samalia. On the other hand, they were afraid not to attend to him. Finally, however, they participated because of Samalia's invocation of the name of their ancestor. Navosavakadua continues to be too important to them to ignore any such claim. They have their own opinions about his meaning in the present day. And they have an interest in knowing what is said about him, partly because, unlike in the colonial era, they have new and now public arenas in which they can debate others' accounts of their ancestor and themselves.

Public Discourse about Navosavakadua in the 1980s

In 1984 Mr. Samalia's meeting in Drauniivi was reported by an Indo-Fijian reporter for the *Fiji Times*. A translation of the article appeared in the Fijian language newspaper *Nai Lalakai*. Several people subsequently wrote letters to the editor of *Nai Lalakai* about the event. A few months later a Vatukaloko man of Wakalou *mataqali* (a much traveled man who asserts leadership in the village when he stays there) began to send in articles about Navosavakadua. He thus initiated the first sustained public discourse about Navosavakadua written by a member of the Vatukaloko people.⁹ In the 1890s in *Na Mata* (The Herald), the government-sponsored Fijian-language gazette, the colonial authorities had presented Navosavakadua and the "Drauniivi people" as objects of government discipline. The Vatukaloko never accepted this construction of their relative and themselves, but they had sought no public forum for an alternative discourse: Jovesa Bavou's book was locally and privately held. His ritual-political explanations of the world were not incorporated by the land commissioners into the synthetic summaries that now constitute the Native Lands Commission "Bibles." But in 1984, thanks to Mr. Samalia, Navosavakadua and Vatukaloko history were again up for scrutiny.

The *Fiji Times* article in English (and the *Nai Lalakai* article, a direct translation) informed its readers that

> The chief *[turaga]* Navosa [is] believed to have come from Drauniivi Village and is said to have possessed powers of prophecy and could perform miracles. He was at his ascendancy *[e a tu sara ga ko koya e na gauna ni nona kaukauwa vakaturaga]* in the 1930s.
>
> Navosa is the short form of Navosavakadua (He-Who-Speaks-Once-Only).

Here Navosavakadua was identified as a "legendary chief" rather than as a priest *(bete)*, reflecting the colonial-Fijian normalization of designation of leadership. Public discourse in Fiji still avoids attributing legitimate leadership to priests because of the missionary and colonial construction of the illegitimate "charlatan priest." In the *Fiji Times* Navosavakadua is further identified for English-speaking readers by a village name (the colonial designation of "Drauniivi people") rather than by *mataqali* Nakubuti or *yavusa* Vatukaloko. Finally, conflated perhaps with Apolosi Nawai, his historical time period is incorrectly given. In response to the articles, and to the meeting convened by Mr. Samalia, Osea Ravai's letters to *Nai Lalakai* reproduce the designation of Navosa as a

---

9. For accounts of the meeting see article by Firoz Shaheem, *Fiji Times* 15 March 1984, and *Nai Lalakai* 22 March 1984; for Osea Ravai's stories and correspondence concerning Navosavakadua see *Nai Lalakai*, weekly May through July 1984, especially 10 May 1984. See also *Siga Rarama* (Fijian language newspaper published by the *Fiji Sun*) from March through September 1984. I thank Vasiti Ritova for translating some of these stories and for checking my translations of others.

chief (indeed, people in Drauniivi are anxious to avoid calling him a priest). However, writing to a Fijian audience, the stories do identify Navosavakadua by *yavusa,* claiming him proudly as a Vatukaloko man. These letters to the readers of *Nai Lalakai* seek to explain the nature of Navosavakadua's miracles and to prove that his power came from God.

> To the Editor
>
> Dear Sir,
>
> In this printed forum I would like to explain to you readers of Nai Lalakai, concerning the wisdom *(vuku)* of this man who is widely known as Navosavakadua.
>
> I would like to clarify his true name.
>
> Navosavakadua was born in the days after the [British] flag was raised and his baptismal name was Moses Dukumoi. He was known later as Navosavakadua because of the miracles *(cakacaka mana)* he performed.
>
> Because of the raising of the flag at Drauniivi a few months ago some people have thought that he returned on that day.
>
> Sir Editor, Navosa didn't promise a day he would return to our ancestors who lived when he did.
>
> And we also don't know who had the flag raised at Drauniivi.
>
> I want to show here that many are writing letters saying that he will come back.
>
> In these letters they say that he and another person called Waicalanavanua will be coming back. This is a very mistaken story, and it is not true.
>
> As it says in the Bible (Isaiah 2:22) "Cease ye from man, whose breath is in his nostrils for wherein is he to be accounted of?" [I.e., don't believe these men, believe only the word of God.]
>
> This man Navosavakadua was a true church believer *(daulotu)* when he was growing up. He was such a strong believer that he worshipped God 28 times a day.
>
> (Osea Ravai, *Nai Lalakai* 10 May 1984, my translation)

Later letters stress that all of Navosavakadua's miracles were accomplished by and accompanied by prayer. For example, after he had caused a crop of yams *(uvi)* to grow in one day the harvested yams were first heaped up and offered to God, and then divided among the owners of the land and the visitors who had accompanied Navosa to plant them.

> When breakfast was finished in the morning of the next day, Navosa then asked the people to turn to the point that faced the sea, the same land where Atunaisa was baked [and came out of the oven alive] to have a prayer.
>
> When their prayer was over, Navosa then made clear to those who were there that the power that he had was the power of God and then he told them again that he was

just a man like them and was enabled to do miracles through the strength of love, truth, and belief.

Among the letters to the Fijian-language newspapers, the reaction to Osea Ravai's tales divided into two contrasting groups. One group replicates in many ways the Fijian-Christian chiefly articulation. These Fijian Christians wrote in to challenge the contention that Navosavakadua was a Christian and that his miracles were made possible by Jehovah. A Seventh Day Adventist wrote to say that it could not be true because he would never have reconstituted a pig to feed his followers since pork is forbidden in the Bible. Another critic wrote a series of letters quoting the Bible to deny that Navosavakadua represented or incarnated god (quoting especially First Timothy 2:5, "For there is one God and one mediator between God and men, the man Jesus Christ"). He also disparaged the alleged miracles. He suggested that Osea go to the market and ask the market gardeners whether bananas (*vudi*) or other produce could be grown in a day, and argued that if Navosa prayed twenty-eight times a day, as claimed, he would be in church every hour. Osea wrote back listing the names of Vatukaloko men of the past generation who were eyewitnesses to the miracles. He explained that Navosa worshipped God during all his activities, not simply in church. He insisted that Navosavakadua was not God, but simply a man who "worshipped the true god," and who truly, through God's grace, could perform these miracles.

In contrast, a Fijian supporter of Mr. Samalia wrote saying that he appreciated the stories and to support Osea against critics. However, he argued for a very different construction of the relation of Navosavakadua and Fijian and Christian gods, resembling the fiercer early twentieth-century version of Tuka of the Bobuco people or Apolosi Nawai's anti-chiefly and anti-European Viti Company. Contradicting Osea, he claimed that Navosavakadua was Jesus (and also Hitler) and that he would be returning to Fiji. He further explained that the religion of the present in Fiji was not a true religion, but one imposed upon Fijians by Tongans and foreigners painted white. He proposed instead a sequential history in which ancestor gods gave way to the Twins who were then displaced by the Christian god.[10] Fijians were descendants, he claimed, of

---

10. He did not include Krishna in his history. This version of events, including a relation of Navosavakadua and Hitler (with Hitler constructed as, like Navosa, an enemy of the colonial British), is close to versions propounded in Ra in the early part of this century, and I think that these are Fijian versions or traditions of Navosavakadua that influenced Mr. Samalia's vision. The vision of religious history in Fiji seen in these letters contains an unusual — for a Fijian — rejection of Jehovah. I felt that talking about these letters made people in Drauniivi uncomfortable.

"the elder line." Where, he asked are the descendants of Jesus? He accused the Fijian-Christian writer of "not being truly a Fijian *[itaukei]*." One of the defenders of the Christian position countered with an equally genealogical argument:

> We Fijians who are members of the Christian faith have this hope in the Bible verse in Galatians 3:29 — "And if ye be Christ's, then are ye Abraham's seed and heirs according to the promise." Therefore my relative, in front of you are two lines of descendants, which are you counted in? The choice is yours, and you are not forced. (Translated by Vasiti Ritova)

In a sense, the two sets of commentaries on Osea Ravai's Navosavakadua stories were inversions of each other. One saw Christianity, a true religion, properly replacing older heathenism. The other saw Christianity replacing a truer religion through conquest and trickery. In contrast to both, the Vatukaloko author asserted that Navosavakadua simply was a Christian.

In all three arguments, colonial-Fijian articulations were revealed, part of an interesting post-colonial dialogue with fundamental definitions in question. The Christian author moved between denying that Navosavakadua was god and being skeptical of the miracles as impossible in nature.[11] The Samalia-connected writer insisted on calling Navosavakadua "Ratu Navosa," using a chiefly honorific generalized in the colonial period to reflect generic "chiefly" status. Yet this account saw him as a countercolonial figure, of political as well as ritual significance, since time was portrayed as a series of stages in which Europeans come to dominate Fijians improperly through tricking them with religion.

In his contrasting account Osea Ravai did not claim Navosa as a chief, but simply as a religious man. The scenes he presented mirror biblical tales of Christ, in which Navosavakadua performs miracles to feed his followers, or answers their questions. Further, though he ostensibly situated him in Christian and colonial time (claiming that he was baptized), he did not address the relation of Navosavakadua and the colonial government. In the letters to *Nai Lalakai* he did not write of the deportation, nor does Navosavakadua engage in any sort of relation with any other group in Fiji (beyond prophesying the arrival of others along with goods and education and opportunities). Instead, the Navosavakadua he portrayed was ultimately a timeless, legendary figure,

---

11. His argument reminds me of that of the then head teacher at the Drauniivi public school, who filled the school with posters quoting the Bible, but could not understand why the Vatukaloko people insisted on "mixing up" things from the Bible with their daily lives, e.g., believing that biblical sites are located in the Kauvadra.

interacting only with Fijians, situated in a Kauvadra setting that the author at least considered to be biblical. He represents an amalgamation of peaceful and bountiful qualities; generating and regenerating products of earth and sea by prayer. These products are offered to god and then used by the people. His leadership embodies "goodness, truth, and love *(loloma)*."

Osea Ravai's letters to *Nai Lalakai* fairly accurately represent a construction of Navosavakadua I found to be held among many of the Vatukaloko. (I have heard versions of them told by older people who probably told them to Osea, and by young people, who might have learned them from the newspaper.) They believe that Navosa's *mana* was from God, and omit "Tuka" completely from any tale of his life and miracles—even when detailing his miraculous escapes and recovery from colonial persecutions. When pressed to discuss "Tuka" or *"luveniwai"* older informants claim that heathen others, such as Sadiri of Tokaimalo (the warrior priest at Nakorowaiwai), led these practices, not Navosa. A grievous mistake was made by the colonial authorities when they blamed Navosa.

But in the village, unlike in the newspaper articles, a range of stories and anecdotes are told which more closely identify Navosa with Jesus. In sermons and prayers people often quote John 1:1 (In the beginning was the Word *(na Vosa)* and the Word was with God, and the Word was God) though they never discuss ancestor gods in the course of church services. Several women told me that a picture of Jesus hanging in the church actually represents Navosa. Further, in the village Navosa as Christian and the nature of his *mana* are understood in the context of a wider articulation in which the Vatukaloko see themselves as people of the land and as chosen people. Navosa is part of the socio-cosmological history, from Jehovah to the Vatukaloko today. Most importantly, as I will discuss in the next chapter, he is the focal means by which the Vatukaloko attempt to encompass their present and create a seamless connection to their past.

The newspaper debate over Navosa ended late in June when someone sent a letter to the newspaper, claiming to write on behalf of the Vatukaloko people. The writer asked the editors to stop printing the stories. It also informed the newspaper that the author of the stories about Navosa was named Osea Ravai, not Ratu Osea Saumaimuri. In Drauniivi, no one would tell me who sent the last letter. It was not publicly sent by the Tui Vatu or the Turaga ni Koro nor was it discussed at a village meeting. Some think that it was sent by a Nasi man who was very skeptical of Mr. Samalia's visit, going so far as to identify the flag he presented to the villagers as the Girmit flag and to suggest that they not fly it. Whoever the writer was, he or she may also have been annoyed that Osea Ravai was presenting himself as the spokesman for the Vatukaloko or the chronicler of Navosavakadua. Or the letter may have been sent by someone entirely unconnected with the Vatukaloko people.

To what extent has Navosavakadua returned? For Mr. Samalia he remained a present and potent force. After 1987 and the military coups Mr. Samalia held several more public rituals, including two "Prayer Meetings" at inland sites associated with Navosavakadua. In Drauniivi in the early 1990s opinion was divided over whether Mr. Samalia was worth taking seriously when he talked about Navosa, or whether he was crazy, and whether it was dangerous to take part in his activities, given the instability of the post-coup governments. Since 1990 the flag he gave the Vatukaloko has not flown. It disappeared "during a storm" people say.

The newspaper debate over Navosavakadua, Christianity, and Fijian custom has also disappeared, following the coups, supplanted by debates more sharply focused on contemporary agents and parties in government and religion. Of course Navosavakadua remains a powerful potential historical resource for would-be leaders. Dr. Bavadra and the Labour Party drew upon general sentiments that link Ra people. And in 1991 Apisai Tora, another Fijian politician from the west of Viti Levu island, also portrayed himself as a "man from Ra." In the period of political negotiation and confrontation preceding the elections of 1992 he raised Navosavakadua's name in a speech on his own behalf, arguing that it was time for western Fijians to take on national leadership. He said, "First there was Navosa, then there was Apolosi Nawai, and now it is the turn of the West again." Future invocations of Navosa are likely. However, in the 1992 election it was Sitiveni Rabuka who became the prime minister. Rabuka who had lead the coups is from an eastern coastal kingdom, though not himself chiefly.

On Routinization, and Unsuccessful Attempts

Mr. Samalia's narrative of Navosavakadua and his national rituals were coherent, even elegant syncretisms. But he was unsuccessful in his attempt to routinize his vision of divinely ordered "racial" interdependence as a prevailing and natural view of order in Fiji. Unlike either Navosavakadua and the Vatukaloko's articulation or the chiefly-colonial articulation, Samalia's ritual-politics convinced no wider community, nor could he force people to accept his terms.

The story of Mr. Samalia's project disrupts any tidy narrative of two sorts of Fijians (people of the land and chiefs) with contrasting colonial experiences resulting in articulations private and quiescent or public, legal, and orthodox. Instead, we have engaged, albeit briefly, in this chapter some of the complexities of colonial and current Fiji and its ethnic dilemmas. Further, we engage complexities for a theory of articulations and their routinization. On the one hand, there is nothing arbitrary about routinization in the sense that some articulations are routinized and become part of lived realities of groups, while others do not. On the other hand, I do not think that we can hope to find a general theory of the patterns or causes of routinization; precisely because it is a cultural phenomenon. Any general account of patterns or causes designed to predict or account for why some articulations are routinized and others are not would have to be either tautological or reductionist. Because cultural systems do change, each conjuncture is a new conjuncture; but because cultural systems are powerful although changing, they inform the very measure of possibility, coherence, convincingness, utility, and necessity of each new articulation. As we have seen, Samalia's coherent articulation was discordant in basic ways with both Indo-Fijian social experience and Fijian-Christian cosmology. This did not simply doom the project to failure, but it makes that failure unsurprising because of the kinds of cultural change that would have been involved for its acceptance.

In contrast, the quiescent resilience of a land-centric Christianity among the Vatukaloko, its private mobilization of Land Commission modalities of organizing evidence, and its creative adaptation to a century of increasingly assertive national-Christian orthodoxy, provide an example of successful routinization of a contesting vision of Fiji's order that is unsurprising only in retrospect.

Mr. Samalia's energetic failure makes the observation of Vatukaloko quiescent success all the more interesting. Navosavakadua has not returned to overturn the order of things. Nonetheless he has continued to hold an important, if muted, place among the Vatukaloko. As we shall see, his presence there is less important than it once was, precisely because his project has succeeded, and is routinized, in a local Vatukaloko cosmology.

8

NAVOSAVAKADUA AMONG THE VATUKALOKO

It is tempting to read the narrative of Navosavakadua in the newspaper debates as a sign of Vatukaloko transformation in compliance with colonial terms. In the narrative Navosa is not a priest *(bete)*, but rather a Christian. Tuka is not mentioned in these accounts. Nor — in the public debate at least — does Navosa oppose any constituted order, whether that of the Tui Vatu, of Bauans, of past missions, colonial rule, or 1980s national government. Here then is a quiescent Navosavakadua. This chapter is about Navosavakadua among the Vatukaloko today. Have the Vatukaloko become nostalgic ritualists? Have they lost the warrior agency of noble allies, the power to make chiefs held by people of the land, in the course of colonial rule? Have they given up their nineteenth-century goal of polity and autonomy? And is Navosavakadua's quiescence in the current narratives the consequence of colonial regulation? Or, can we read it as a triumph of his own articulation of Christian gods and the gods of the people of the land? Or, is it both?

Navosavakadua among the Vatukaloko

One consequence of Mr. Samalia's big meeting in Drauniivi was that Navosavakadua visited the Vatukaloko, briefly. He inspired a young man of Nakubuti *mataqali* (kin group) who went out one day to feed the pigs and came back and told his family that he had seen an ancestor god *(vu)* who was, in fact,

Navosa. His brothers wondered if he had gone mad. News of his experience spread quickly. For a while, as one informant put it, "he was really in power." Sick people came to live near him, to have him massage them and pray for them.¹ He sometimes prescribed Fijian medicinal cures, or identified the root of illness in breaches of kinship obligations. He also located lost objects. Once a deputation of people came from Nakorosule, an inland village, asking why wild pigs were eating their crops and their children were sick. He told them that this was the consequence of their ancestors having taunted Navosa while he was held prisoner by the British. They returned to formally apologize *(soro)*.

Navosavakadua had returned, but only briefly, and not to overturn the world.² He had not come to challenge the post-colonial polity, nor to found a new religion. And I wondered, why? Was it because the Vatukaloko had come to accept chiefly-colonial domination in its post-colonial forms, to participate in a hegemonic chiefly-colonial construction of what power, agency, and effectiveness could be in Fiji? Was it because the Vatukaloko had become Christian that Navosavakadua could no longer lead a ritual mobilization? Had Navosa been transformed like other gods of the land in Fiji (described in chapter 6) who became marginalized, no longer gods of polity and war, but concerned instead now with individuals, their health, luck, or finances? I think that at least part of our answer is to know more about the powers, agencies, and possibilities in the lives of the Vatukaloko today. There is more to their lives than their connection to this famous ancestor.

Quiescent People of the Land?
The Vatukaloko Social Landscape in the 1980s

Here I want to describe some aspects of the lives of the Vatukaloko people living at Drauniivi, ninety years after their deportation, seventy years after their exile ended, as a routinized articulation of a particular Fijian and colonial conjuncture. Let us begin with a bird's-eye view, or at least an anthropologist's, of the social landscape of the Vatukaloko when I was there in the 1980s and in 1991.

---

1. Massage and prayer are techniques commonly used by seers who consult other ancestor deities, and by those who seek assistance from the Christian god. Special prayer sessions are held weekly at the Methodist church, in which women ask God for help with specific ailments and difficulties that affect villagers and kin.

2. After several months of cures, three of the sick people who were staying in the village to be treated died. This coincided with the diminution of the young man's powers, which did not return to him in any substantive way in the 1980s.

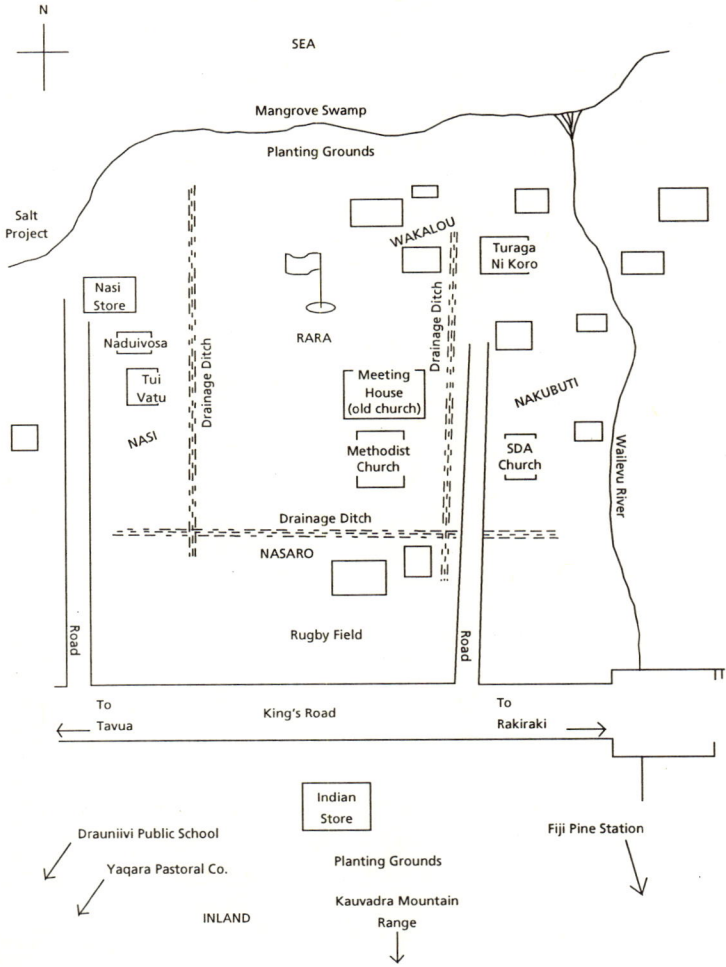

Figure 13. Drauniivi Village in the 1980s: author's sketch (not to scale; not all buildings shown).

Within the heart of the village *(e loma ni koro)* at one end of the central ritual space, the village green *(rara),* stand the Methodist church and the meeting house *(sue ni soqo).* At the other end of the green stands a flagpole. Erected in 1984, from 1984 to 1990 it flew the flag some claimed was Navosa's, brought to them by the Indo-Fijian visionary. Sometime around 1990 the flag vanished, but the flagpole is still there. Also near to the edge of the central green is a village cooperative store, built in 1985.

It will be recalled that the Vatukaloko had come to describe themselves, to the Native Lands Commissioners in 1918, as a *yavusa* made up of three *mataqali* groups, and three *mataqali* only are listed in official published records. By the 1980s the three *mataqali* had become four. I was told that at some point a small group of people from Wakalou *mataqali* split off to form a fourth separate group called Nasaro. The three main groups, with their long, complex histories, continue to define their relationship with one another in the terms stated publicly and privately in 1918: Nasi as chiefly group, Wakalou as the warrior allies of Nasi, and Nakubuti as the installing people. The village of Drauniivi in the 1980s still mapped these divisions onto the land (see my sketch, figure 13). To the left side of the village (if one stands with one's back to the interior mountain range, facing north to the sea) is Nasi's area. Among the houses are the concrete house of the Tui Vatu, who was installed in 1993, the big thatched house called Naduivosa ("the different languages"), and a prosperous concrete house called Kabukilagi where I stayed.

In Nakubuti space on the right border of the village, where there are so many houses that they have spilled over onto Wakalou land (in the center of the village), the custodian of Jovesa Bavou's book of genealogies lives in Taivesi Mamaqa's old house, where the flag of Apolosi's Viti Kabani was raised in the 1910s. A beautiful new Seventh Day Adventist church stands on the outside edge of Nakubuti land. By 1985 the house of the seer *(dau rai)* who briefly found his powers after Mr. Samalia's visit to the village in 1984, was no longer crowded with the sick. In the Wakalou *mataqali* space, in the center of the village, is a thatched house belonging to another seer with powers not immediately connected to Navosa. Among the houses in Nasaro *mataqali* space (at a right angle to the three main *mataqali*, to the inland) are that of the late village pastor and the thatched house of the old lady who was born in Kadavu.

In each space is a house that is that of the head of the *mataqali* group. But each group also has elected two representatives to the Village Committee. They, like the Turaga ni Koro (headman), take the active role in the projects of the village. They conduct business, as does the Turaga ni Koro, in the central meeting house, where meetings of all the people of the village are held every few weeks. Other ritual events are held in Naduivosa or the Tui Vatu's house. Following the death of the last Tui Vatu in the late 1970s the collective endeavors of the village were not directed by the Tui Vatu line, but by another elder from Nasi *mataqali*, though this is likely to change since the chiefly heir was installed by the Nakubuti people in 1993. Colonial codifications notwithstanding, the Vatukaloko are still a people among whom chiefly leadership is importantly mediated by concerns and projects of people of the land. Major rituals take place on the *rara,* the central village green, weekly church services in the Methodist and Seventh Day Adventist churches.

One edge of the village is on the coast. On the side near Nasi, the ground has been cleared, pits and pools dug, and an engine installed for a salt-making project. It belongs to Nasi *mataqali* alone, since the various development agents, including two successive Peace Corps couples who have supervised the salt-making project, could not get the people of the four *mataqali* groups to cooperate. It was a flourishing concern in the mid-1980s, but in 1991 salt was not being made in Drauniivi. At the edges of Wakalou and Nakubuti there are planting grounds, then mangroves, then the sea. The mangrove area is full of crabs, which women catch to sell. But to fish, women must walk a long way from the village to get to the clear coast.

Between the village and the King's Road is a field now used for rugby. Two separate short roads run into the village. One comes down to Nakubuti, passing the new one-room dispensary with the toilet at the back built under the direction of the Peace Corps volunteers. I always wondered whether they thought this would dissuade villagers from seeking healing from ancestor gods and their seers. The other leads down along the edge of Nasi. On this road, on the edge of Nasi, stands the Nasi cooperative store, solvent since the late 1970s. Until 1985 it competed only with a small store run by the Methodist pastor's wife, and with the Indo-Fijian–owned store, across the main King's Road, beyond the rugby field. In 1991 a village cooperative store, a store run by a Seventh Day Adventist family in Nakubuti and a billiards hall (a house with a billiards table in it) have been added to the village public buildings. The Indo-Fijian storekeeper drives a cane lorry as well. Cane lorries also come down the two roads into the village during cutting season, to pick up young men who work on cane gangs, cutting mainly for Indo-Fijian farmers, though in the village several Fijian families also grow cane.

Inland *(i yata)* across the King's Road are the Indo-Fijian–owned store, the Drauniivi Public School (unusual because it is a "mixed" school, with both Fijian and Indo-Fijian pupils), and the planting grounds of the people of Drauniivi. What land they still own is used for subsistence crops (especially cassava), and some is used for cash crops (peanuts and some sugar cane). But most of the land across the road is occupied by the Fiji Pine Station (part of the nationally owned timber industry) and Yaqara Pastoral Company (a nationally owned cattle ranch and farm). These government lands were once Vatukaloko polity *(vanua)* lands, alienated to settlers like Thomas and Burness and eventually sold to the Colonial Sugar Refinery. They became government owned when the sugar industry was nationalized at independence. Until 1986 the farm manager at Yaqara was a Rotuman man; by happy coincidence he is related to Navosavakadua, from Navosa's marriage in Rotuma. Because of his enthusiastic and sincere participation in important local rituals *(soqo vakavanua)* and his genuine appreciation of the particular and miraculous history of the Vatukaloko and other Ra and interior peoples, the government ownership of Yaqara and the fences on the land were less oppressive than they might have been. Moreover, opportunities to work at Yaqara, whether permanent or temporary, were inflected by the kin relationship to the manager. More recently, an expatriate has been manager of Yaqara. Inside the bounds of Yaqara are many sacred spots, especially Korowaiwai, site of the defeat by the Bauans in 1873, and Vale Lebo, which was Navosavakadua's pilgrimage site. Further inland still are the Kauvadra sites, many of which are now considered to be biblical sites. Stretching from Drauniivi inland to the Kauvadra mountain range and then even farther inland are the villages in which dwell the people of the old Vatukaloko polity who are now referred to as the "Twelve Tribes."

Stretching along the King's Road are the Fijian villages of Togavere (to the southeast) and Rabulu (to the west). Those who live there are closely connected with the Vatukaloko, still belying the colonial stereotype of "one village — one kin group *(yavusa)*." The Namacuku people were living at Togavere when the Vatukaloko came down from the hills to intermarry with and, in the mid-nineteenth century, to rule over them. The people at Rabulu are closely connected to Nakubuti, and several of Navosavakadua's direct descendants live there. Inland from the King's Road there are Indo-Fijian settlements as well, such as Caboni and Nakinawai which are built on land alienated to white planters in the 1860s. Along the King's Road run buses southeast to Rakiraki and west to Tavua in Ba province. Although Tavua is closer, people still prefer to go to Rakiraki to use the post office or hospital, having closer ties of kinship or respect for Rakiraki, or feeling the pull of custom (and colonial regulation) to go to the center of Ra province. Throughout the province and adjoining provinces are sugar cane fields, and many Vatukaloko young men hire out as cane cutters in the milling season. The roads go farther, all the way around the island, to Suva the capital in the southeast, and to Nadi the airport town on the western side, where many Vatukaloko people have gone to work and some have settled. Vatukaloko people have gone to work at the Vatukoula gold mine, at tourist resorts, and in the cities too. Some are wage laborers and "house girls," others have training and education and are permanent employees at the airport, in banks, journalism, industry, and teaching.

The road connects to airports and wharves, and thereby to places beyond the islands. Through the airport, and the capital city, Fijians are connected with the world. In 1985 the son of the late Methodist pastor was in the Middle East, as part of the United Nations multinational peacekeeping forces. Of course the world comes more directly into the village, for example, in the form of money, consumer goods (above all tinned fish), and on radio broadcasts both from Suva the capital, and Radio West, another branch of the national broadcasting service. By the mid-1980s just about everyone in Drauniivi had seen videotaped movies, especially action films, on rented televisions and VCRs, and the debated advent of broadcast television is one of the major social and political topics of Fiji of the 1990s.

What organizes life within this social landscape? Do old polity relations of land people *(itaukei)* and chiefs *(turaga)*, interior and coast, still matter in people's lives? What about the Twelve Tribes? What of European orderings, including mission circuits and colonial districts? What of the projects of development that brought the market to Drauniivi explicitly, with missionary zeal, and the forces of the market that more subtly inflect all Fijians' lives? What of the (ostensible) multiracialism of Independent Fiji (1970–1987), and the Fijian nationalist projects of the Republic of Fiji of the 1987 coups era? How do the Vatukaloko articulate these systems, or live with their contradictions?

Some nineteenth-century ritual-political relations straightforwardly continue to order some aspects of life in the village. Others have changed radically. The Vatukaloko are no longer warriors protecting their standing as noble allies against Rakiraki chiefs, or challenging the might of Bau by killing a labor recruiter. This is not to say, however, that they have given up narratives of ritual authority and precedence over far-flung descendants of junior lines. A Nakubuti man insisted on this when, following Mr. Samalia's visit, he told me the story about the discussion of Degei, ancestor to Rakiraki and other coastal peoples, between his father and the Lands Commissioners in 1918 (here I repeat the story told in chapter 2).

> Yes, that is true. He [Degei] was the youngest one. His older brother was born first, then some in the middle, he was the younger brother. It was given to him the power to sit at the stone [at the summit of Kauvadra]. Then he married. He had one hundred wives. His oldest son was the ancestor of the Bauans. They say that Degei was the oldest but he wasn't.
>
> When the Lands Commission came to Nanukuloa, Mr. Maxwell opened the Lands Commission, together with a Fijian, Savenaca Komaisavai, and the representatives from every part of Ra met. Then it was finished. Then Savenaca Komaisavai and Mr. Maxwell said "Now it's time for the representative from Vatukaloko to

speak." Then Jovesa Bavou spoke. But when he stood up to prepare to testify, Savenaca Komaisavai said "Jovesa, there's just one question we have for you." They asked him the thing I've made clear to you. "What about Degei?"

And then he said to them both, "Degei was the third person in relation to me." It was heard there as I have explained it. Leka, Qisoya, Degei [the three ancestor gods]. Leka [the Vatukaloko ancestor] the oldest, then Qisoya. The two older brothers then gave Degei the power to sit on the stone, which, as I have told you, was made by Jehovah. To watch over it, to keep it and every thing. Then Degei got married to one hundred women and his eldest was born, and his descendants are Bau. The name of this eldest was Vueti, born of the first woman he took. It is thus that they are saying that they are descendants of the first born.

"What about Degei?" Jovesa Bavou said "He is the third man after me." This means, I am the oldest. If you listen to people throughout Tailevu they will call "Hey, older brother *(tuakaqu)*." Ratu George Cakobau, the former Governor General, calls us "the elders" *(na qase)* or "my older brother." Because we are the oldest, they are the younger. The descendants of Vueti are the people of Bau. They were given the rule to hold by their brothers.

Then my informant discussed Mr. Samalia's claim that the government would be overthrown and that a new flag would be raised, assuming that it meant that the elder brothers would take back the rule. He immediately added:

> But that Indian man, we don't know him. Had never seen him. But he wrote and said the flag should be raised . . . and he said "I know it is Sunday. The Sunday that Jesus rose again. It is also the day I want to raise the flag. This is the flag of the land, of Fiji. Don't be afraid." . . . But if you go to explain this at Bau they will be angry with jealousy. They will come and they will shoot us. When we say this that we are the older brothers. But they know it. They are the younger brothers of men.

In this complex passage the Nakubuti man claimed ritual precedence or authority in the face of "Bauan" power. What Jovesa Bavou in the 1910s recorded as a socio-cosmological and genealogical claim is here (because of Mr. Samalia's prediction of a new government) amplified momentarily into a vision of conflict between the Vatukaloko and the "Bauans." But the storyteller believed that such a conflict (even making the claim publicly) would result immediately in the punishment of the Vatukaloko. Read without the superposition of Mr. Samalia's message of impending governmental change, the Vatukaloko vision of their ritual authority is claimed with conviction, and disseminated freely, but without intent to put it to any political use in the wider fields of Fijian polity relations, or the nation. In this sense, then, nineteenth-century ritual-political relations, in which people of the land were warriors made invulnerable by gods, have attenuated in the lives of the Vatukaloko.

But at the more local level, the ritual-politics of land and sea may have more ongoing practical salience. The separation and relationships of the three founding ancestors of the three main *mataqali*, self-consciously mapped into village space in 1909 at the direction of the then Tui Vatu, continued to organize questions of ritual-political leadership in the 1980s, notably a creative balance between installers and the chiefly line, in which a Nakubuti man even used the colonially created Turaga ni Koro office, like Taivesi Mamaqa at the turn of the century, as a position from which to represent a strong installing *mataqali*. Further, as "Drauniivi" has become identified with "Navosavakadua" in the view of outsiders (from colonial authorities to other Fijians), his descendants among the Nakubuti people who have a more direct genealogical tie to him are to some degree thrust into a position of spokesmanship. Nonetheless, the Tui Vatu line kept a place for chiefly ritual leadership, especially in 1993 with the installation of the new Tui Vatu.

Nineteenth-century polity relations from the wider Vatukaloko polity, nowadays known as the "Twelve Tribes," are also currently invoked to organize rituals *(soqo vakavanua)* of wider scale. At the funeral of the last Tui Vatu and the installation of his successor, the Nasoqo people, borderers to the Vatukaloko polity since the nineteenth century, came to "carry the clubs," the ritual function that denotes noble ally *(bati)* status. Other such land *(vakavanua)* relations of alliance in war or through marriage are invoked for village rituals, and at various less elaborate life cycle rituals. The peoples of the Twelve Tribes ritual polity are easily called together, for example, for the visit of Mr. Samalia, or the installation of the Tui Vatu.

In all four *mataqali* (though especially in Nakubuti) houses are named after the older village sites and origin sites *(yavutu)* which are inland. The ancestor gods too are still associated with the Kauvadra range, inhabiting and watching over their old sites. They are at least acknowledged, and sometimes invoked and drawn down into the village through kava *(yaqona)* ceremonies, sometimes by seers *(dau rai)*. They appear in dreams and visions to give advice and to warn when social rules are transgressed. The landscape between the Kauvadra range and the coast is full of this living history of the ancestor gods. But without contradiction for many Vatukaloko people this living history is also conceived as Christian. This articulation is again routinized in the very landscape. Biblical sites are identified with or located among those of the ancestor gods. In Jovesa Bavou's version, Jehovah created the first man and woman at the place called Vatukaloko in the Kauvadra range. Following the articulation initiated by Navosavakadua, the Vatukaloko have established Jehovah as a god of the land.

Moreover, nowadays colonial codification of space and identity into villages, districts, and provinces are also constructed as customary relations "in the way of the land" *(vakavanua)*. In the colonial period units of Fijian administration (province, district, and village) and the concomitant designations of kingdom, chiefdom, tribe, lineage, and family or household (*matanitu, vanua, yavusa, mataqali,* and *tokatoka*) were codified in the process of ruling Fijians and, importantly, assuring them the ownership of their land. These units from the colonial project have been retained in the post-colonial nation, in the separate Fijian Administration. As we have seen in chapter 6, they have become inextricably linked with Fijian identity as owners of the land *(itaukei)*. Similarly the offices and requirements of indirect rule have been established as part of the way of the land. Through routinization of colonial rule these are now Fijian categories, part of the Fijian polity within a polity, distinct from the units of classification, offices, and activities of Indo-Fijians and Europeans, marking the special nature of Fijians as indigenes and landowners. Thus the office of village headman (Turaga ni Koro) is considered traditional, the meeting house *(sue ni soqo)* is a "land" space, and communal responsibilities to the district and province, even including money levied for the provincial fundraising festivals, are regarded not so much as duties to the government, but to the collective people of Ra.[3]

But if the way of the land has been articulated with Christian god and colonial bounds (and in turn been altered and reified by them), relations with the post-colonial nation are more complex. On the one hand, in the post-colonial government from independence in 1970 to 1987 Lauans, Bauans, and other chiefs of the Alliance Party were held to represent the interests of all Fijians in opposition to Indo-Fijians. On the other hand, many among the Vatukaloko have been supporters of alternative political parties.

In the 1970s and early 1980s support for the Alliance Party came despite memory of Bauan encroachment which is etched into the landscape at the old

---

3. To avoid painting too completely synthetic a picture I should note that sometimes the village of Drauniivi does not fulfill its provincial obligations. Moreover there can be resentment when the District Officer comes around to inspect the cook houses and village cleanliness. Although he is now a Fijian, his recommendations in 1984 almost exactly replicate the sanitary concerns of British District Officers' reports from the early part of this century. Nonetheless, the basis of his authority is in some sense conceived "traditional," especially among an older generation (forty and above) who nostalgically describe the mid-nineteenth-century colonial days as an orderly period in which there was less crime, drinking, unmarried pregnancy, etc.

site of the Battle of Nakorowaiwai. As I noted previously, in 1986, months before the national election, the Vatukaloko were able to successfully appeal to Alliance politicians and the Governor General (all high eastern chiefs) for use of lands, long claimed, that fall within the bounds of government-owned Yaqara Pastoral Company. In the multi-ethnic national context, these high chiefs were acceptable leaders to the people of the land, largely because they presented themselves as the alternative to purported Indo-Fijian domination.[4]

The bounds of the village exclude most Indo-Fijians. They enter occasionally to sell vegetables or, more occasionally, to attend a ritual, for example to bring down some *yaqona* (kava) as a token of respect if there has been a death in the village. Schoolchildren see their Indo-Fijian classmates daily in the school across the road, but the Indo-Fijian children do not come into the village to play. Mostly, Indo-Fijians are encountered outside the village, in stores, at the markets in the nearby towns, in public projects such as raising money for the public school. These relationships (never coherently envisioned by nineteenth-century colonial rulers, or the "ruling chiefs" at the time of Cession) are carried out in colonial and post-colonial public spaces. In general, Vatukaloko folk have seen themselves as very different from their Indo-Fijian fellow citizens, a point on which I will say more below.

While the eastern Fijian national political leaders had their support from the Vatukaloko in the new multi-racial political field, other Fijian leaders also were popular. The Fijian Nationalist Party, headed by a virulently anti–Indo-Fijian spokesman, interested many in the village. Most important, in 1987 other issues cross-cut the political hegemony of Eastern Fijian national leaders and their rhetoric of racial division. The Fiji Labour Party, founded in 1985, was headed by a commoner, a medical doctor from Viseisei in the west of Viti Levu. Dr. Bavadra of the Labour Party was "a child of Ra" as one Drauniivi villager described him. The Labour Party received substantial support from Drauniivi voters. Bavadra's government, formed in a coalition dependent on the Indo-Fijian National Federation Party, was ousted by the military coups of 1987. Rule returned in the interim to the Alliance Party eastern coastal chiefs, and then in the elections of 1992, Lieutenant Colonel (now Brigadier Gen-

---

4. Concomitant with the changed relationship with Bauan chiefs are Vatukaloko reconstructions of the role of Fijian officials in their deportation history. People have told me, for example, that the turn-of-the-century Roko Tui Ra, Ratu Jone Madraiwiwi, saved the Vatukaloko from an unfairly long period of exile in Nanukuloa and sent them on to Drauniivi, or that his son Ratu Sukuna was empowered by the ancestor deity Kalinamolikula, younger brother of the Twins, who helped him become the most important Fijian in the colonial government.

eral) Rabuka, the commoner from Vanua Levu who led the coups, became Prime Minister. Political possibilities seem more open now in Drauniivi, since in the past few years they have experienced national leadership by chiefs, by Dr. Bavadra and the Labour Party, by the military, and now by another commoner, General Rabuka. All the leaders they envision, however, are Fijian. In any case, this is ensured by the post-coups constitution.[5]

As to the market, it is clear that the Vatukaloko have long depended for their subsistence on money and consumer goods, gained through theirs and their relatives' wage labor. In addition money is necessary for obligations such as school fees, and ongoing Christian and customary ritual obligations. Vatukaloko support for the Labour Party owed much to political-economic reasoning by people who are hard pressed for land to cultivate and fair wages when they can find work. But in the 1980s an argument for a better place for the Vatukaloko within a capitalist political-economic system, the kind of argument made by the Labour Party on behalf of many Fijians, existed side by side with an older and perhaps more powerful narrative, a narrative part argument and part lament. In this narrative, Fijians are different from others in Fiji because they are *not* part of the market economy. They are different, and perhaps morally superior, because they live "life in the way of the land" or (as it is said in Drauniivi) life in the way of *loloma* or kindly love.

Life in the way of *loloma* is idealized as communal, rural,[6] Christian, and customary. *Loloma* is generally glossed as kindly love, but it also commonly means a freely given gift (Capell 1971). When I began fieldwork in Drauniivi *loloma* was the aspect of Fijian life that my family was most concerned to communicate. Frequently at meals they would say "when we Fijians eat, if we see anyone walk by, a stranger, a relative, a friend, we must call out to them 'come and eat' or 'come drink tea.' This is the meaning of *loloma*." *Loloma* is a contemporary indigenous characterization and reification of a whole Fijian ritual, political, and economic system of "generalized reciprocity" (Sahlins 1972; cf. Thomas 1991). But it is also the word the missionaries used to translate Christ's grace. On the one hand, therefore, *loloma* is associated with

---

5. Support for Labour may have changed since Dr. Bavadra, the "child of Ra," no longer heads the party (he died of a heart attack in 1989). Other politicians from the west of Viti Levu, or others with a powerful nationalist or evangelical rhetoric, may be particularly appealing.

6. The characterization of Fijians as "pre"-capitalist, rural, and communal, was, of course, a central feature of the colonial social-evolutionary view of them. The Native Administration routinized this characterization by keeping Fijians in villages, just as the Native Lands system assigned land to kin groups.

Jesus, the kindly and interceding aspect of the Christian god. And on the other hand, it is explicitly conceived nowadays as a defining characteristic of Fijians, as central to their very nature. That nature is Christian and rejects money, or at least the values associated with it.

If autochthony, Christianity, and *loloma* are so bound together, then it is implied that foreigners, and those who use money, are in some senses "heathen." One of my Fijian brothers made this point when he asked me "What god do you [Americans] worship in America?" I answered that different Americans have different religions including Methodism, Catholicism, Judaism, there are even some Muslims and Hindus. "I think you worship money," he said, "the Indians here worship money and idols and live in the world of business. You Americans live in the world of business and so I think you must worship money. We Fijians worship Jesus *(na kalou dina).*"[7]

But though they may conceive the village as the locus of *loloma* in opposition to town or city, money and consumer goods do go all the way into the village, and the people of Ra, including ancestors of the Vatukaloko, have long gone out to work for money as well.[8] However, as I described in chapter 6, there are routine ritual forms *(soli)* with which to transform money for use in the world of *loloma,* and these are ways in which urban Fijians and wage laborers too can identify themselves with life in the way of *loloma.* Urban-

---

7. In a fascinating momentary conjuncture — and contradiction — of Christian, Hindu, and Fijian systems, a Fijian lady once warned me against one of the Indian schoolteachers. The teacher consulted with a Hindu ritual expert who propitiated a local, *Fijian* god, in fact, the snake god, Degei. "They worship demons," the Fijian lady told me. In this view, Degei must be either revered ancestor god (with the emphasis on ancestor) or devil. Others in Drauniivi resolve the contradiction by conceiving Degei to have been created as ancestor god by Jehovah, and to be made of spirit as Jehovah is. (The typical analogy is that the ancestor gods were like angels.) But the Indian Hindu mode of worship for the snake deity is unacceptable within this framework, a judgment perhaps as much consequence as cause of the view that the Hindus are heathens.

8. One way the world of money comes into Drauniivi is from the top down. "Development" was implemented in this way in the mid-1980s, and the local Peace Corps workers (unwittingly echoing the horrified Mr. Carew) complained that the kin groups would not work together, lacking a "proper chief like down the road in Vunitogaloa village." In the face of requests from the participants in their salt-making project that money be paid to each *mataqali* group, they insisted on paying individuals. This contravened a principle which is prevalent (but increasingly challenged) among the Vatukaloko: that payment should not derive from labor and time spent by an individual but rather accrues properly to groups, or to individuals according to their rank, and is to be used either communally or according to status and obligations. One solution, for the Vatukaloko, has been to redefine "development" as a mobilization to collect money for things that those in the village desire. This can be done through *soli* fundraising festivals, rather than the forms of business the Peace Corps required.

dwelling Fijians retain membership (patrilineally) in the kin groups reified in the "Bibles" of ownership of land held at the Native Lands Commission. Thus they too are firmly tied and codified as special indigenes. They can assert these ties by participation in village-centered rituals, and by giving money at village fundraising events. In this way they too partake in life in the way of kindly love, the life of Fijians, as different from other groups in the current national context.[9]

The Boat from Rotuma Appears: Navosa among the Vatukaloko, Again

It was at one such *soli* ritual in 1984 that I heard Navosa invoked as his name flashed up in a brief moment of memory and then receded. This ritual occupied several months of planning at the end of the year of Mr. Samalia's visit. The goal of the *soli,* called the Queen of the Land Festival ("Adi Vanua"), was to raise money for village projects. It was also a self-conscious celebration by the Vatukaloko people of themselves as Vatukaloko. The culmination of the preparations, which began early in the year, took place on Christmas Day and the day following.

The form of the ritual, a "Queen" *(Adi)* fundraising festival *(soli)* originated in colonial days. It combines forms from redistributive rituals in service to chiefs *(solevu),* and colonial elements such as the honored guests who open and close the festival, and the "Queens," who are women who represent the various divisions who compete to raise the most money.[10] In this version, rather than inviting chiefs to open and close, the village residents invited relatives living in Suva, the capital city, to open, and relatives from Nadi, the airport town, to close. Unlike other fundraising festivals which are typically initiated, even required, by outside authorities such as province, church, or local public

---

9. "Life in the way of *loloma*" is an articulation of Fijian nature that works well with some aspects of the Labour Party agenda, especially in its skepticism of profit-making. But because it associates money with non-Fijians it works equally well with other Fijian nationalist agendas that claim for Fijians a unique morality.

10. The "Queen" (Adi) ritual form is shared with non-Fijian urban groups as well. The city of Lautoka has the Sugar Queen festival, the city of Suva has the Hibiscus Queen. Here businesses sponsor contestants who actually compete to be crowned "Queen." They are judged on "beauty pageant" standards, perhaps with influence exerted by prominent families, businesses, etc. A Charity Queen who raises the most money is also selected. The surrounding festivities are a tourist attraction and bring business to the city, concessionaires, and local businesses.

school, this festival was organized voluntarily by the village. It was named and referred to as the "Adi Vanua" or "Queen of the Land," and some also called it a "development" project.

On the first day, Christmas itself, the Turaga ni Koro opened the festival with a Christian prayer. Half an hour later, the desk to receive money was opened. (Deposits received over the two days were announced on a loudspeaker.) In preparation, the women of the village assembled the hundreds of mats they had woven and presented them to the elder men of the village, who accepted them on behalf of the village, in preparation for giving them to the relatives who had come to donate. Then those who were not preparing food, or welcoming guests went to church, where the sermon was preached on John 1:1 ("In the beginning was the word"). Before and after church, visiting relatives were busy offering *sevusevu* of kava to their elders to mark their re-entrance into the village. They gave money to their families, in small household and *mataqali soli*, and then also gave again as members of the "opening" and "closing" guest groups.

Mid-afternoon, the festival was formally opened. The visiting relatives from Suva were seated in a covered shed on the central green, and were welcomed with *veiqaravi vakavanua* (chiefly ceremonies of respect), including offerings of whales' teeth, kava, and foods, to which they responded with appropriate exchanges. After they had donated, the "Queens" representing each *mataqali* came out and deposited the money collected by their various *mataqalis,* and were seated in the shed with the honored Suva relatives. Then, the women of the village emerged dramatically in a line from across the village green, each carrying a mat, which they heaped up as gifts to the relatives. The atmosphere moved from solemn to exuberant as a group of seated older ladies began to sing and chant, and the women who had brought the mats entertained their relatives with gesture chants and dances.

Similar chiefly ceremonies of respect were performed for the relatives from Nadi on the second day when they donated as the closing guests for the festival. In the early evening, the winner among the Queens was announced. She was the representative of Nasi, the chiefly *mataqali*. As dancing and celebration began, the Turaga ni Koro closed the ceremonies with a final prayer. The fundraising generated over Fijian $4,000. Nasi had won the internal *mataqali* fundraising competition, but competition was then subsumed in cooperation, as it was decided to use the money to establish a village cooperative store.[11]

11. For a more detailed account of this *soli* see Kaplan (1988).

As I learned at the Queen of the Land festival, in the 1980s the Vatukaloko people of Drauniivi had projects and desires that were very different from those in the days of their famous ancestor. At the Adi Vanua, I saw a mobilization that articulated Christian, colonial, chiefly, and land forms. It was carried out with an attention and self-consciousness typical of the way in which the Vatukaloko organize such projects, whether locally motivated or required from above. They have become, through colonial inquiries and deportations, and through routinizations of visions such as that of Jovesa Bavou, hypercorrect in their life in the way of the land.

In 1984 the Vatukaloko twice mobilized their kin and themselves to participate in large-scale rituals of particular importance; first for the meeting called by Mr. Samalia early in the year and second for the Queen of the Land festival at the end. At Mr. Samalia's instigation they called upon people from throughout the old Vatukaloko polity to come together in anticipation of some message from their ancestor Navosavakadua. But without Mr. Samalia as catalyst no similar large-scale rituals had centered directly on Navosavakadua since the 1930s. In contrast to the ceremonies led by Mr. Samalia, the quiescent Queen of the Land festival far more accurately represents the inheritance from Navosavakadua that the Vatukaloko people have been given, and have chosen to claim. In it, we can see the land-centric Christianity in which they construct Navosa, and which can be read as a continuant of his claim that Jehovah and Jesus were Fijian gods. In fact, in the course of the Queen of the Land festival, two texts invoked Navosavakadua, not as central focus of the ritual, but as part of the Vatukaloko heritage. The first text was the biblical passage John 1:1, "In the beginning was the Word (Na Vosa)" which many believe refers to their ancestor, which was the text for the sermon on Christmas Day. The second was a gesture chant *(meke)* sung by the elderly ladies of the village while the women of the land danced to entertain their honored guests.

On the day before the Queen of the Land festival (Christmas Eve) the women who were to dance and entertain the honored guests held a *meke* (gesture chant) practice. They began by presenting kava to the "owner" of the main gesture chant they planned to use. The main *meke* sung at the Adi Vanua was chosen because it had been received from the ancestor gods and performed before at another auspicious *soli* in the 1950s when men of the village returned from Ba where they had gone to cut sugar cane to raise money, which they then gave to build the Methodist Church. The *meke* was received in a dream by the father of the ritual head of Nasi, the leader of the *bete* (priest) subdivision of Nasi who was a noted *dau ni vucu* (person who is taught *meke* by ancestor deities, while asleep or in a trance).

The main *meke* moves between the world of the ancestor gods *(vu)* and the occasion of the first performance of the *meke* itself in Drauniivi in the 1950s. The initial segments tell how Tui Bokadrala, an ancestor god, awoke and was given kava by the women, who were asking for the *meke*. He gives it to them, and observes them as they begin to step and sway to it, instructed by him and a lady ancestor, wishing the women good luck as they return to their village. This main *meke* was a part of the process by which, several decades ago, the money made in Ba was brought back to the village and made useful for land purposes, for the building of the village Methodist Church. In the words of the *meke,* and in the process of its creation, the ancestor gods themselves came into the land to celebrate the building of the church.

But on the day before the festival, when they had offered the kava to the "owner" of the main *meke,* the women also sang a short, ending *vucu* (a short segment which is sung only during the practice to invite the ancestor gods and the people and to notify them that the *meke* is being practiced). The *vucu* sung at this practice was a segment of a longer *meke* about Navosavakadua received by a man in Nayaulevu, Tokaimalo many years ago.

> I was visiting on the coast of gold.
> And our land will be split open.
> That they may split it up into different pieces.
> They join together at the coast of Gold.
> The youths are foolish.
> They leave and forget the gestures and verses of the *meke*.
> The fish of the sea twist and change.
> They meet at the point of the land.
> Someone calls "sail ho," here comes a canoe.
> The boat from Rotuma appears.
> My *meke* is swaying very slowly.
> Adi Lebakula [an ancestor goddess] is watching.
> They have left and forgotten the content of my *meke*.
> The sea dries up.
> Our land is shaken up.
> Eee i yaa.

Only this first verse was sung as the ending *vucu* at the practice. Intrigued by the sudden allusion to Navosavakadua, returning from exile in Rotuma ("the boat from Rotuma appears"), after the practice I asked the performers to tell me about the *meke,* and they chanted for me a fuller version. The *meke* continues:

The coast of gold trembles.
I enter into the sticky [?] house.
I jump into the house that is dry with a good roof overhead.
The elders are meeting.
The law giver stands up.
His name is Navosavakadua.
The old laws will be put away.
And we will learn new laws.
Agree to these laws in his name.
He stood up and issued it out.
Leave all things behind.
Join the Viti Kabani.
To sign up for our work.
Authorization is given.
To you who are gathered here.
As your ears hear and your eyes look.
I have said my *meke* already.
My duty is to issue out (the news).
[Chorus:]
Alas, Navosa shoots a gun.
Fires a double mouthed gun.
The bullets spread all over the world.

(*Translated by Vasiti Ritova*)

These last lines are a metaphor for Navosavakadua's laws and prophecies which spread throughout the world. In this twentieth-century *meke*, Navosavakadua endorses Apolosi Nawai's Viti Kabani.

The short segment flashed up like a powerful memory, then vanished in the midst of the Queen of the Land festival. It represents Navosavakadua as he was in the late nineteenth century: a prophet who formed a new ritual polity, who shook the world and overturned it. But, no sooner mentioned, he was gone.[12] Just as the Vatukaloko do not nowadays initiate large-scale rituals to

---

12. I asked the elderly ladies in the village about other *meke*, they said there are none about Navosavakadua that were received by Vatukaloko *dau ni vucu*. No *meke* or any other rituals are performed that are attributed to Navosa, except of course for Christian prayer. Nor do the Vatukaloko cherish any "Tuka" *meke* or invocations, though some were recorded among other Colo peoples by colonial officers early in this century. They learned this *meke* about Navosavakadua at Tokaimalo along with other *meke* taught by a *dau ni vucu* there because the last Tui Vatu was *vasu* (sister's child) to Nayaulevu in Tokaimalo. His widow leads the elderly ladies who sing and play the *meke*, and she chose this segment.

invoke Navosavakadua, so too during the Queen of the Land festival they did not use a *meke* to him as a central motif. Despite Mr. Samalia's flag then waving on the village green, Navosavakadua is no longer the focus of Vatukaloko projects. Instead, when the Vatukaloko invoke him, as in the *vucu* segment of the *meke* practice, it is as a special local, particularly effective, ancestral deity. When he is invoked in the Bible verse quoted in the sermon (John 1:1) he is part of their particular land-Christian articulation.

This is not to say that Navosavakadua may not lead Fijians again someday, toward some more dramatic goal. Given the shock dealt by the 1987 coups to the sometimes tenuous articulations and syntheses through which Fijian systems of authority are constructed, it is possible, though I know of no signs of it, that a Vatukaloko or other Twelve Tribes leader could mobilize an active project that would draw national attention of the sort drawn by Apolosi Nawai. Certainly this was Mr. Samalia's intention, thoroughly unsuccessful. And as Labour Party successes show, Navosa remains a potent historical resource for other would-be leaders who wish to call upon the people of Ra (and north and western Viti Levu more generally).

But there is a sense in which Navosavakadua need not return, since crucial aspects of what he sought to do (though not all of them) have already come to organize the ritual and political lives of the Vatukaloko today. Believing Fiji and the Kauvadra to be the origin of divinity and power in the world, Navosa identified the effective foreign god as an indigenous god. Nowadays the Vatukaloko explain that the world is the way it is, because Navosa predicted and enabled the events that followed him. At Navosa's pilgrimage site, Vale Lebo, inland near Nakorowaiwai, are a series of stone circles. In 1986 Vatukaloko informants said that they are stone pools *(tobu ni vatu)* in which Navosa showed his followers the future.

> There is a *tobu ni wai* (pool of water) near the old village where people met to learn about the future from Navosa. It was like going to the movies or video. There they could see the things that were going to happen in the future. They could see the signs and proofs of the future in that pool. Ships, submarines, everything that has happened, they already saw here. The ancestor [Navosavakadua] would say "this will happen, these things will be in our land." Some others wanted to *tell* their own versions of the story but Navosa *showed* them what would happen in this pool. Nowadays the ancestors are gone, but we their descendants see these things that he predicted. [Did people come to ask specific questions about the future?] No, you ask that kind of question to a different kind of people, such as a seer *(dau rai)*, but he was doing a different kind of work, because he actually did it right in front of the people;

showed them thereby the things they wanted to know to prove to them, because he was not doing the work of humans or of ancestor gods, but rather the work of God.

This story likens Navosavakadua to Christ. He knows he will be betrayed (just as he knows the future of Fiji) but also that his doctrine or truths will eventually rise again. Certainly Christ's life is a model for a claim of ritual authority misunderstood and persecuted by the secular authorities of the time. But while the Vatukaloko clearly articulate Navosavakadua and his fate to Christ, there is a further emphasis, on prediction, that does not simply flow from an adaptation of the Christian story. By predicting the future, Navosa enabled the events to occur. Thus the changes in Fiji's history (generally portrayed as incursions of people and goods) are signs and proofs of his *mana* (power and effectiveness).

In a final example, we can see the way this current, quiescent understanding of Navosa understands his ritual politics and sees the Vatukaloko present as their successful result. It is said that when Jehovah created the world he first made the stone that sits at the summit of the mountain called Uluda (folk etymology: "our heads") in the Kauvadra range. A stone is also identified as the original "Vatukaloko" (rock clock) which is explained through folk etymology as formerly having been named *"vatu ni gauna"* (rock of time), since *"kaloko"* (clock or watch) is a European word. (Clearly the whole etymology developed in the contact period, since it depends on the contrast with the English-derived word *kaloko*.) In the tale of Degei and his two older brothers told above, the ancestors of the Vatukaloko and of the other inland people give the rock to Degei, ancestor of the Bauans. He is to lie upon it, and to protect it. It represents Fiji, and the protection of Degei represents "Bauan" chiefly dominance and governance over Fiji.[13] In Osea Ravai's tale, Navosavakadua manipulates another rock, again signifying Fiji, at the top of Navicomaca mountain to portray the future of Fiji.

> First he stepped on it to sink it down into the soil. Then he rose up and the ground closed to cover it. He told his followers that when the stone rose again, there would be new people and new goods in the land. When it reached a certain height, Fijians would be good and wise and surpass their ancestors. However, when it reached a further height they would forget their customs, government would be greedy, people would live like animals and behave in slatternly ways. And today, the stone stands

13. I have seen the stone. It is surrounded by small fragments of seashells, brought up and left in earlier days. The version I heard told in 1984 elaborates on the version in Jovesa Bavou's book written c. 1918.

at that very level, the author warned his readers. (Summarized from *Nai Lalakai* 21 June 1984, my translation)[14]

Here Navosavakadua, like Jehovah, creates the world to come. As such he has the status of the "maker of the land" *(bulibulivanua)*. He makes "the land, the chiefs, and the rule" (as a Nakubuti informant told me). The creation is accomplished through the power of his word, his prophecies, or through his manipulation of the land itself. These tales implicitly construct Navosavakadua and the people of the land as agents of God's will and authors of their own destiny. They insist on an interpretation of authority and effectiveness in the world in which the past constitutes the present. In both Fijian and colonial-Fijian contexts, these myths can express an authoritative account of that past because they conjoin the nineteenth-century Fijian ascription of originating and constituting authority to ancestral gods of the land and the colonial insistence on "custom" as the foundation of Fijian life. Thus in repeating and elaborating Navosavakadua's miracles the Vatukaloko find the present in their past.

The Vatukaloko World

In conclusion, in the nineteenth century, Navosavakadua, through the power of his *mana,* challenged the European and Bauan claims about the Christian god and claimed all sources of truly effective power to be Fijian. At stake were ritual-political authority and autonomy, based in founding relations by ancestor gods and access to gods of the land. Nowadays, beginning with Jovesa Bavou in 1918, the Vatukaloko can tell the story of their history without reference to Navosavakadua, for they have resolved this conflict over the source of effective power. In Jovesa Bavou's socio-cosmological genealogy, Jehovah is the undisputed agent, the founding ancestor and ultimate source, of relations among gods and peoples today. In the nineteenth century, it was Navosa who claimed these Christian gods as gods of the land in the pivotal ritual-political confrontation. Today, with that aspect of his land-centric project routinized in Vatukaloko land-centric Christianity, Jehovah is now the constituting figure, and Navosavakadua cannot be seen as its revolutionary author. Rather, he is conceived to be, like Christ, an intermediary. When the present-day Vatuka-

14. In later conversations with Osea Ravai, he informed me that the stone was in effect a moral-economic clock for Fijians. Just as Europeans wear watches to order their sleeping, waking, and eating, the stone clock ordered the important epochs of Fiji, he said.

loko historians describe him, they stress that he was "given a task by god." He is no longer a constituting, founding agent. He has been reconstructed as quiescent, within a prior framework constituted by god. "Archaic" forms, such as the *meke,* are embedded in present-day life. They may be used, but they do not energize new projects.

Because Navosavakadua constructed the Christian god as Fijian, the Vatukaloko now conceive their world to have been created by Jehovah. That world includes officials colonial and post-colonial, from Lands Commissioners to Special Branch. The Vatukaloko have come to accept colonial, Christian, and national systems. They received the high chiefs when they visited the province, they accept communion from their circuit's ordained minister, they respond to the District Officer when he tells them to fence the village. They did not deny the authority of the Peace Corps couple who organized the salt project or construct a dispensary in the village in an attempt to combat the seer's popularity as a healer. But simultaneously they seek to envision this larger world of different articulating systems as the working out of their land-centric system. In forms from Jovesa Bavou's book to 1980s compliant quiescence to police inspection, the Vatukaloko have not overtly resisted official claims, but rather have accepted outside authority, *on their own terms.* In a post hoc vision, they live in the world Navosavakadua and the colonial encounter turned on its head, and construct it as continuous with the past.

But have the Vatukaloko simply been transformed from active warrior-allies, creators of their own small but expanding Vatukaloko polity, led by invulnerable war priests and later by Navosavakadua, into disenfranchised peripheral peoples with only "ritual" representations of their past claims? Have the mission and colonial disengagement of the indigenous Fijian political ritual from the structures of national politics made the Vatukaloko into archaic conjurers on the margins of society? Yes, on the one hand, "land" political authority is no more and the Vatukaloko are disenfranchised, while "Bauans" and others have assumed the "political" leadership of the nation of Fiji. But this is not to suggest that because the Vatukaloko continue to assert their ritual authority that they continue a "cult" while the rest of Fiji has become a "modern," "western," or "rational" nation-state.

Throughout Fiji, indigenously and in colonial and post-colonial days, plural articulations of cultural systems and projects have been attempted. Some are more dominant than others, but none has been the inevitable end point of some fixed trajectory. The colonial state had its own ritual forms of authority, commissions, and "Bibles" among them. And in the present day, so does the post-colonial state. Just as the Vatukaloko disenfranchisement is a product of the colonial, Christian, and chiefly syntheses, so too the leaders of the Fijian nation have been created and create their leadership within an articulation of these categories. In the ruling chiefly system, effective leadership is authorized through relations to divinity — to Jehovah, the Christian god, and through a claim that the "way of the land" means respecting chiefs (the early claim of the Coups), or authorizing only Fijian leadership in a multiethnic state (a later result of the Coups). On such bases these leaders of the Fijian state construct, disseminate, and deploy their own cultural visions of relations in Fiji and the world. Quite like the Vatukaloko they have attempted to impose their own seamless socio-cosmological view on Fiji. My point, then, is that the Vatukaloko are in no way unusual in their insistence on a ritual politics to organize their world.

9

CONCLUSION:

DO CULTS EXIST?

DO STATES EXIST?

From Sadiri to Navosavakadua to "Ratu Navosa," from the Twins to Jehovah, from struggles for autonomy in a Fijian ritual-political system to visions of the nation in post-colonial Fiji. This narrative of Navosavakadua and Tuka has been one of turbulent conjunctures and struggles to control the sign in the making of a colonial society. In each case, Fijians, colonizers, and Fiji citizens have worked to routinize, or to delegitimize, visions of polity and order. Such contests can be found in the internal Fijian struggles between major chiefly polities and the hinterland groups, in the contest between Navosavakadua's project and the emerging colonial polity, in the contrast between current Vatukaloko constructions of Fijian Christianity and more orthodox versions, in the making of a new nation through decolonization and constitution and through coups, and in efforts to invoke Navosavakadua's name to create a nation.

If this narrative seeks to show the power of colonized people to articulate and routinize new systems, to make their own history, it also recognizes colonial power in the history of Fiji, and tries to understand both its effects and limits. In this turbulent, uneven, and sometimes painful colonial dialogue, categories and meanings have been made and remade, often, but not always, "from the top down." While it is surely wrong to read Tuka simply as a continuant of indigenous practices, completely encompassing the novel, it is wrong, also, to see Tuka as an incitement in a system of power already constituted from above, taking its shape only from colonial spaces for order and disorder.

Yet it is hard to argue a simple relativist position, to claim that the quiescent Vatukaloko articulation of Navosavakadua as Methodist has the same power, the same authority, the same effectiveness *(mana)* as the dominant, central articulation of Jehovah and colonial authority wielded in the national capital by eastern coastal chiefs. In the 1870s the Vatukaloko people killed Koroi i Latikau, but "sa samu ko Nakorowaiwai" (Nakorowaiwai was destroyed utterly) as Bauan troops and European muskets destroyed their fortified village. In the 1880s Navosavakadua sought to create a new ritual polity, but the agents of the new colonial polity deported him and his Vatukaloko followers. Nowadays the Vatukaloko ask for the return of their land alienated a century ago, and the central authorities have the power to give it. What is the nature of that difference of power? It is not simply force, but authority, legitimacy, effectiveness, the power to routinize and to control. It is the power to designate self as constituted authority and other as cult. But this power is not stable — as Fiji's recent coups have shown. What is its scope and what are its limits? In this conclusion, I want to think more about "cults" and "states."

Do Cults Exist?

Ontologically no, historically yes.[1] If we do not look for intrinsic characteristics linking "cargo cults" and "millenarian movements" — finding that task too much akin to colonial juxtapositions of Tuka, freemasonry, and the Maori Hau Hau — I think we can best understand our common sense of "cult" as unusual, marginal, powerful, and dangerous phenomena by seeing cults as constructed as antitheses by centralizing, organizing orthodoxies, for example, churches, states, colonial states. In Fiji, "Tuka" came into being as criminal disorder in face of the colonial ordering "civilizing" project. Navosavakadua and his people were not disorderly, of course. We can read their motives in an understanding of what they understood and upheld to be the autonomy and authority of people of the land. Nor did Navosavakadua's narrative of power lack coherence, but colonial authorities conceived and treated it as irrational.

The narrative of Tuka as negative tradition and of cults as the opposite of an orthodoxy in the making has many parallels in other colonial societies: the (British) colonial imagination of millenarianism in colonial Malawi and Zambia from 1900 to 1925 analyzed by Fields (1985), sixteenth- and seventeenth-

---

1. I borrow this phrase from Christine Jourdan (in press) who is talking about nations. See the Preface for my general argument concerning the senses in which cults do and do not exist.

century Spanish men making Andean women into witches in an intertwined process of Catholic inquisition and the imposition of colonial state control (Silverblatt 1987). A similar narrative can be written for Europe: the invention of witchcraft through inquisition in the Italian Friuli region in the sixteenth and seventeenth centuries when agrarian fertility rites were turned to satanic inversions of Catholic practice in the church's imagination and in consequence disenchanted in the practitioners' lives as well (Ginzburg 1983, but see also Holmes 1989:160–63), or in England where cunning men and wise women became marginal and dangerous witches with the rise first of the church and then scientific orthodoxies (Thomas 1971).[2] In each case, a "cult" — a marginal, dubious deviant activity — is brought into being in the imagination not of its practitioners (who have other understandings of what they do) but of its inquisitors, the central authorities. In the process of inquiry, criminal codification, or extirpation the new "cult" may be refracted into the practice and categories of the colonized as well.

This narrative of the creation of cults sees "cults" as intrinsically tied to states. To understand cults, we also need to tell the story of the rise of a state, or an institution such as the church, that deploys and depends on centralizing, routinizing technologies. It is above all official, claiming to itself the power of truth. It operates through centralizing and routinizing, and simultaneously marginalizes, criminalizes, charges as deviant all that does not fit its ordering categories. It works not simply through force, but through knowledge and meaning. Hegemonically it constructs the real. No one has told this narrative more convincingly, of course, than Michel Foucault in his accounts of the forms of power of the modern European state.[3]

---

2. From J. P. S. Uberoi comes an ironic recasting of Europe's disenchantment, as positivist cosmological "wrong turn" in 1529 when Ulroth Zwingli debated Martin Luther over the nature of the Eucharist. "Zwingli insisted that in [Christ's] utterance 'This is my body' (Hoc est corpus meum), the existential word 'is' (est) was to be understood, not in a real, literal and corporeal sense, but only in a symbolical, historical or social sense (significat, symbolum est, or figura est).... Dualism or double monism was fixed in the world-view and the life world of the modern age, which was thereby ushered in" (Uberoi 1978:31). In this moment, he argues, Europe came to imagine a separation of the truly real from the symbolic, science from religion. Uberoi is less concerned with the church, academic, and state institutions that routinized the separation; his interest is the consequences for understanding that result when ritual, religion, the symbolic are marginalized as less real: notably the consequence is an inability to understand non-European systems that do not make this same distinction.

3. The overarching point of *Discipline and Punish* is the transformation from "power over death" to "power over life." In his essay "Governmentality" Foucault foregrounds a transformation that is three-part, from sovereignty to disciplinary society to society of government and/through statistics

In general, the anthropological parallel narrative to this widely accepted vision of the trajectory of power, in Europe and in colonial societies, has been to seek to show the agency of the colonized in the face of this (accepted as real) enforced trajectory, from closed to open, magic to scientific, traditional to modern, indigenous to colonized, other to westernized, and so on. This narrative argues that while the cargo cult or millenarian movement may be temporary, it is worthy of respect. In cults and movements are the phenomena in which anthropology has sought out otherness, respected its enchantment, even while posing it as temporary. I can read my own chapters on oracle-priests and people of the land, the insistence on Navosavakadua's ritual-political authority, as such a narrative—though I do not believe that the Vatukaloko will ever be folded into the trajectory of transformation some other scholars assert. But I hope that this is not all that my narrative does. Because here I want to pose some questions about the narrative of the state, the trajectory of power that Foucault and others trace so convincingly.

Is state power so absolute that it utterly defines that which it has marginalized, the criminal, the deviant, the cult? Is the only agency of others the power to incite orthodoxy's own fears? And if we follow the narrative of the power of the European state, the colonial state, the orthodox institution to create cults, are we agreeing with its own (European) image of itself that it is "real" and "political," not "symbolic" and "religious"? Is the state itself disenchanted? If we have wondered whether cults exist, shouldn't we also ask: Do states exist?

Does the State Exist?

What hubris! My real goal here is to consider the colonial state, in a place like Fiji. Does the colonial state exist? I will argue, ontologically, no, historically, yes, but first let us consider the possibilities: the arguments of Taussig following Abrams of ways in which the state does not exist, and Michel Foucault's depiction of technologies of power, seen indeed to exist, and making the uniquely modern European state.

(1991:102). *Discipline and Punish* also contains similar three-stage schemes, e.g., in forms of punishment, from the ceremonial punishment by the sovereign to judicial punishment, still exemplary, to the most subtle era of punishment as coercion, the creation through training of docile bodies (1977:129–31). Two stages or three, the trajectory presumes a history in which others look all too similar to Europe's past.

That which we call the state has its own enchantments, or, according to Taussig (1992), its own sorceries *(maleficium)*. From Philip Abrams (1998 [1977]) and Michael Taussig (1992) comes a powerful argument that The State does not exist. In the face of centuries of argument over definitions, over the intrinsic characteristics of Leviathan, these scholars argue that it does not exist as a positive entity, that it is reified when imagined as a real thing. Rather, it is the form that people, classes, and interests use to figure, and cloak, their agency. As Abrams concludes,

> The State is not the reality which stands behind the mask of political practice. It is itself the mask which prevents our seeing political practice as it is. It is one could almost say, the mind of a mindless world, the purpose of purposeless conditions, the opium of the citizen. There *is* a state-system in Milibands's sense; a palpable nexus of practice and institutional structure centered in government and more or less extensive, unified and dominant in any given society. And its sources, structure and variations can be examined in fairly straight-forward empirical ways. There *is*, too a state-idea, projected, purveyed and variously believed in different societies at different times. And its modes, effects and variations are also susceptible to research. The relationship of the state system and the state-idea to other forms of power should and can be central concerns of political analysis. We are only making difficulties for ourselves in supposing that we have also to study the state — an entity, agent, function or relation over and above the state-system and the state-idea. The state comes into being as a structuration within political practice; it starts its life as an implicit construct; it is then reified — as the *res publica*, the public reification, no less — and acquires an overt symbolic identity progressively divorced from practice as an illusory account of practice. The ideological function is extended to a point where conservatives and radicals alike believe that their practice is not directed at each other but at the state; the world of illusion prevails. The task of the sociologist is to demystify; and in this context that means attending to the senses in which the state does not exist rather than to those in which it does. (1988:82)

The state is real because the state-idea is made real in political practice, including (perhaps *beginning*, some scholars would argue) in colonialism.

For Taussig, the issue is "state fetishism": "the existence and reality of the *political power* of this *fiction*, its powerful insubstantiality" (1992:113). Abrams urges us to demystify the state; Taussig finds interstitial figures such as Jean Genet most powerful in unmasking the fetish, just as he read South Americans who worship the devil in the tin mines to be unmasking a commodity fetishism those who live in capitalism take for granted. Perhaps we could read in Navosavakadua's creative practice an insight into the constructed nature of the "good order under God and the Queen" that Gordon and Thurston so believed in. In his belief that he could make a polity, did he not fabricate, and thus show the constructed nature of the state-system too, countering the colonial establishment of courts, laws, police with his own hierarchy of truth as "He who speaks but once and is effective"? Did he not establish his own "power over life" when, as the story goes, the colonial scissors meant to cut his hair (making docile his body) were unable to do the task? But perhaps, instead, like Gordon and Thurston, Navosavakadua was no demystifying Genet. I think it more likely that he too believed in a form of the state, the ritual polity he sought to found.

The weight of past European scholarship (radical and conservative) before and during the recent deconstructive turn, has of course believed in the state. In this tradition, we could insist that what Abrams calls the state-system ("a palpable nexus of practice and institutional structure centered in government") is the "real" aspect of the state in any society. Empiricists, and those seeking general laws, would prefer this narrative. And so too would those morally angered when terms like "constructions," "fetishes," and the like are used to describe political-economic colonizing processes involving the violence of muskets, handcuffs, and floggings, and the compulsions of plantation labor, land alienation, and the infiltration of commodities into noncapitalist modes of production or systems of exchange. In response we might note that political-economic discourse might have its own orthodoxies and masks for the real. Taussig and others have argued that political-economic analyses of these processes mistakenly take capitalist assumptions as their very ground of analysis (Kelly 1991, 1992, Sahlins 1976; see also Taussig 1989 and Mintz and Wolf 1989).

Less engaged in the debate over whether states exist, a third group of scholars seek simply to examine the processes by which self-described colonial states (whose founders were not always troubled by ontological and epistemological nightmares) have been made. These colonial states are understood in Foucauldian terms. They may even anticipate the European state, and as Barney Cohn has argued, be the site of origin of some of its technologies of power, notably statistics (see Cohn and Dirks 1988). They depend on objectification. The panopticon, Jeremy Bentham's rationalized prison that is Foucault's favorite example of modern penal discipline, looms large as metaphor (and sometimes actual bricks and mortar) in accounts of the making of colonies (see Mitchell 1988 on "colonizing Egypt," but also Kaplan in press [b]). They run on "rituals and routines of rule" (the phrase is Corrigan and Sayer's). They centralize, officialize, codify, count, classify, and chronicle. In domains from schools to medicine to law to the writing of history they monopolize the truth. They work through what Foucault has called "power over life." In the subtle establishment of this hegemony, this colonizers' power to make the true, the real, the natural, and the necessary, the colonized often become hegemonized participants. It is easy to recognize and refuse handcuffs, harder to see the subtle bonds in a sanitation project in Fiji (see Thomas 1990) or a census. (But see also Guha [1989] who argues that India was not hegemonized because the British could not acknowledge the full social presence of the Indians.)

It is very convincing to read Fiji's colonizing as an instance of the making of such a modern state-idea. Indirect rule, the Lands Commissions, and the Native Administration proceeded by means of centralization, codification, classification, the modes of authority establishment intrinsic to making the state seem real. And what of the Fijian response? Did it mirror the colonial rituals and routines? What of the scrap of paper found by Joske, *"na iwiliwili ni koro,"* the list of Tuka villages? Mirror to colonial district lists or censuses? Are the *tobu ni vatu,* the stone circles that Vatukaloko people now say Navosavakadua built to see past, present, and future, a parallel panopticon? (If not for Navosavakadua, then are they understood as such by his descendants, after a century of colonial scrutiny?)

But we are at risk of conceding all agency to colonial power. Paradoxically, to claim that the state does not exist intrinsically can make explanation of the power of its name produce narratives that focus on colonial power to the exclusion of others' agency. And note also that these narratives may depend on a distinction between the premodern and the modern, the colonized and the colonizer. For Mitchell (1988) the colonizers of Egypt herald the modern, for Todorov (1984) Cortez, manipulator of signs, is the first modern man, for Cohn and Dirks (1988) it is the European states and European colonizers who invent civil society, with its dependence on what Foucault calls "power over life." This is Foucault's trajectory, from kingdoms and states where power was ritual, costly, display, paradigmatically the public beheading, "power over death" to the modern state where power is subtle, calculating, and bureaucratized, paradigmatically the panopticon, power over life (Foucault 1977). But as I have noted above there are problems with Foucault's trajectory.

First, it was from a colonial trajectory assuming European temporal difference from others that the concept of cult emerged. Of course Foucault and these other scholars reverse the valence, they do not celebrate the rise of the modern state with its power over life. But like cult theorists celebrating the enchantment and resistance in cults before their agents are inevitably drawn into modernity, they endorse a trajectory that, instead, we ought to question.

Are European states (or European colonial states) the only polities to depend on objectification and power over life? It is tempting to read a transformation in Fijian practice from Sadiri the warrior priest who had the power of invulnerability to the Methodist concern with salvation and immortality. We would see in Cakobau's old kingdom a ritual state working through lavish ritual, display, and cannibal sacrifice, supplanted by Gordon's colonial state depending on despatches, commissions, and deportations. But isn't Hocart correct when he writes of the Fijian chief as the source of life: fertility, increase, of people, land and sea, for which he was held accountable? Isn't there a similarity between the control over knowledge, the claims to truth, made by the Europe state and the Fijian paramount's claim to *mana* (miraculous effectiveness)? *"Mana e dina"* (mana is true) go the words at the end of Fijian kava ceremonies, celebrating and instituting Fijian chiefly power. Were the calculations and predictions of oracle-priests, the rituals of royal sacrifice, land insemination, and redistribution, assuring chiefly control over life and truth, so very different from the censuses, sanitation projects, and administrative and Methodist circuits? Technologies not as impressive, nor as centralizing, perhaps, but nonetheless, power over life.

And were European states and European colonizing states so free of the costly, theatrical ritual of power over death? As Vivekananda once pointed out, who was it who brought extraordinary means of destruction to the colonial world? Who killed Sadiri the oracle priest? Whose guns and fire destroyed Nakorowaiwai? Who wanted to "make an example" of Navosavakadua and the Drauniivi people?

Finally and most important, I think that histories such as Navosavakadua's are far too complex culturally to fit these dichotomies and trajectories. Max Weber wrote of routinization as the tragic and inevitable fate of authentic charisma, when institutionalized religion smooths its own forward passage. Foucault's interest in technologies of making truth and power reverses the image: truth production and maintenance is immanent in the technologies; the routinizing powers do not enervate authentic charisma, but hide their own mana by celebrating their authorities. Foucault sees the reality in the officializer and his method, not the officialized and his charismatic genius. But what this leaves out are what Weber would have called the irreducible value orientations, so crucial to culture. Even if we reject the privilege for the authentic original, if we give up the idea of an untouched indigenous system, is the message reducible to the medium? Are states their technologies? Are all states the same?

Even if we were to concede that there is a difference between modern states and other operations of coercion and suasion, specifically a unique set of technologies of power, and even if we concede that these technologies led their deployers to control of a new and overwhelming sort, the technologies are insufficient to define what the new colonial and post-colonial states will be. They do not all parallel Foucault's modern, bourgeois France. The colonial state and post-colonial state in Fiji was and is not simply capitalist in either land or labor policies. It has never been democratic. It does not run on principles of free market (does anywhere?), nor on formal egalitarianism. It is not a bourgeois state. It is in many ways an aristocratic state.[4] The closest European comparison to the Fijian landholding system, where genealogically defined groups hold bounded lands, are the estates of nobles. But even this comparison is not very close. Fiji is a hybrid state — and not just because the British made it so. Yes, the British wrote selected parts of their past onto the Fijian landscape. But it was not just the British who did the selecting, and Europe was not the only source for imagination of what a polity could be in Fiji.

If we accept Foucault's trajectory, his insistence on two (or three) kinds of power, arranging it in temporal hierarchy, we write narratives in which "state" power, made by those who believe in states, is the most compelling force on the colonial landscape. Yet is this the history of colonial societies? Surely not always and not everywhere. However compelling state power, however useful a technique like census taking, others can create, articulate plural systems and innovate, and can routinize. Navosavakadua's *tobu ni vatu* stone pools were never simply a panopticon. Nor were they only recapitulations of the kava dishes in which older Fijian oracle-priests had seen the past, present, and future. I believe they were both, and more, just as "Navosavakadua" was oracle-priest, Moses, chief justice, and someone powerful and new. And is it not ironic that the property relations as authorized by colonial power are captured in the orthodox Fijian imagination as a Bible? Could Mr. Samalia's vision of Navosa as avatar someday be routinized? Or, to take a more probable example, if the Labour Party survives the coups into the next few decades, might not Navosavakadua's story become a founding trope to rival, and remake, Cession?

---

4. Even when commoner Brigadier General Rabuka became prime minister in 1992 aristocracy remained crucial; the Great Council of Chiefs had legitimized his coups and authorized the new post-coups constitution of the Republic of Fiji.

Of course predicting anything about the future of the state and the nation in Fiji is now very difficult, in the wake of the four or five major breaks in sovereignty (decolonization and new constitution at independence, coup, proposed government of national unity, second coup, second constitution) that we have seen since 1970. I would rather end with a final look at the articulation and routinization of difference by and for the Vatukaloko themselves. Jovesa Bavou's private book, and the kindred Vatukaloko techniques for holding and using knowledge about their ritual politics and ancestor, were no threat (perhaps by design) to the routinizing, standardizing center, yet they maintained Vatukaloko difference in the face of those standardizing practices. And it takes little risk to predict that Vatukaloko history-making will persist through multiple future imaginings and reorderings of the sovereign state in the Fiji islands.

BIBLIOGRAPHY

Abrams, Philip. 1988 [1977]. "Notes on the Difficulty of Studying the State." *Journal of Historical Sociology.* 1 (1): 58–89.
Asad, Talal. 1973. "Two European Images of Non-European Rule." In *Anthropology and the Colonial Encounter,* ed. Talal Asad, pp. 103–18. London: Ithaca Press.
Brewster, Adolph B. (previously A. Brewster Joske). n.d.a. "Chronicles of Noemalu." Manuscript. Photocopy in National Archives of Fiji, Suva.
———. n.d.b. Papers. Fiji Museum, Suva.
———. 1891. "Superstition in Fiji." *The Australasian.* 17 October 1891. Sydney.
———. 1922. *The Hill Tribes of Fiji.* London: Seeley, Service and Co., Ltd. Reprinted 1967, New York: Johnson Reprint Corporation.
Burridge, Kenelm. 1969. *New Heaven, New Earth.* Oxford: Basil Blackwell.
Calvert, Rev. James. 1983. *Fiji and the Fijians,* vol. 2, *Mission History.* Suva: Fiji Museum. Originally published 1858.
Capell, A. 1973. *A New Fijian Dictionary.* Suva: Government Printer.
Cato, A. C. 1947. "A New Religious Cult in Fiji." *Oceania* 18 (1): 146–56.
Clammer, John. 1975. "Colonialism and the Perception of Tradition in Fiji." In *Anthropology and the Colonial Encounter,* ed. Talal Asad, pp. 199–220. London: Ithaca Press.
Clifford, James, and George E. Marcus, eds. 1986. *Writing Culture: Poetics and Politics of Ethnography.* Berkeley: University of California Press.
Clunie, Fergus. 1977. "Fijian Weapons and Warfare." Suva: Fiji Museum Bulletin 2.
Cohn, Bernard. 1983. "Representing Authority in Victorian India." In *The Invention of*

Tradition, ed. Eric Hobsbawm and Terrence Ranger, pp. 165–210. Cambridge: Cambridge University Press.

———. 1987. *An Anthropologist among the Historians and Other Essays.* Delhi: Oxford University Press.

Cohn, Bernard S., and Nicholas B. Dirks. 1988. "Beyond the Fringe: The Nation State, Colonialism and the Technologies of Power." *Journal of Historical Sociology* 1 (2): 224–29.

Comaroff, Jean. 1985. *Body of Power, Spirit of Resistance.* Chicago: University of Chicago Press.

Corrigan, Philip, and Derek Sayer. n.d. "From 'The Body Politic' to 'The National Interest': English State Formation in Comparative and Historical Perspective. An Argument concerning 'Politically Organized Subjection.'" Manuscript.

———. 1985. *The Great Arch: English State Formation as Cultural Revolution.* Oxford: Basil Blackwell.

Counts, David, and Dorothy Counts. 1976. "Apprehension in the Backwaters." *Oceania* 46 (4): 283–305.

Deering, J. W. 1962. "The Seaqaqa War." *Transactions of the Fiji Society* 9:113–19. Issued 1968.

De Marzan, Pere Jean. 1907–1913 Papers. Manuscripts in Catholic Archives, Suva. See also Thomas (1987).

Derrick, R. A. 1950. *A History of Fiji.* Suva: Government Press.

Fabian, Johannes. 1979. "The Anthropology of Religious Movements: From Explanation to Interpretation." *Social Research* 46:4–25.

Fields, Karen E. 1985. *Revival and Rebellion in Colonial Central Africa.* Princeton: Princeton University Press.

Fison, Rev. Lorimer. 1867. "From Another of Our Missionaries in Fiji." *Wesleyan Missionary Notices* 1(38): 599–600. Tippett Reference Collection, St. Marks Library, Canberra.

Foucault, Michel. 1977. *Discipline and Punish: The Birth of the Prison.* London: Penguin Books.

———. 1991. "Governmentality." In *The Foucault Effect: Studies in Governmentality,* ed. Graham Burchell, Colin Gordon, and Peter Miller, pp. 87–104. Chicago: University of Chicago Press.

France, Peter. 1966. "The Kaunitoni Migration: Notes on the Generation of a Fijian Tradition." *Journal of Pacific History* 1:107–13.

———. 1969. *The Charter of the Land: Custom and Colonization in Fiji.* Melbourne: Oxford University Press.

Geertz, Clifford. 1973. "Thick Description: Toward an Interpretive Theory of Culture." In Clifford Geertz *The Interpretation of Cultures,* pp. 3–30. NY: Basic Books.

Gillion, K. L. 1962. *Fiji's Indian Migrants.* Melbourne: Oxford University Press.

———. 1977. *The Fiji Indians: Challenge to European Dominance 1920–1946.* Canberra: Australian National University.

Ginzburg, Carlo. 1983. *Night Battles: Witchcraft and Agrarian Cults in the Sixteenth and Seventeenth Centuries.* New York: Penguin.

Gordon, Sir Arthur Hamilton (later Lord Stanmore). 1879a. *Letters and Notes Written during the Disturbances in the Highlands (Known as the "Devil Country") of Viti Levu, Fiji, 1876,* vols. 1 and 2. Edinburgh: Privately printed by R. and R. Clark. Newberry Library, Chicago.

———. 1879b. *Paper on the System of Taxation in Force in Fiji: Read before the Royal Colonial Institute 18 March, 1879.* London: Harrison and Sons. Newberry Library, Chicago.

Guha, Ranajit, ed. 1982. *Subaltern Studies I: Writings on South Asian History and Society.* Delhi: Oxford University Press.

———. 1989. "Dominance without Hegemony and Its Historiography." In *Subaltern Studies Writings on South Asian History and Society,* ed. Ranajit Guha, pp. 210–309. Delhi: Oxford University Press.

Hobsbawm, Eric, and Terence Ranger. 1983. *The Invention of Tradition.* Cambridge: Cambridge University Press.

Hocart, A. M. n.d.a. "The Heart of Fiji." Manuscript in the Turnbull Library, Wellington. Microfilm in Regenstein Library, University of Chicago.

———. n.d.b. "Field Notes." Manuscript. Microfilm in Regenstein Library, University of Chicago.

———. 1912. "On the Meaning of Kalou and the Origin of Fijian Temples." *Journal of the Royal Anthropological Institute of Great Britain and Ireland* 42: 437–39.

———. 1929. "Lau Islands, Fiji." *Bernice P. Bishop Museum Bulletin* 62. Honolulu: Bishop Museum.

———. 1950. *Caste.* New York: Russell and Russell.

———. 1969. *Kingship.* Oxford: Oxford University Press. Reissue of 1927 edition.

———. 1970. *Kings and Councillors.* Chicago: University of Chicago Press. Originally published 1936.

Holmes, Douglas. 1989. *Cultural Disenchantments: Worker Peasantries in Northeast Italy.* Princeton: Princeton University Press.

Hooper, Anthony, and Judith Huntsman, eds. 1985. "Transformations of Polynesian Culture." *Polynesian Society Memoir,* No. 45. Auckland: Polynesian Society.

Howard, Michael C. 1991. *Fiji: Race and Politics in an Island State.* Vancouver: University of British Columbia Press.

Jourdain, Christine. In press. "Stepping Stones to National Consciousness: the Solomon Islands Case." In *Nation-Making in Postcolonial Melanesia.* Robert J. Foster, ed. Ann Arbor: University of Michigan Press.

Kaplan, Martha. 1988. "Land and Sea and the New White Men: A Reconsideration of the Fijian Tuka Movement." Ph.D. dissertation, Department of Anthropology, University of Chicago.

———. 1989a. "Luveniwai as the British Saw It: Constructions of Custom and Disorder in Colonial Fiji." *Ethnohistory* 36 (4): 349–71.

———. 1989b. "The Dangerous and Disaffected Native in Fiji: British Colonial Constructions of the Tuka Movement." *Social Analysis* 26:20–43.

———. 1990. "Christianity, People of the Land, and Chiefs in Fiji." In *Christianity in Oceania: Ethnographic Perspectives*. ASAO Monograph No. 12, ed. John Barker, pp. 7–147. Lanham, MD: University Press of America.

———. In press(a). "Blood on the Grass and Dogs will Speak: Ritual Politics and the Nation in Fiji." Forthcoming in *Nation-Making in Postcolonial Melanesia*, Robert J. Foster, ed. Ann Arbor: University of Michigan Press.

———. In press(b). "Panopticon in Poona." *Cultural Anthropology*, 10 (1): 85–98.

Kaplan, Martha, and John D. Kelly. 1994. "Rethinking Resistance: Dialogics of Disaffection in Colonial Fiji." *American Ethnologist* 21 (1): 123–51.

Kaplan, Martha, and Mara Rosenthal. 1993. "Battlements, Temples and the Landscape of *Tuka:* The Archaeological Record of a Cultural Transformation in 19th Century Fiji." *Journal of the Polynesian Society* 102 (2): 121–45.

Keesing, Roger M. 1988. Melanesian Pidgin and the Oceanic Substrate. Stanford, CA: Stanford University Press.

Kelly, John D. 1988a. "From Holi to Diwali in Fiji: An Essay on Ritual and History." *Man* (n.s.) 23:40–55.

———. 1988b. "Fiji Indians and Political Discourse in Fiji: From the Pacific Romance to the Coups." *Journal of Historical Sociology* 1 (4): 399–422.

———. 1988c. "Bhakti and the Spirit of Capitalism in Fiji." Ph.D. dissertation, University of Chicago.

———. 1991. *A Politics of Virtue: Hinduism, Sexuality and Counter-Colonial Discourse in Fiji*. Chicago: University of Chicago Press.

———. 1992. "Fiji Indians and 'Commoditization of Labor.'" *American Ethnologist* 19:97–120.

Lal, Brij V. 1988. *Power and Prejudice: The Making of the Fiji Crisis*. Wellington: New Zealand Institute of International Affairs.

———. 1992. *Broken Waves: A History of the Fiji Islands in the Twentieth Century*. Honolulu: University of Hawaii Press.

Lan, David. 1985. *Guns and Rain: Guerrillas and Spirit Mediums in Zimbabwe*. Berkeley: University of California Press.

Lawry, Rev. Walter. 1850. *Friendly and Feejee Islands*. London: Charles Gilpin.

Legge, J. D. 1958. *Britain in Fiji, 1858–1880*. London: Macmillan & Co., Ltd.

Lester, R. H. 1941. "Magico-Religious Secret Societies of Viti Levu, Fiji." *Transactions of the Fiji Society* 2: 117–134. Issued December 1953.

Linnekin, Jocelyn. 1983. "Defining Traditions: Variations on the Hawaiian Identity." *American Ethnologist* 10:241–52.

Lyth, Rev. R. B. n.d. Papers, including Voyaging Journal c. 1849. Manuscript in Mitchell Library, Sydney. Microfilm BV112 reel 3: 1008, Regenstein Library, University of Chicago.

Macnaught, Timothy. 1971. "The Subjugation of the Hill Tribes of Fiji." B.A. Honours thesis, Macquarie University.

———. 1979. "Apolosi R. Nawai: The Man from Ra." In *More Pacific Islands Portraits,* ed. Deryck Scarr, pp. 173–93. Canberra: Australian National University Press.

———. 1982. *The Fijian Colonial Experience: A Study of the Neotraditional Order under British Colonial Rule prior to World War II.* Pacific Research Monograph 7 Canberra: Australian National University.

McDowell, Nancy. 1988. "A Note on Cargo Cults and Cultural Constructions of Change." *Pacific Studies* 11 (2): 121–34.

Mintz, Sidney, and Eric Wolf. 1989. "Reply to Michael Taussig." *Critique of Anthropology* 9 (1): 25–31.

Mitchell, Timothy. 1988. *Colonising Egypt.* Berkeley: University of California Press.

Nayacakalou, R. R. 1975. *Leadership in Fiji.* Melbourne: Oxford University Press.

Quain, Buell. 1948. *Fijian Society.* Chicago: University of Chicago Press.

Ritova, Vasiti. 1993. "Vatukaloko Crowns Its King." *Daily Post,* Suva. 16 October 1993.

Rokowaqa, Epeli. 1935. *Ai Tukutuku kei Viti.* National Archives of Fiji, Suva.

Routledge, David. 1985. *Matanitu: The Struggle for Power in Early Fiji.* Suva: University of the South Pacific.

Rutz, Henry J. 1987. "Capitalizing on Culture: Moral Ironies in Urban Fiji." *Comparative Studies in Society and History* 29 (3): 533–57.

Sahlins, Marshall. 1972. *Stone Age Economics.* Chicago: Aldine-Atherton.

———. 1976. *Culture and Practical Reason.* Chicago: University of Chicago Press.

———. 1981. *Historical Metaphors and Mythical Realities: Structure in the Early History of the Sandwich Islands Kingdom.* ASAO Special Publication 1. Ann Arbor: University of Michigan Press.

———. 1985. *Islands of History.* Chicago: University of Chicago Press.

———. 1988. "Cosmologies of Capitalism: The Trans-Pacific Sector of 'The World System.'" *Proceedings of the British Academy* 74: 1–51.

———. 1992. *Historical Ethnography.* Vol. 1 of Patrick V. Kirch and Marshall Sahlins, *Anahulu: The Anthropology of History in the Kingdom of Hawaii.* Chicago: University of Chicago Press.

Said, Edward. 1978. *Orientalism.* New York: Vintage Books.

Sayes, Shelley Ann. 1984. "The Paths of the Land: Early Political Hierarchies in Cakaudrove, Fiji." *Journal of Pacific History* 19:3–20.

Scarr, Deryck. 1970. "A Roko Tui for Lomaiviti: The Question of Legitimacy in the Fijian Administration, 1874–1900." *Journal of Pacific History* 7:3–31.

———. 1980. *Viceroy of the Pacific: The Majesty of Colour, A Life of Sir John Bates Thurston*. Canberra: Australian National University.

———. 1984. *A Short History of Fiji*. Sydney: George Allen and Unwin.

Scott, James. 1990. *Domination and the Arts of Resistance*. New Haven: Yale University Press.

Silverblatt, Irene. 1987. *Moon, Sun, and Witches: Gender Ideologies and Class in Inca and Colonial Peru*. Princeton: Princeton University Press.

Smythe, S. M. 1864. *Ten Months in the Fiji Islands: With an Introduction and Appendix by Col. W. J. Smythe*. Oxford: Henry and Parker.

Stoler, Ann L. 1989. "Making Empire Respectable: The Politics of Race and Sexual Morality in 20th Century Colonial Cultures." *American Ethnologist* 16 (4): 634–60.

Sukuna, Ratu Sir Lala. 1983. *Fiji: The Three-legged Stool*, ed. Deryck Scarr. London: Macmillan Education.

Sutherland, William. 1910. "The Tuka Religion." *Transactions of the Fiji Society*. Suva: Fiji Society. Photocopy at National Archives of Fiji.

Taussig, M. 1980. *The Devil and Commodity Fetishisms in South America*. Chapel Hill: University of North Carolina Press.

———. 1987. *Shamanism, Colonialism, and the Wild Man: A Study in Terror and Healing*. Chicago: University of Chicago Press.

———. 1989. "History as Commodity: In Some Recent American (Anthropological) Literature." *Critique of Anthropology* 9 (1): 7–23.

———. 1992. "Maleficium: State Fetishism." In *The Nervous System*, ed. Michael Taussig, pp. 111–41. New York: Routledge.

Thomas, Keith. 1971. *Religion and the Decline of Magic*. New York: Charles Scribner's Sons.

Thomas, Nicholas, trans. 1987. Jean de Marzan, *Customs and Beliefs in Upland Viti Levu: Papers from Anthropos 1907–1913*. Domodomo: Bulletin of the Fiji Museum, pp. 28–62.

———. 1988. *Planets around the Sun: Contradictions and Dynamics of the Fijian Matanitu*. Oceania Monograph 31. Sydney: University of Sydney.

———. 1990. "Sanitation and Seeing." *Comparative Studies in Society and History* 32:149–70.

———. 1991. *Entangled Objects: Exchange, Material Culture, and Colonialism in the Pacific*. Cambridge, Mass.: Harvard University Press.

Thompson, E. P. 1963. *The Making of the English Working Class*. NY: Random House.

Thompson, Laura. 1940. *Southern Lau: An Ethnography*. Bernice P. Bishop Museum Bulletin 232. Honolulu: Bishop Museum.

Thomson, B. 1895. "The Kalou Vu (Ancestor Gods) of the Fijians." *Journal of the Royal Anthropological Institute* 24:340–59.

Todorov, Tzvetan. 1984. *The Conquest of America: The Question of the Other*. New York: Harper and Row.

Toren, Christina. 1988. "Making the Present, Revealing the Past: The Mutability and Continuity of Tradition as Process." *Man* (n.s.) 23 (4): 696–717.
Uberoi, J. P. S. 1978. *Science and Culture*. Delhi: Oxford University Press.
Valeri, Valerio. 1985. *Kingship and Sacrifice: Ritual and Sacrifice in Ancient Hawaii*. Chicago: University of Chicago Press.
Waterhouse, Rev. Joseph. 1868. *The King and People of Fiji*. London: Wesleyan Conference.
Weber, Max. 1978. *Economy and Society*. Berkeley: University of California Press.
Williams, Francis E. 1977. *"The Vailala Madness" and Other Essays*. Ed. Eric Schwimmer. Honolulu: University Press of Hawaii.
Williams, Rev. Thomas. 1858. *Fiji and the Fijians,* vol. 2, *The Islands and Their Inhabitants*. Suva: Fiji Museum. Reprinted 1982.
Wolf, Eric. 1982. *Europe and the People without History*. Berkeley: University of California Press.
Worsley, Peter. 1968. *The Trumpet Shall Sound*. New York: Schocken Books.
Wright, Georgius. 1901. "Fiji in the Early Seventies." *Transactions of the Fiji Society*. Issued in 1916, pp. 17–43. Suva: The Fiji Society. Photocopy at National Archives of Fiji.

INDEX

Abrams, Philip, 204, 205
Adi Sovanatabua, 152, 155, 164
Agency, 1, 13, 15, 91, 121, 179, 207; of colonized, 204; of states, 204. *See also* Colonial power
Alliance Government, 167
Alliance Party, 169, 170, 187
Alternative government, 133
Ancestor gods (*kalou vu*), 49, 109, 140; and church building, 194; as devils, 106; visits from, 150
Apolosi Nawai, 129, 133–39, 176, 181, 195. *See also* Viti Kabani
Articulations, 98, 100, 121–23, 133, 190n; of authority in contemporary Fiji, 196; defined, 15–16, 176; of Fiji's orthodoxies, 159; in Fijian postcolonial dialogue, 174; Fijian-Christian chiefly, 173, 300; land-Christian, 196; plural, 199; unroutinized, 176; Vatukaloko, 184
Asad, Talal, 13, 16
Assemblies of God, 157n

Autochthony, 28, 111, 190

Back-sliding, 128
Baker, Thomas, 42, 79
Bati (warrior allies), 26, 36, 186
Bau, 19, 25–26, 39–41, 103, 150–51, 154; on map, xii–xiii. *See also* Cakobau
Bavadra, Timoci, 188–89, 189n
Bavou, Jovesa, 102, 133, 145, 148, 171, 181, 193, 197; book of, 149–59
Beche de mer, 39, 77n
Bentham, Jeremy, 206
Bete (priests), 23, 26, 32, 47, 109–10, 112; defined 49–50
Bible, 174, 192–93; Fijian, 140, 144, 147, 191
Biblical sites, 156
Blackbirding (labor trade), 73
Bobuco, 33n, 118–21, 132, 141, 157; on map, 20
Body disciplines, 115
Body politic, British notions of, 109

INDEX

Brewster, A. B., 3n. *See also* Joske
Bulibulivanua, 29–30, 145–51; in genealogy, 152
Buli (local district official), 84; and Tuka, 119
Bure kalou (temple), 46–49, 67, 87, 89, 112, 117
Burness, T. F., 23, 44, 53, 131
Burridge, Kenelm, xi–xii, 136n

Cakobau, 3, 22, 31, 54, 71, 74, 84, 105, 109, 156; conversion, 75; government of, 22, 38, 40–43, 93n, 208. *See also* Bau
Cakobau, George, 164
Cannibalism: Navosavakadua and, 114–15; rumors of, 135; as sacrifice, 76n, 80
Capitalism: counter-colonial, 136; and the Vatukaloko, 162, 189–91
Carew, Walter S., 63–66, 80, 103, 118, 120, 190; obsession with Na Bisiki, 84
Cargo cults, xi–xiv, 1n, 2, 96, 202–204. *See also* Cult
Catholics, 87, 96, 120, 141
Cato, A. C., 131
Census, 43
Cession, 45, 55, 70, 76, 105, 140, 209
Charisma, 16n, 208
Chiefdom (*vanua*), 24–26
Chiefly centrism 116
Chiefs (*turaga*), 26–28, 49, 104, 108; in colonial imagination, xii, 77; and colonial transformations, 124, 140; and goods, 137. *See also* Great Council of Chiefs
Christ. *See* Jesus
Christianity, xii, 4, 11, 39–45, 62, 75–76, 81, 141; contesting views of, 173–75; conversion between denominations, 157n; conversion to, 44–45, 76, 105, 140; Fijian, 189–91; land-centric, 193; routinized, 76, 139–44. *See also* Lotu, Methodism, Missionaries
Christmas, 192
Churches, Vatukaloko building of, 125, 181, 194
Clifford, James, 2, 14
Cohn, Bernard, xi, 206
Colonial anxieties, incitement of, 113
Colonial boundaries, 54–55, 89, 149; become customary 187; map of, xiii
Colonial capitalism, 138
Colonial constructions: of loyal Christian Fijians, 75–78; of Navosavakadua, 50; of rebellious inland people, 43–45; of "Tuka" 62–97
Colonial dialogue, 201
Colonial history, 1–3, 12–16
Colonial power, 2, 15, 158, 199, 201, 207. *See also* Agency
Colonial project, xiv, 61, 72, 109; heterogeneity of, 70
Colonial reification: of cults, xii–xiv, 69; of Fijian social groups 24
Colonial Secretary's Office, 5n, 133n, 142n
Colonial state, 204–210; forms of ritual authority, 199
Colonial Sugar Refining Co., 138, 146
Commissions, 144
Confederations (*matanitu*), 24–26
Confidential files, 133n. *See also* Colonial Secretary's Office
Conversion. *See* Christianity
Corrigan, Philip and Derek Sayer, 72, 206
Cosmology, 159; of Navosavakadua, 100; of Samalia, 166
Cotton, 38
Coups, 11, 158, 188, 210; predictions of, 164
Cult, xi–xiv, 1n, 18, 161, 202–204, 207. *See also* Cargo Cult

Cultural difference, 12, 15
Cultural change, 177
Curing. *See* Healing
Custom: arbiters of, 86; codification of, 140, 146–147. *See also* Negative tradition; Vakavanua

Dead, controversy over treatment of, 127–28. *See also* Resurrection
Deed of Cession. *See* Cession
Degei, 30, 69, 79, 145, 151, 154, 184, 197; and Indo-Fijians, 190n; and Jehovah, 105, 190n; narratives of, 100–103
DeMarzan, Jean, 50
Democracy, 209
Deportation, 63, 85, 117, 188n
Development, 139, 190n
Disaffection, 60, 70, 81–92; 1887 ordinance against, 66, 85; as negative tradition, 78, 96
Disorder, projection of, 93, 96, 135–36, 143, 202
District Commissioners, 133
Divine kingship. *See* Chiefs
Divine power: in Fijian imagination, 140; perspectives on, 158
Drauniivi village, xi, 5, 63, 67, 161, 167, 169, 187n; arrests of people of, 6, 24; on map, xii, 20, 21, 180; in the 1980s, 180; rebuilding of, 29, 131–32, 156; as research site, xiv–xv
Drauniivi Public School, 182
Dugamoi (or Dukumoi). *See* Navosavakadua

Enchantment, 208
European Stipendiary Magistrates, 133

Fields, Karen, 202

Fiji: concept of, 156; as nation, 164; map of, xii
Fiji Company. *See* Viti Kabani
Fiji Girmit Association, 160, 167
Fiji Indians. *See* Indo-Fijians
Fiji Labour Party, 170, 188
Fiji Pine Station, 182
Fiji Times, 160, 162n, 168
Fijian Administration, 187
Fijian Nationalist Party, 188
Fijian social groups, 24–25
Fison, Lorimer, 50–51, 60, 88, 108, 109
Flags, 15, 125, 133, 139, 161–69, 175, 180
Flogging, 67, 88
Foreigners (*vulagi*): chiefs as, 26; as heathen, 190; twins as, 102
Foucault, Michel, 2, 13, 203–204, 207–208
France, Peter, 71, 145
Freemasonry, 91, 96

Ganilau, Penaia, 170
Genealogies, 150–55
Generalized reciprocity, 136, 189. *See also* Loloma, Soli
Germans: and Apolosi, 134; sympathizers 95, 143. *See also* Hitler
Ginzburg, Carlo, 78, 203
Gods. *See* Degei, Jehovah, Jesus, Kauvadra, Krishna, Lakshmi, Twins
Gordon, Arthur (Governor), 62, 71, 73, 77, 79, 132n, 136, 206, 208; background, 73; on Na Bisiki, 84; vision of social evolution, 73
Gramsci, Antonio, 2, 13
Great Council of Chiefs, 52, 56, 59n, 135, 142, 209n
Guha, Ranajit, 13, 207

Handcuffs, 83
Healing, 107n, 167, 179, 182

Heathen, as classification, 41, 43, 90, 174, 190
Hierarchy: British, 70–74; and civilizability, 76–78, 93; Fijian, 26–27; lack of in Ra, 83
Hill people, stereotypes of, 41–43, 79
Hitler, 11, 143, 163, 166
Hobsbawn, Eric and Terence Ranger, 78
Hocart, Arthur Maurice, 25, 28, 48, 107, 108, 142n, 208
Houses, named, 186

Immortality, 91, 106–12, 208. *See also* Invulnerability; Resurrection
Im Thurn, Everard, 132, 132n
Incitement, 204; of colonial anxiety 113, 135; of fear among Vatukaloko, 127
Indirect rule, 62–97, 207. *See also* Gordon, Arthur
Indo-Fijians, 3n, 11, 124, 132, 137, 139, 147, 159, 160–61, 162; and Alliance Party, 165; and caste, 74; and Drauniivi village, 182, 188; "free," 144n; religions of, 11; in Vatukaloko imagination, 170
Inspections, 132
Installation ceremonies, 27, 140, 186
Invention of tradition, 71, 78
Invulnerability, 106–12, 208; rituals of, 49–50, 60. *See also* Immortality
Isikeli, of Viwa, 39–41, 54–57, 89
Itaukei. *See* People of the Land

Jehovah, 61, 143, 198; and Apolosi Nawai, 133, 138; in Bavou's book, 150–59, 186–87; as Fijian God, 10, 102–106, 131n; rejection of, 173n. *See also* Christianity
Jehovah's Witnesses, 141
Jesus: as Fijian God, 10, 102–106, 131n; like Apolosi, 138; and loloma, 189–191; as Navosavakadua, 163, 197
John 1:1, 192–93

Joske, A. B. (aka A. B. Brewster), 3, 3n, 10, 63, 66, 88, 92, 94, 103, 106, 118, 131

Kadavu, 5, 68, 93, 124, 131, 155; on map, xii
Kai colo, 42–43, 76
Kalou rere, 46–53, 56–62, 68, 82, 88, 95, 99, 101, 107n, 108, 110. *See also Luve ni wai*
Kalou vu. *See* Ancestor Gods
Kaplan, Martha: goes to Drauniivi, 162; in Drauniivi, 181
Kauvadra, 3, 100–11, 141, 155–56; 174; Biblical sites in, 106, 141, 186–87; gods of, 100–11, 142, 150–56, 186; on map, xii, xiii, 21. *See also* Adi Sovanatabua, Degei, Twins
Kava (*yaqona*), 47, 49, 65, 110, 116, 168, 188, 192, 193, 208; changing use of, 107
Kelly, John, 206
Koroi i Latikau, 19, 24, 27, 45
Korowaiwai, 19–45, 49, 146, 183
Krishna, 11, 162–67

Labor recruiting, 19, 40–43
Labour Party, 176, 188–89
Labour Government, 11
Lakshmi, 164
Lala (work levy), 127–30, 137
Land-centric polity, 111–16
Land policy. *See* Native Land Commission
Leba (virgin women attending Navosa), 65, 87, 111, 113, 119
Lewa (rule), 27
Lewanavanua, 29–30, 145–51; in genealogy, 152
Linnekin, Jocelyn, 78
Little War, 80–83
Loloma (kindly love), 137, 162, 175; defined, 189–91
Lotu (religion), 44–45, 75–76, 90

Luve ni wai, 46–53, 56–62, 68, 126, 132, 134, 142; charges of, 128; 1887 ordinance against, 85; prosecutions of, 95. *See also Kalou rere*
Lyth, R. B., 37, 79

Macnaught, Timothy, 135
Madraiwiwi, Joni, 105, 125, 188n
Mamaqa, Taivesi. *See* Taivesi Mamaqa
Mana, 10, 202; of Apolosi, 136–38; European, 105; of Navosavakadua, 52–53, 57, 106–11, 175, 196–98. *See also* Miracles
Maori Hau Hau, 96
Mara, Kamisese, 9, 169–70
Marcus, George, 2, 14
Marie Louise (ship), 22
Marx, Karl, 138
Matana, Maciu, 21
Matanitu, 90. *See also* Confederations
Mataqali: defined, 25; as landholding unit, 144; of Vatukaloko, 29, 151–55, 180–82. *See also* Nasi, Nakubuti, Nasaro, Wakalou
Mats, 192
Maxwell, G. V., 144, 147, 150
McDowell, Nancy, xiii
Measles epidemic, 45
Meke (gesture chant), 192–96
Methodism, 74, 141; in Drauniivi, 156–57; as established church, 75. *See also* Christianity
Military coups. *See* Coups
Millenarian movements. *See* Cult; Cargo Cult
Mintz, Sidney, 206
Minute papers. *See* Colonial Secretary's Office
Miracles, 8, 10, 48, 57, 98, 108, 114, 115, 172
Missionaries, 72–79; and colonial project, 109; as deceitful, 101; on eternal life, 109; Roman Catholic, 93; Wesleyan Methodist, 39–40
Mitchell, Charles, 66
Modernity, 207
Monckton, 133–35
Money: Vatukaloko and, 162, 189–90; and sacrifice, 137
Moses, 60, 99, 111
Mudu, 82–83
Muslims, 11
Mystification, 138

Na Bisiki, 81–84, 90
Nabuya, 157n; on map, 21
Nadrau, 33n, 141; on map, 20
Naereere, 34–37
Nai Lalakai, xv, 115, 158, 171, 174
Naivalulevu, 38, 125, 129; in genealogy, 34
Nakorowaiai, 7, 19–48, 79, 146; on map, 21
Nakubuti, 29–34, 129, 148, 154–55, 181; on map, 180
Na Mata, 125, 156, 171
Nanukuloa, 125
Narratives, 12–18, 160–77
Narratography, 15
Nasaro, 181; on map, 180
Nasi, 29–34, 48, 129, 148, 154, 181; on map, 180
Nasoqo, 33, 64, 118–21, 146, 186; on map, 20
National Archives of Fiji, xvi
National Federation Party, 188
Nation, narratives of, 164, 169, 176
Native Administration, 71, 78, 123, 207
Native Lands Commission, 7, 33, 36, 71, 123, 140, 144–49, 181, 184, 191, 207; access to records of, 147; records as Bible, 171
Native Lands Trust Board, archives of, xvi

Navosavakadua: among the Vatukaloko, 178–99; arrests of, 6, 58; attitudes toward, 87; as avatar, 162; as bulibulivanua, 10, 198; as chief, 171; as Christ, 175, 197; as Christian, 172–75; colonial comments on, 50; cosmology, 100; as countercolonial, 174; dangerous and disaffected native, 62–97; death of, 1897, 68; as Dugamoi (or Dukumoi), 4, 7–8, 47; flag of, 11; founds ritual polity, 98, 110; on future as return, 111; genealogies of, 47, 50; as Hitler, Krishna, 163; invocations of, in 1990, 176; and land-centric ritual policy, 61; as local ancestral deity, 196; as martyr, 119; and Na Bisiki, 90; narratives of, xvi, 6–11; in 1980s, 170; as oracle priest (*bete*), 10; priest of the land, 46–61; not like Sadiri or Saro Saro, 60; proclamation of return, 160; prophesies of, 98, 111, 196; return of, 163, 172, 176, 178; routinized in Vatukaloko cosmology, 167, 176; successors to, 117; "of Tuka Movement fame," xi; Vatukaloko narratives of, 175, 198; as warrior priest, 59
Negative tradition, 78, 85
New Guinea, xiv, 1n

Panopticon, 206–207
Peace Corps, 182, 199; and Mr. Carew, 190n
People of the land (*itaukei*), xv, 19, 26–31, 78, 96, 104, 124, 133–45, 187; as commoners, 74
Pigs, white, 69, 111, 114
Plantations, 39, 41
Planters. *See* White settlers
Political economy, 2, 13, 70, 189, 206
Portugal, 155
Power: of colonized people, 1–2, 176–77, 201, 207–210; over death, 108, 115, 208; over life, 109, 115, 206–208. *See also* Colonial power
Prayer, 172, 179n
Priests. *See Bete*
Public discourse, 170–76
Public rituals, 176
Public spaces: and race, 188; in village, 182

Qali (subject people), 27, 36
Qaliyalatina, 118–21; on map, 20
Quiescence, 177–79, 191, 193, 197–99

Rabuka, Sitiveni, 158, 176, 189, 209
Rabulu, 183; on map, 20
Race, in Fiji, 162n
Racial war, prophesy of, 164
Raicula, 118
Rainmaking, 103, 110
Rakiraki, 26–37, 40, 50–61, 149; chiefs, genealogy of, 35; on map, xiii, 20
Rara (village green), 182
Ravai, Osea, 170–75, 197
Ravunakana, 51–52; in genealogy, 35
Recrudescence, theory of, 94
Reflexivity, 2, 14, 114n
Religion Eight, 141
Resistance. *See* Agency
Resurrection, 107, 114–15; of the ancestors, 112. *See also* Immortality
Reversal, 116
Rewa, 25, 154
"Rituals and routines of rule," 206
Ritual experts, 48–49, 179
Ritual politics, 26–31; in colonial imagination, 77
Robinson, Hercules, 71
Roko (Provincial head), 54
Roko Tui Kadavu, 127–28
Roko Tui Ra, 54–63, 125, 135, 144n; and Navosavakadua, 88

Rotuma, 4, 92, 183, 194
Routinization, 111, 123, 167, 176, 187, 193, 198, 208; of articulating systems, 15, 159; defined, 15–16, 176; failed attempts, 159, 161, 165n; by Navosavakadua, 100; by states, 203

Sabbath, 157, 166
Sacrifice, 111–16
Sadiri, 21–23, 44–45, 49, 52, 60, 79, 99, 208
Sahlins, Marshall, xi, 2, 12, 16, 26–28, 48, 102n, 136, 206
Sailosi Ratu, 132, 141, 143
Sakiusa Qarau, 156; in genealogy, 34
Samalia, Harigyan, 160–70, 193, 209
Sandalwood, 39, 77n
Sanitation, 187, 207–208
Saro Saro, 3–4, 50–53, 60
Saumaimuri, 29–30, 145–51; in genealogy, 152
Scarr, Deryck, 51, 60, 135
Scott, James, 13
Settlers. *See* White settlers
Seventh Day Adventists, 8, 141, 157, 181–82
Siga Rarama, 135
Silverblatt, Irene, 203
Soli, 137, 139, 150n, 190–94
Soro, 179
Sovereignty, breaks in, 210
State, 18, 72, 199–210
St. John, Samuel Avery, 38, 42
Stranger kings, 26–31, 104, 111
Structure and history, 2, 12
Subaltern Studies, 13
Sukuna, Lala, 135, 139, 144n, 146–47
Sutherland, William, 94–95, 114, 131
Swanston, 20, 89
Syria monument, 164–65

Tabua (whales' teeth), 5, 19, 23, 47, 58, 87, 88, 166, 192
Taivesi Mamaqa, 33, 126–34, 139, 143, 150n, 155, 181
Talatala, 140
Tamata dina (true men), 56, 86
Tanganyika, 28
Tanoa (kava bowl), 114
Taukei. *See* People of the Land
Taussig, Michael, 2, 13, 204–206
Tauvu, 155
Tavakece, of Rakiraki, 57–58, 61; in genealogy, 35
Tavakece Rareba of the Vatukaloko, 38, 57n; in genealogy, 34
Technologies of power, 208–209
Temples. *See Bure kalou*
Tevoro, 75, 143
Thomas brothers, 38, 131
Thomas, Keith, 203
Thompson, Edward P., 74n
Thurston, John Bates, 3, 63–68, 76–77, 88–89, 93–97, 125–127, 131, 141, 206; on the True God, 67
Todorov, Tzvetan, 207
Togavere, 23, 54, 64, 89, 146, 183; on map, 20–21
Tora, Apisai, 176
Tui Navitilevu (Rakiraki chief). *See* Rakiraki
Tui Vatu (Vatukaloko chief), 29–30, 38, 129, 146, 148, 154, 181, 186; genealogy of, 34
Tuiwai, Jone, 7–10, 150n
Tuka, xi, 3–7, 46–47, 57, 132; colonial constructions of, 6, 62–70, 85–97; as continuant of indigenous practice, 52, 60, 69, 201; as disease, 94; as disorder, 69, 85–97; immortality and, 87; as negative tradition, 95–97, 201–203; 1980s ac-

Tuka (*cont.*)
  counts, 6–9, 173–75; revival in 1891, 66–68, 92, 118–21; revival in 1914, 68–69, 118–21; as ritual polity, 98–122; in scholarly narratives, xii–xiii, 69, 96. *See also* Wai ni tuka
Turaga. See Chiefs
Turaga ni koro (village headman), 7, 129, 131, 166, 192
Twelve Tribes, 8, 33, 33n, 98, 111, 116, 125, 166, 183, 186, 196
Twins (Nacirikaumoli and Nakausabaria), 56, 69, 91, 100–104, 131, 155; and Apolosi, 138; in Bible, 101; as Christian gods, 103–104; marry women in England, 155

Uberoi, J. P. S., 203n
Udreudre, 34–37, 40, 53, 61

Vakavanua, 127–30, 143–47, 158. *See also* Custom
Vale Lebo, 46–47, 53, 111, 117, 125, 157n; on map, 21
Vanua. See Chiefdom
Vatukaloko, xv, 6, 22–34, 40, 111, 148; as bati, 26–31, 36–37, 59, 99, 184; chiefs, genealogy, 34; churches of, 125, 181, 193–94; 1891 deportation to Kadavu, 67–68, 124–33; and Kauvadra gods, 48; land, 54n, 146–47, 170, 180–83; 1980s, 179–99; 1980s narratives of Navosavakadua, 7–10, 172–76, 194–98; 1990s, 181, 198–200; old polity, 20–21, 31–34, 89; as people of the land, 26–31; and Rakiraki, 35–37
Veiqaravi, 114, 166, 192

Verata, 25, 150, 153–54
Video, 184
Virginity, eternal, promise of, 111. *See also* Leba
Viti Kabani (Fiji Company), 129, 133–39, 181, 195. *See also* Apolosi Nawai
Vivekananda, 208
Viwa, 26, 39–41; on map, xii, 20. *See also* Isikeli
Vugala, 36–37, 141; on map, 21
Vutoni, 57; in genealogy, 35

Wai ni tuka (water of immortality), 3, 51–52, 98, 106–13
Wakalou, 29–34, 148, 154, 181; on map, 180
Waqalevu, 37, 40, 51–52; in genealogy, 35
Waterhouse, Joseph, 102–103, 105n, 108–109
Weber, Max, 16n, 208
Whales' teeth. *See Tabua*
White settlers, 22–24, 37–39, 41–43, 54n, 73, 79–82, 90, 136
Wilkinson, David, 54–59, 86, 100–103, 110
Williams, Thomas, 13, 79
Witchcraft. *See* Tevoro
Wolf, Eric, 2, 206
Woods, George, 38
World wars, 135, 143
Worsley, Peter, xi, xii
Wright, Georgius, 23

Yaqara pastoral company, 146n, 170, 182–83
Yaqona. See Kava

Martha Kaplan is Assistant Professor of Anthropology at Vassar College.

Library of Congress Cataloging-in-Publication Data

Kaplan, Martha, 1957-
Neither cargo nor cult : ritual politics and the colonial
imagination in Fiji / Martha Kaplan.
p.   cm.
Includes bibliographical references and index.
ISBN 0-8223-1578-5 (cl.). — ISBN 0-8223-1593-9 (pbk.)
1. Cargo cults — Fiji. 2. Navosavakadua. 3. Fiji — Politics and
government. 4. Fiji — Biography. 5. Colonialism — British. I. Title.
GN671.F5K37 1995
306'.099611 — dc20   94-38508   CIP